"BE·MUCH OCCUPIED
WITH
JESUS"

SEA HARP PRESS

The Christian's
Secret of
a Happy Life

The Christian's Secret of a Happy Life by Hannah Whitall Smith

This edition copyright © 2022—Sea Harp
An imprint of Nori Media Group
P.O. Box 310, Shippensburg, PA 17257-0310
"Be Much Occupied with Jesus"

Cover design and interior page design copyright 2022.

All rights reserved.

Cover design by Christian Rafetto

Cover artwork by Jan Luyken, "Woman holds her hand over her eyes when looking at the sun"

Foreword by Eugene Luning

This book and all other Sea Harp books are available at Christian bookstores and distributors worldwide.

For more information on foreign distributors, call 717-532-3040.

Reach us on the Internet: www.seaharp.com

ISBN 13 TP: 978-0-7684-6440-5

ISBN 13 eBook: 978-0-7684-6441-2

For Worldwide Distribution

1 2 3 4 5 6 7 8 / 26 25 24 23 22

Contents

Foreword

THE TONE OF THIS WORK is so completely natural, so conversational, so robust with hints of the writer's smile, that one is tempted almost to imagine it as a personal tête-à-tête. Say, you and Hannah Whitall Smith sitting at table, sharing a pot of tea, speaking of your spiritual journeys. The authoress leans forward to you, over her lace-doilied tabletop. She says, smiling:

> *I suppose that you have trusted the Lord Jesus for the forgiveness of your sins, and know something of what it is to belong to the family of God, and to be made an heir of God through faith in Christ?*

> You nod, *yes.*

> *And now you feel springing up in your soul the longing to be conformed to the image of your Lord?*

Again, you nod, *yes*.

In order for this, you know there must be an entire surrender of yourself to Him, that He may work in you all the good pleasure of His will; and you have tried over and over to do it, but hitherto without any apparent success...

Then the eyes of this woman across from you narrow. She whispers: *At this point it is that I desire to help you...*

We at Sea Harp believe that one of the reasons for the enduring quality of *The Christian's Secret of a Happy Life* is how effectively the "voice" of Mrs. Smith comes through on every page. One almost feels as if she's becoming one's close friend. The simple richness of her writings lead to constant affirmations of God's goodness, His love for His children, and practicable steps to walk more nearly with Him.

It is with a smile of joy that we offer up this timeless work.

Thank you for being part of the Sea Harp Family!

SEA HARP PRESS

Preface

THIS IS NOT a theological book. I frankly confess I have not been trained in theological schools, and do not understand their methods nor their terms. But the Lord has taught me experimentally and practically certain lessons out of His Word, which have greatly helped me in my Christian life, and have made it a very happy one. And I want to tell my secret, in the best way I can, in order that some others may be helped into a happy life also.

I do not seek to change the theological views of a single individual. I dare say most of my readers know far more about theology than I do myself, and perhaps may discover abundance of what will seem to be theological mistakes. But let me ask that these may be overlooked, and that my reader will try, instead, to get at the experimental point of that which I have tried to say, and if that is practical and helpful, forgive the blundering way in which it is expressed. I have tried to reach the absolute truth which lies at the foundation of all "creeds" and "views," and to bring the soul into those personal relations with God which must exist alike in every form of religion, let the expression of them differ as they may.

I have committed my book to the Lord, and have asked Him to counteract all in it that is wrong, and to let only that which is true find entrance into any heart. It is sent out in tender sympathy and yearning love for all the struggling, weary ones in the Church of Christ, and its message goes right from my heart to theirs. I have given the best I have, and could do no more. May the blessed Holy Spirit use it to teach some of my readers the true secret of a happy life!

Hannah Whitall Smith
Germantown, Pennsylvania

I

God's Side and Man's Side

IN INTRODUCING THIS SUBJECT of the life and walk of faith, I desire, at the very outset, to clear away one misunderstanding which very commonly arises in reference to the teaching of it, and which effectually hinders a clear apprehension of such teaching. This misunderstanding comes from the fact that the two sides of the subject are rarely kept in view at the same time. People see distinctly the way in which one side is presented, and, dwelling exclusively upon this, without even a thought of any other, it is no wonder that distorted views of the whole matter are the legitimate consequence.

Now there are two very decided and distinct sides to this subject, and, like all other subjects, it cannot be fully understood unless both of these sides are kept constantly in view. I refer, of course, to God's side and man's side; or, in other words, to God's part in the work of sanctification, and man's part. These are very distinct and even contrastive, but are not contradictory; though, to a cursory observer, they sometimes look so.

This was very strikingly illustrated to me not long ago. There were two teachers of this Higher Christian Life holding meetings in the same place, at alternate hours. One spoke only of God's part in the work, and the other dwelt exclusively upon man's part. They were both in perfect sympathy with one another, and realized fully that they were each teaching different sides of the same great truth; and this also was understood by a large proportion of their hearers. But with some of the hearers it was different, and one lady said to me, in the greatest perplexity, "I cannot understand it at all. Here are two preachers undertaking to teach just the same truth, and yet to me they seem flatly to contradict one another." And I felt at the time that she expressed a puzzle which really causes a great deal of difficulty in the minds of many honest inquirers after this truth.

Suppose two friends go to see some celebrated building, and return home to describe it. One has seen only the north side, and the other only the south. The first says, "The building was built in such a manner, and has such and such stories and ornaments." "Oh, no!" says the other, interrupting him, "you are altogether mistaken; I saw the building, and it was built in quite a different manner, and its ornaments and stories were so and so." A lively dispute would probably follow upon the truth of the respective descriptions, until the two friends discover that they have been describing different sides of the building, and then all is reconciled at once.

I would like to state as clearly as I can what I judge to be the two distinct sides in this matter; and to show how the looking at one without seeing the other, will be sure to create wrong impressions and views of the truth.

To state it in brief, I would just say that man's part is to trust and God's part is to work; and it can be seen at a glance how contrastive these two parts are, and yet not necessarily contradictory. I mean this. There is a certain work to be accomplished. We are to be delivered from the power of sin, and are to be made perfect in every good work to do the will of God. "Bcholding as in a glass the glory of the Lord," we are to be actually "changed into the same image from glory to glory, even as by the Spirit of the Lord." We are to be transformed by the renewing of our minds, that we may prove what is that good and acceptable and perfect will of God. A real work is to be wrought in us and upon us. Besetting sins are to be conquered. Evil habits are to be overcome.

Wrong dispositions and feelings are to be rooted out, and holy tempers and emotions are to be begotten. A positive transformation is to take place. So at least the Bible teaches. Now somebody must do this. Either we must do it for ourselves, or another must do it for us. We have most of us tried to do it for ourselves at first, and have grievously failed; then we discover from the Scriptures and from our own experience that it is a work we are utterly unable to do for ourselves, but that the Lord Jesus Christ has come on purpose to do it, and that He will do it for all who put themselves wholly into His hand, and trust Him to do it. Now under these circumstances, what is the part of the believer, and what is the part of the Lord? Plainly the believer can do nothing but trust; while the Lord, in whom he trusts, actually does the work intrusted to Him. Trusting and doing are certainly contrastive things, and often contradictory; but are they contradictory in this case? Manifestly not, because it is two different parties that are concerned. If we should say of one party in a transaction that he trusted his case to another, and yet attended to it himself, we should state a contradiction and an impossibility. But when we say of two parties in a transaction that one trusts the other to do something, and that that other goes to work and does it, we are making a statement that is perfectly simple and harmonious. When we say, therefore, that in this higher life, man's part is to trust, and that God does the thing intrusted to Him, we do not surely present any very difficult or puzzling problem.

The preacher who is speaking on man's part in this matter cannot speak of anything but surrender and trust, because this is positively all the man can do. We all agree about this. And yet such preachers are constantly criticized as though, in saying this, they had meant to imply there was no other part, and that therefore nothing but trusting is done. And the cry goes out that this doctrine of faith does away with all realities, that souls are just told to trust, and that is the end of it, and they sit down thenceforward in a sort of religious easy-chair, dreaming away a life fruitless of any actual results. All this misapprehension arises, of course, from the fact that either the preacher has neglected to state, or the hearer has failed to hear, the other side of the matter; which is, that when we trust, the Lord works, and that a great deal is done, not by us, but by Him. Actual results are reached by our trusting, because our Lord undertakes the thing trusted to Him, and accomplishes it. We do not do anything, but He does it; and it is all the more effectually done because of this. The puzzle as to the preaching of faith disappears entirely as soon as this is clearly seen.

On the other hand, the preacher who dwells on God's side of the question is criticized on a totally different ground. He does not speak of trust, for the Lord's part is not to trust, but to work. The Lord does the thing intrusted to Him. He disciplines and trains the soul by inward exercises and outward providences. He brings to bear all the resources of His wisdom and love upon the refining and purifying of that soul. He makes everything in the life and circumstances of such a one subservient to the one great purpose of making him grow in grace, and of conforming him, day by day and hour by hour, to the image of Christ. He carries him through a process of transformation, longer or shorter, as his peculiar case may require, making actual and experimental the results for which the soul has trusted. We have dared, for instance, according to the command in Romans 6:11, by faith to reckon ourselves "dead unto sin." The Lord makes this a reality, and leads us to victory over self, by the daily and hourly discipline of His providences. Our reckoning is available only because God thus makes it real. And yet the preacher who dwells upon this practical side of the matter, and tells of God's processes for making faith's reckonings experimental realities, is accused of contradicting the preaching of faith altogether, and of declaring only a process of gradual sanctification by works, and of setting before the soul an impossible and hopeless task.

Now, sanctification is both a sudden step of faith, and also a gradual process of works. It is a step as far as we are concerned; it is a process as to God's part. By a step of faith we get into Christ; by a process we are made to grow up unto Him in all things. By a step of faith we put ourselves into the hands of the Divine Potter; by a gradual process He makes us into a vessel unto His own honor, meet for His use, and prepared to every good work.

To illustrate all this: suppose I were to be describing to a person, who was entirely ignorant of the subject, the way in which a lump of clay is made into a beautiful vessel. I tell him first the part of the clay in the matter, and all I can say about this is that the clay is put into the potter's hands, and then lies passive there, submitting itself to all the turnings and overturnings of the potter's hands upon it. There is really nothing else to be said about the clay's part. But could my hearer argue from this that nothing else is done, because I say that this is all the clay can do? If he is an intelligent hearer, he will not dream of doing so, but will say, "I understand. This is what the clay must do; but what must the potter do?" "Ah," I answer, "now we come to the important part. The potter takes the clay thus abandoned to his working, and begins to mold and fashion it according to his own will. He kneads and works it, he tears it apart and presses it together again, he wets it and then suffers it to dry. Sometimes he works at it for hours together, sometimes he lays it aside for days and does not touch it. And then, when by all these processes he has made it perfectly pliable in his hands, he proceeds to make it up into the vessel he has purposed. He turns it upon the wheel, planes it and smooths it, and dries it in the sun, bakes it in the oven, and finally turns it out of his workshop, a vessel to his honor and fit for his use."

Will my hearer be likely now to say that I am contradicting myself; that a little while ago I had said the clay had nothing to do but lie passive in the potter's hands, and that now I am putting upon it a great work which it is not able to perform; and that to make itself into such a vessel is an impossible and hopeless undertaking? Surely not. For he will see that, while before I was speaking of the clay's part in the matter, I am now speaking of the potter's part, and that these two are necessarily contrastive, but not in the least contradictory, and that the clay is not expected to do the potter's work, but only to yield itself up to his working.

Nothing, it seems to me, could be clearer than the perfect harmony between these two apparently contradictory sorts of teaching on this subject. What can be said about man's part in this great work, but that he must continually surrender himself and continually trust?

But when we come to God's side of the question, what is there that may not be said as to the manifold and wonderful ways in which He accomplishes the work intrusted to Him? It is here that the growing comes in. The lump of clay would never grow into a beautiful vessel if it stayed in the clay-pit for thousands of years. But once put into the hands of a skillful potter, and, under his fashioning, it grows rapidly into a vessel to his honor. And so the soul, abandoned to the working of the Heavenly Potter, is changed rapidly from glory to glory into the image of the Lord by His Spirit.

Having, therefore, taken the step of faith by which you have put yourself wholly and absolutely into His hands, you must now expect Him to begin to work. His way of accomplishing that which you have intrusted to Him may be different from your way. But He knows, and you must be satisfied.

I knew a lady who had entered into this life of faith with a great outpouring of the Spirit, and a wonderful flood of light and joy. She supposed, of course, this was a preparation for some great service, and expected to be put forth immediately into the Lord's harvest field. Instead of this, almost at once her husband lost all his money, and she was shut up in her own house, to attend to all sorts of domestic duties, with no time or strength left for any Gospel work at all. She accepted the discipline, and yielded herself up as heartily to sweep, and dust, and bake, and sew, as she would have done to preach, or pray or write for the Lord. And the result was that through this very training He made her into a vessel "meet for the Master's use, and prepared unto every good work."

Another lady, who had entered this life of faith under similar circumstances of wondrous blessing, and who also expected to be sent out to do some great work, was shut up with two peevish invalid nieces, to nurse, and humor, and amuse them all day long. Unlike the first lady, this one did not accept the training, but chafed and fretted, and finally rebelled, lost all her blessing, and went back into a state of sad coldness and misery. She had understood her part of trusting to begin with, but not understanding the divine process of accomplishing that for which she had trusted, she took herself out of the hands of the Heavenly Potter, and the vessel was marred on the wheel.

I believe many a vessel has been similarly marred by a want of understanding these things. The maturity of Christian experience cannot be reached in a moment, but is the result of the work of God's Holy Spirit, who, by His energizing and transforming power, causes us to grow up into Christ in all things. And we cannot hope to reach this maturity in any other way than by yielding ourselves up utterly and willingly to His mighty working. But the sanctification the Scriptures urge as a present experience upon all believers does not consist in maturity of growth, but in purity of heart, and this may be as complete in the babe in Christ as in the veteran believer.

The lump of clay, from the moment it comes under the transforming hand of the potter, is, during each day and each hour of the process, just what the potter wants it to be at that hour or on that day, and therefore pleases him. But it is very far from being matured into the vessel he intends in the future to make it.

The little babe may be all that a babe could be, or ought to be, and may therefore perfectly please its mother, and yet it is very far from being what that mother would wish it to be when the years of maturity shall come.

The apple in June is a perfect apple for June. It is the best apple that June can produce. But it is very different from the apple in October, which is a perfected apple.

God's works are perfect in every stage of their growth. Man's works are never perfect until they are in every respect complete.

All that we claim then in this life of sanctification is, that by a step of faith we put ourselves into the hands of the Lord, for Him to work in us all the good pleasure of His will; and that by a continuous exercise of faith we keep ourselves there. This is our part in the matter. And when we do it, and while we do it, we are, in the Scripture sense, truly pleasing to God, although it may require years of training and discipline to mature us into a vessel that shall be in all respects to His honor, and fitted to every good work.

Our part is the trusting, it is His to accomplish the results. And when we do our part, He never fails to do His, for no one ever trusted in the Lord and was confounded. Do not be afraid, then, that if you trust, or tell others to trust, the matter will end there. Trust is only the beginning and the continual foundation; when we trust, the Lord works, and His work is the important part of the whole matter. And this explains that apparent paradox which puzzles so many. They say, "In one breath you tell us to do nothing but trust, and in the next you tell us to do impossible things. How can you reconcile such contradictory statements?" They are to be reconciled just as we reconcile the statements concerning a saw in a carpenter's shop, when we say at one moment that the saw has sawn asunder a log, and the next moment declare that the carpenter has done it. The saw is the instrument used, the power that uses it is the carpenter's. And so we, yielding ourselves unto God, and our members as instruments of righteousness unto Him, find that He works in us to will and to do of His good pleasure; and we can say with Paul, "I labored; yet not I, but the grace of God which was with me." For we are to be His workmanship, not our own (Ephesians 2:10). And in fact, when we come to look at it, only God, who created us at first, can re-create us, for He alone understands the "work of His own hands." All efforts after self-creating result in the marring of the vessel, and no soul can ever reach its highest fulfillment except through the working of Him who "worketh all things after the counsel of His own will."

In this book I shall of course dwell mostly upon man's side in the matter, as I am writing for man, and in the hope of teaching believers how to fulfill their part of the great work. But I wish it to be distinctly understood all through, that unless I believed with all my heart in God's effectual working on His side, not one word of this book would ever have been written.

II

The Scripturalness of This Life

WHEN I APPROACH THIS SUBJECT of the true Christian life, that life which is hid with Christ in God, so many thoughts struggle for utterance that I am almost speechless. Where shall I begin? What is the most important thing to say? How shall I make people read and believe? The subject is so glorious, and human words seem so powerless! But something I am impelled to say. The secret must be told. For it is one concerning that victory which overcometh the world, that promised deliverance from all our enemies, for which every child of God longs and prays, but which seems so often and so generally to elude their grasp. May God grant me so to tell it that every believer to whom this book shall come may have his eyes opened to see the truth as it is in Jesus, and may be enabled to enter into possession of this glorious life for himself.

For sure I am that every converted soul longs for victory and rest, and nearly everyone feels instinctively, at times, that they are his birthright. Can you not remember, some of you, the shout of triumph your souls gave when you first became acquainted with the Lord Jesus, and had a glimpse of His mighty saving power? How sure you were of victory then! How easy it seemed, to be more than conquerors, through Him that loved you. Under the leadership of a Captain who had never been foiled in battle, how could you dream of defeat? And yet, to many of you, how different has been your real experience. The victories have been but few and fleeting, the defeats many and disastrous. You have not lived as you feel children of God ought to live. There has been a resting in a clear understanding of doctrinal truth, without pressing after the power and life thereof. There has been a rejoicing in the knowledge of things testified of in the Scriptures, without a living realization of the things themselves, consciously felt in the soul. Christ is believed in, talked about, and served, but He is not known as the soul's actual and very life, abiding there forever, and revealing Himself there continually in His beauty. You have found Jesus as your Savior and your Master, and you have tried to serve Him and advance the cause of His kingdom. You have carefully studied the Holy Scriptures and have gathered much precious truth therefrom, which you have endeavored faithfully to practice.

But notwithstanding all your knowledge and all your activities in the service of the Lord, your souls are secretly starving, and you cry out again and again for that bread and water of life which you saw promised in the Scriptures to all believers. In the very depths of your hearts you know that your experience is not a scriptural experience; that, as an old writer says, your religion is "but a talk to what the early Christians enjoyed, possessed, and lived in." And your souls have sunk within you, as day after day, and year after year, your early visions of triumph have seemed to grow more and more dim, and you have been forced to settle down to the conviction that the best you can expect from your religion is a life of alternate failure and victory; one hour sinning, and the next repenting; and beginning again, only to fail again, and again to repent.

But is this all? Had the Lord Jesus only this in His mind when He laid down His precious life to deliver you from your sore and cruel bondage to sin? Did He propose to Himself only this partial deliverance? Did He intend to leave you thus struggling along under a weary consciousness of defeat and discouragement? Did He fear that a continuous victory would dishonor Him, and bring reproach on His name? When all those declarations were made concerning His coming, and the work

He was to accomplish, did they mean only this that you have experienced? Was there a hidden reserve in each promise that was meant to deprive it of its complete fulfillment? Did "delivering us out of the hands of our enemies" mean only a few of them? Did "enabling us always to triumph" mean only sometimes; or being "more than conquerors through Him that love us" mean constant defeat and failure? No, no, a thousand times no! God is able to save unto the uttermost, and He means to do it. His promise, confirmed by His oath, was that "He would grant unto us, that we, being delivered out of the hand of our enemies, might serve Him without fear, in holiness and righteousness before Him, all the days of our life." It is a mighty work to do, but our Deliverer is able to do it. He came to destroy the works of the devil, and dare we dream for a moment that He is not able or not willing to accomplish His own purposes?

At the very outset, then, settle down on this one thing, that the Lord is able to save you fully, now, in this life, from the power and dominion of sin, and to deliver you altogether out of the hands of your enemies. If you do not think He is, search your Bible, and collect together every announcement or declaration concerning the purposes and object of His death on the cross. You will be astonished to find how full they are.

Everywhere and always His work is said to be, to deliver us from our sins, from our bondage, from our defilement; and not a hint is given anywhere, that this deliverance was to be only the limited and partial one with which the Church so continually tries to be satisfied.

Let me give you a few texts on this subject. When the angel of the Lord appeared unto Joseph in a dream, and announced the coming birth of the Savior, he said, "And thou shalt call His name Jesus, for He shall save His people from their sins."

When Zacharias was "filled with the Holy Ghost" at the birth of his son, and "prophesied," he declared that God had visited His people in order to fulfill the promise and the oath He had made them, which promise was, "That He would grant unto us, that we, being delivered out of the hands of our enemies, might serve Him without fear, in holiness and righteousness before Him, all the days of our life."

When Peter was preaching in the porch of the Temple to the wondering Jews, he said, "Unto you first, God, having raised up His Son Jesus, sent Him to bless you in turning away every one of you from his iniquities."

When Paul was telling out to the Ephesian church the wondrous truth that Christ had loved them so much as to give Himself for them, he went on to declare, that His purpose in thus doing was, "that He might sanctify and cleanse it by the washing of water by the word, that He might present it to Himself a glorious church, not having spot or wrinkle, or any such thing; but that it should be holy and without blemish."

When Paul was seeking to instruct Titus, his own son after the common faith, concerning the grace of God, he declared that the object of that grace was to teach us "that denying ungodliness and worldly lusts, we should live soberly, righteously, and godly in this present world"; and adds, as the reason of this, that Christ "gave Himself for us that He might redeem us from all iniquity, and purify us unto Himself a peculiar people, zealous of good works."

When Peter was urging upon the Christians, to whom he was writing, a holy and Christ-like walk, he tells them that "even hereunto were ye called because Christ also suffered for us, leaving us an example that ye should follow His steps: who did no sin, neither was guile found in His mouth"; and adds, "who His own self bare our sins in His own body on the tree, that we, being dead to sins, should live unto righteousness; by whose stripes ye were healed."

When Paul was contrasting in the Ephesians the walk suitable for a Christian, with the walk of an unbeliever, he sets before them the truth in Jesus as being this, "that ye put off concerning the former conversation the old man, which is corrupt according to the deceitful lusts; and be renewed in the spirit of your mind; and that ye put on the new man, which after God is created in righteousness and true holiness."

And when, in Romans 6, he was answering forever the question as to continuing in sin, and showing how utterly foreign it was to the whole spirit and aim of the salvation of Jesus, he brings up the fact of our judicial death and resurrection with Christ as an unanswerable argument for our practical deliverance from it, and says, "God forbid. How shall we, that are dead to sin, live any longer therein? Know ye not that so many of us as were baptized into Jesus Christ were baptized into His death? Therefore we are buried with Him by baptism into death; that like as Christ was raised up from the dead by the glory of the Father, even so we also should walk in newness of life." And adds, "Knowing this, that our old man is crucified with Him, that the body of sin might be destroyed, that henceforth we should not serve sin."

Dear Christians, will you receive the testimony of Scripture on this matter? The same questions that troubled the Church in Paul's day are troubling it now: first, "Shall we continue in sin that grace may abound?" And second, "Do we then make void the law through faith?" Shall not our answer to these be Paul's emphatic "God forbid"; and his triumphant assertions that instead of making it void "we establish the law"; and that "what the law could not do, in that it was weak through the flesh, God sending His own Son in the likeness of sinful flesh, and for sin, condemned sin in the flesh: that the righteousness of the law might be fulfilled in us who walk not after the flesh, but after the Spirit"?

Can we suppose for a moment that the holy God, who hates sin in the sinner, is willing to tolerate it in the Christian, and that He has even arranged the plan of salvation in such a way as to make it impossible for those who are saved from the guilt of sin to find deliverance from its power?

As Dr. Chalmers well says, "Sin is that scandal which must be rooted out from the great spiritual household over which the Divinity rejoices...Strange administration, indeed, for sin to be so hateful to God as to lay all who had incurred it under death, and yet when readmitted into life that sin should be permitted;

and that what was before the object of destroying vengeance, should now become the object of an upheld and protected toleration. Now that the penalty is taken off, think you that it is possible the unchangeable God has so given up His antipathy to sin, as that man, ruined and redeemed man, may now perseveringly indulge under the new arrangement in that which under the old destroyed him? Does not the God who loved righteousness and hated iniquity six thousand years ago, bear the same love to righteousness and hatred to iniquity still?...I now breathe the air of loving-kindness from Heaven, and can walk before God in peace and graciousness; shall I again attempt the incompatible alliance of two principles so adverse as that of an approving God and a persevering sinner? How shall we, recovered from so awful a catastrophe, continue that which first involved us in it? The cross of Christ, by the same mighty and decisive stroke wherewith it moved the curse of sin away from us, also surely moves away the power and the love of it from over us."

And not Dr. Chalmers only, but many other holy men of his generation and of our own, as well as of generations long past, have united in declaring that the redemption accomplished for us by our Lord Jesus Christ on the cross at Calvary is a redemption from the power of sin as well as from its guilt, and that He is able to save to the uttermost all who come unto God by Him.

A quaint old divine of the seventeenth century says:

"There is nothing so contrary to God as sin, and God will not suffer sin always to rule his masterpiece, man. When we consider the infiniteness of God's power for destroying that which is contrary to Him, who can believe that the devil must always stand and prevail? I believe it is inconsistent and disagreeable with true faith for people to be Christians, and yet to believe that Christ, the eternal Son of God, to whom all power in heaven and earth is given, will suffer sin and the devil to have dominion over them.

"But you will say no man by all the power he hath can redeem himself, and no man can live without sin. We will say, Amen, to it. But if men tell us, that when God's power comes to help us and to redeem us out of sin, that it cannot be effected, then this doctrine we cannot away with; nor I hope you neither.

"Would you approve of it, if I should tell you that God puts forth His power to do such a thing, but the devil hinders Him? That it is impossible for God to do it because the devil does not like it? That it is impossible that anyone should be free from sin because the devil hath got such a power in

them that God cannot cast him out? This is lamentable doctrine, yet hath not this been preached? It doth in plain terms say, though God doth interpose His power, it is impossible, because the devil hath so rooted sin in the nature of man. Is not man God's creature, and cannot He new make him, and cast sin out of him? If you say sin is deeply rooted in man, I say so, too, yet not so deeply rooted but Christ Jesus hath entered so deeply into the root of the nature of man that He hath received power to destroy the devil and his works, and to recover and redeem man into righteousness and holiness. Or else it is false that 'He is able to save to the uttermost all that come unto God by Him.' We must throw away the Bible, if we say that it is impossible for God to deliver man out of sin.

"We know when our friends are in captivity, as in Turkey, or elsewhere, we pay our money for their redemption; but we will not pay our money if they be kept in their fetters still. Would not anyone think himself cheated to pay so much money for their redemption, and the bargain be made so that he shall be said to be redeemed, and be called a redeemed captive, but he must wear his fetters still? How long? As long as he hath a day to live.

"This is for bodies, but now I am speaking of souls. Christ must be made to me redemption, and rescue me from captivity. Am I a prisoner any where? Yes, verily, verily, he that committeth sin, saith Christ, he is a servant of sin, he is a slave of

sin. If thou hast sinned, thou art a slave, a captive that must be redeemed out of captivity. Who will pay a price for me? I am poor; I have nothing; I cannot redeem myself; who will pay a price for me? There is One come who hath paid a price for me. That is well; that is good news, then I hope I shall come out of my captivity. What is His name, is He called a Redeemer? So, then, I do expect the benefit of my redemption, and that I shall go out of my captivity. No, say they, you must abide in sin as long as you live. What! must we never be delivered? Must this crooked heart and perverse will always remain? Must I be a believer, and yet have no faith that reacheth to sanctification and holy living? Is there no mastery to be had, no getting victory over sin? Must it prevail over me as long as I live? What sort of a Redeemer, then, is this, or what benefit have I in this life, of my redemption?"

Similar extracts might be quoted from Marshall, Romaine, and many others, to show that this doctrine is no new one in the Church, however much it may have been lost sight of by the present generation of believers. It is the same old story that has filled with songs of triumph the daily lives of many saints of God throughout all ages; and is now afresh being sounded forth to the unspeakable joy of weary and burdened souls.

Do not reject it, then, dear reader, until you have prayerfully searched the Scriptures to see whether these things be indeed so. Ask God to open the eyes of your understanding by His Spirit, that you may "know what is the exceeding greatness of His power to usward who believe, according to the working of His mighty power, which He wrought in Christ, when He raised Him from the dead, and set Him at His own right hand in the heavenly places." And when you have begun to have some faint glimpses of this power, learn to look away utterly from your own weakness, and, putting your case into His hands, trust Him to deliver you.

In Psalms 8:6, we are told that God made man to "have dominion over the works of His hand." The fulfillment of this is declared in 2 Corinthians 2, where the apostle cries, "Thanks be unto God which always causeth us to triumph in Christ." If the maker of a machine should declare that he had made it to accomplish a certain purpose, and if upon trial it should be found incapable of accomplishing that purpose, we would all say of that maker that he was a fraud.

Surely then we will not dare to think that it is impossible for the creature whom God has made, to accomplish the declared object for which he was created. Especially when the Scriptures are so full of the assertions that Christ has made it possible.

The only thing that can hinder is the creature's own failure to work in harmony with the plans of his Creator, and if this want of harmony can be removed, then God can work. Christ came to bring about an atonement between God and man, which should make it possible for God thus to work in man to will and to do of His good pleasure. Therefore we may be of good courage; for the work Christ has undertaken He is surely able and willing to perform. Let us then "walk in the steps of that faith of our father Abraham," who "staggered not at the promise of God through unbelief; but was strong in faith, giving glory to God; being fully persuaded that what He had promised, He was able also to perform."

III

The Life Defined

IN MY LAST I tried to settle the question as to the scripturalness of the experience sometimes called the Higher Christian Life, but which to my own mind is best described in the words, the "life hid with Christ in God." I shall now, therefore, consider it as a settled point that the Scriptures do set before the believer in the Lord Jesus a life of abiding rest and of continual victory, which is very far beyond the ordinary line of Christian experience; and that in the Bible we have presented to us a Savior able to save us from the power of our sins, as really as He saves us from their guilt.

The point to be next considered is as to what this hidden life consists in, and how it differs from every other sort of Christian experience.

And as to this, it is simply letting the Lord carry our burdens and manage our affairs for us, instead of trying to do it ourselves.

Most Christians are like a man who was toiling along the road, bending under a heavy burden, when a wagon overtook him, and the driver kindly offered to help him on his journey. He joyfully accepted the offer, but when seated, continued to bend beneath his burden, which he still kept on his shoulders. "Why do you not lay down your burden?" asked the kind-hearted driver. "Oh!" replied the man, "I feel that it is almost too much to ask you to carry me, and I could not think of letting you carry my burden too." And so Christians, who have given themselves into the care and keeping of the Lord Jesus, still continue to bend beneath the weight of their burden, and often go weary and heavy-laden throughout the whole length of their journey.

When I speak of burdens, I mean everything that troubles us, whether spiritual or temporal.

I mean, first of all, ourselves. The greatest burden we have to carry in life is self. The most difficult thing we have to manage is self. Our own daily living, our frames and feelings, our especial weaknesses and temptations, and our peculiar temperaments, our inward affairs of every kind, these are the things that perplex and worry us more than anything else, and that bring us oftenest into bondage and darkness. In laying off your burdens, therefore, the first one you must get rid of is yourself. You must hand yourself and all your inward experiences, your temptations, your temperament, your frames and feelings, all over into the care and keeping of your God, and leave them there. He made you, and therefore He understands you and knows how to manage you, and you must trust Him to do it. Say to Him, "Here, Lord, I abandon myself to thee. I have tried in every way I could think of to manage myself, and to make myself what I know I ought to be, but have always failed. Now I give it up to thee. Do thou take entire possession of me. Work in me all the good pleasure of thy will. Mould and fashion me into such a vessel as seemeth good to thee. I leave myself in thy hands, and I believe thou wilt, according to thy promise, make me into a vessel unto thine honor, 'sanctified, and meet for the Master's use, and prepared unto every good work.'" And here you must rest, trusting yourself thus to Him continually and absolutely.

Next, you must lay off every other burden,—your health, your reputation, your Christian work, your houses, your children, your business, your servants; everything, in short, that concerns you, whether inward or outward.

Christians always commit the keeping of their souls for eternity to the Lord, because they know, without a shadow of a doubt, that they cannot keep these themselves. But the things of this present life they take into their own keeping, and try to carry on their own shoulders, with the perhaps unconfessed feeling that it is a great deal to ask of the Lord to carry them, and that they cannot think of asking Him to carry their burdens too.

I knew a Christian lady who had a very heavy temporal burden. It took away her sleep and her appetite, and there was danger of her health breaking down under it. One day, when it seemed especially heavy, she noticed lying on the table near her a little tract called "Hannah's Faith." Attracted by the title, she picked it up and began to read it, little knowing, however, that it was to create a revolution in her whole experience. The story was of a poor woman who had been carried triumphantly through a life of unusual sorrow. She was giving the history of her life to a kind visitor on one occasion, and at the close the visitor said, feelingly, "O Hannah, I do not see how you could bear so much sorrow!" "I did not bear it," was the quick reply; "the Lord bore it for me." "Yes," said the visitor "that is the right way. You must take your troubles to the Lord." "Yes," replied Hannah, "but we must do more than that; we must leave them there. Most people," she continued, "take their burdens to Him, but they bring them away with them again, and are just as worried and unhappy as ever. But

I take mine, and I leave them with Him, and come away and forget them. And if the worry comes back, I take it to Him again; I do this over and over, until at last I just forget that I have any worries, and am at perfect rest."

My friend was very much struck with this plan and resolved to try it. The circumstances of her life she could not alter, but she took them to the Lord, and handed them over into His management; and then she believed that He took it, and she left all the responsibility and the worry and anxiety with Him. As often as the anxieties returned she took them back; and the result was that, although the circumstances remained unchanged, her soul was kept in perfect peace in the midst of them. She felt that she had found out a blessed secret, and from that time she tried never again to carry her own burdens, nor to manage anything for herself.

And the secret she found so effectual in her outward affairs, she found to be still more effectual in her inward ones, which were in truth even more utterly unmanageable. She abandoned her whole self to the Lord, with all that she was and all that she had, and, believing that He took that which she had committed to Him, she ceased to fret and worry, and her life became all sunshine in the gladness of belonging to Him. And this was the Higher Christian

Life! It was a very simple secret she found out. Only this, that it was possible to obey God's commandment contained in those words, "Be careful for nothing, but in everything by prayer and supplication, with thanksgiving, let your requests be made known unto God"; and that, in obeying it, the result would inevitably be, according to the promise, that the "peace of God which passeth all understanding shall keep your hearts and minds through Christ Jesus."

There are many other things to be said about this life hid with Christ in God, many details as to what the Lord Jesus does for those who thus abandon themselves to Him. But the gist of the whole matter is here stated, and the soul that has got hold of this secret has found the key that will unlock the whole treasure-house of God.

And now I do trust that I have made you hunger for this blessed life. Would you not like to get rid of your burdens? Do you not long to hand over the management of your unmanageable self into the hands of One who is able to manage you? Are you not tired and weary, and does not the rest I speak of look sweet to you?

Do you recollect the delicious sense of rest with which you have sometimes gone to bed at night, after a day of great exertion and weariness? How delightful was the sensation of relaxing every muscle, and letting your body go in a perfect abandonment of ease and comfort. The strain of the day had ceased for a few hours at least, and the work of the day had been thrown off. You no longer had to hold up an aching head or a weary back. You trusted yourself to the bed in an absolute confidence, and it held you up, without effort, or strain, or even thought on your part. You rested.

But suppose you had doubted the strength or the stability of your bed, and had dreaded each moment to find it giving away beneath you and landing you on the floor; could you have rested then? Would not every muscle have been strained in a fruitless effort to hold yourself up, and would not the weariness have been greater than not to have gone to bed at all?

Let this analogy teach you what it means to rest in the Lord. Let your souls lie down upon IIis sweet will, as your bodies lie down in your beds at night. Relax every strain and lay off every burden. Let yourselves go in perfect abandonment of ease and comfort, sure that when He holds you up you are perfectly safe.

Your part is simply to rest. His part is to sustain you, and He cannot fail.

Or take another analogy, which our Lord Himself has abundantly sanctioned, that of the child-life. For "Jesus called a little child unto Him, and set him in the midst of them, and said, Verily I say unto you, Except ye be converted and become as little children, ye shall not enter the kingdom of Heaven."

Now, what are the characteristics of a little child and how does he live? He lives by faith, and his chiefest characteristic is thoughtlessness. His life is one long trust from year's end to year's end. He trusts his parents, he trusts his caretakers, he trusts his teachers, he even trusts people often who are utterly unworthy of trust, because of the confidingness of his nature. And his trust is abundantly answered. He provides nothing for himself, and yet everything is provided. He takes no thought for the morrow, and forms no plans, and yet all his life is planned out for him, and he finds his paths made ready, opening out to him as he comes to them day by day, and hour by hour. He goes in and out of his father's house with an unspeakable ease and abandonment, enjoying all the good things it contains, without having spent a penny in procuring them. Pestilence may walk through the streets of his city, but he regards it not. Famine and fire and war may rage around him, but under his father's tender care he abides in utter unconcern and perfect rest. He lives in the present moment, and receives his life without question as it comes to him day by day from his father's hands.

I was visiting once in a wealthy house, where there was one only adopted child, upon whom was lavished all the love and tenderness and care that human hearts could bestow or human means procure. And as I watched that child running in and out day by day, free and light-hearted, with the happy carelessness of childhood, I thought what a picture it was of our wonderful position as children in the house of our Heavenly Father. And I said to myself, "If nothing could so grieve and wound the loving hearts around her, as to see this little child beginning to be worried or anxious about herself in any way, about whether her food and clothes would be provided for her, or how she was to get her education or her future support, how much more must the great, loving heart of our God and Father be grieved and wounded at seeing His children taking so much anxious care and thought!" And I understood why it was that our Lord had said to us so emphatically, "Take no thought for yourselves."

Who is the best cared for in every household? Is it not the little children? And does not the least of all, the helpless baby, receive the largest share? As a late writer has said, the baby "toils not, neither does he spin; and yet he is fed, and clothed, and loved, and rejoiced in," and none so much as he.

This life of faith, then, about which I am writing, consists in just this; being a child in the Father's house. And when this is said, enough is said to transform every weary, burdened life into one of blessedness and rest.

Let the ways of childish confidence and freedom from care, which so please you and win your hearts in your own little ones, teach you what should be your ways with God; and leaving yourselves in His hands, learn to be literally "careful for nothing"; and you shall find it to be a fact that "the peace of God which passeth all understanding shall keep (as in a garrison) your hearts and minds through Christ Jesus." Notice the word "nothing" in the above passage, as covering all possible grounds for anxiety, both inward and outward. We are continually tempted to think it is our duty to be anxious about some things. Perhaps our thought will be, "Oh, yes, it is quite right to give up all anxiety in a general way; and in spiritual matters of course anxiety is wrong; but there are things about which it would be a sin not to be anxious; about our children, for instance, or those we love, or about our church affairs and the cause of truth, or about our business matters. It would show a great want of right feeling not to be anxious about such things as these." Or else our thoughts take the other tack, and we say to ourselves, "Yes, it is quite right to commit our loved ones and all our outward affairs to the Lord, but when it comes to our inward lives, our religious experiences, our temptations, our besetting sins, our growth in grace, and all such things, these we ought to be anxious about; for if we are not, they will be sure to be neglected."

To such suggestions, and to all similar ones, the answer is found in our text,—

"In NOTHING be anxious."

In Matthew 6:25-34, our Lord illustrates this being without anxiety, by telling us to behold the fowls of the air and the lilies of the field, as examples of the sort of life He would have us live. As the birds rejoice in the care of their God and are fed, and as the lilies grow in His sunlight, so must we, without anxiety, and without fear. Let the sparrows speak to us:—

"I am only a tiny sparrow,
     A bird of low degree;
My life is of little value,
     But the dear Lord cares for me.

"I have no barn nor storehouse,
     I neither sow nor reap;

God gives me a sparrow's portion,
    But never a seed to keep.

"I know there are many sparrows;
    All over the world they are found;
But our heavenly Father knoweth
    When one of us falls to the ground.

"Though small, we are never forgotten;
    Though weak, we are never afraid;
For we know the dear Lord keepeth
    The life of the creatures he made.

"I fly through the thickest forest,
    I light on many a spray;
I have no chart nor compass,
    But I never lose my way.

"And I fold my wing at twilight
    Wherever I happen to be;
For the Father is always watching,
    And no harm will come to me.

"I am only a little sparrow,
    A bird of low degree,
But I know the Father loves me;
    Have you less faith than we?"

IV

How to Enter In

HAVING TRIED TO SETTLE the question as to the scripturalness of the experience of this life of full trust, and having also shown a little of what it is, the next point is as to how it is to be reached and realized.

And first, I would say that this blessed life must not be looked upon in any sense as an attainment but as an obtainment. We cannot earn it, we cannot climb up to it, we cannot win it; we can do nothing but ask for it and receive it. It is the gift of God in Christ Jesus. And where a thing is a gift, the only course left for the receiver is to take it and thank the giver. We never say of a gift, "See to what I have attained," and boast of our skill and wisdom in having attained it; but we say, "See what has been given me," and boast of the love and wealth and generosity of the giver. And everything in our salvation is a gift. From beginning to end, God is the giver and we are the receivers; and it is not to those who do great things, but to those who "receive abundance of grace, and of the gift of righteousness," that the richest promises are made.

In order, therefore, to enter into a realized experience of this interior life, the soul must be in a receptive attitude, fully recognizing the fact that it is to be God's gift in Christ Jesus, and that it cannot be gained by any efforts or works of our own. This will simplify the matter exceedingly; and the only thing left to be considered then will be to discover upon whom God bestows this gift, and how they are to receive it. And to this I would answer in short, that He bestows it only upon the fully consecrated soul, and that it is to be received by faith.

Consecration is the first thing. Not in any legal sense, not in order to purchase or deserve the blessing, but to remove the difficulties out of the way and make it possible for God to bestow it. In order for a lump of clay to be made into a beautiful vessel, it must be entirely abandoned to the potter, and must lie passive in his hands. And in order for a soul to be made into a vessel unto God's honor, "sanctified and meet for the Master's use, and prepared unto every good work," it must be entirely abandoned to Him, and must lie passive in His hands. This is manifest at the first glance.

I was once trying to explain to a physician, who had charge of a large hospital, what consecration meant, and its necessity, but he seemed unable to understand. At last I said to him, "Suppose, in going your rounds among your patients, you should meet with one man who entreated you earnestly to take his case under your especial care in order to cure him, but who should at the same time refuse to tell you all the symptoms, or to take all your prescribed remedies; and should say to you, 'I am quite willing to follow your directions as to certain things, because they commend themselves to my mind as good, but in other matters I prefer judging for myself and following my own directions.' What would you do in such a case?" I asked. "Do!" he replied with indignation,—"do! I would soon leave such a man as that to his own care. For of course," he added, "I could do nothing for him, unless he would put his whole case into my hands without any reserves, and would obey my directions implicitly." "It is necessary then," I said, "for doctors to be obeyed, if they are to have any chance to cure their patients?" "Implicitly obeyed!" was his emphatic reply. "And that is consecration," I continued. "God must have the whole case put into His hands without any reserves, and His directions must be implicitly followed." "I see it," he exclaimed,—"I see it! And I will do it. God shall have His own way with me from henceforth."

Perhaps to some minds the word "abandonment" might express this idea better. But whatever word we use, we mean an entire surrender of the whole being to God; spirit, soul, and body placed under His absolute control, for Him to do with us just what He pleases. We mean that the language of our soul, under all circumstances, and in view of every act, is to be, "Thy will be done." We mean the giving up of all liberty of choice. We mean a life of inevitable obedience.

To a soul ignorant of God, this may look hard. But to those who know Him, it is the happiest and most restful of lives. He is our Father, and He loves us, and He knows just what is best, and therefore, of course, His will is the very most blessed thing that can come to us under all circumstances. I do not understand how it is that Satan has succeeded in blinding the eyes of the Church to this fact. But it really would seem as if God's own children were more afraid of His will than of anything else in life; His lovely, lovable will, which only means loving-kindnesses and tender mercies, and blessings unspeakable to their souls. I wish I could only show to everyone the unfathomable sweetness of the will of God. Heaven is a place of infinite bliss because His will is perfectly done there, and our lives share in this bliss just in proportion as His will is perfectly done in them. He loves us, and the will of love is always blessing for its loved one. Some of us know what it is to love, and we know that could we only have our way, our beloved ones would be overwhelmed with blessings. All that is good, and sweet, and lovely in life would be poured out upon them from our lavish hands, had we but the power to carry out our will for them. And if this is the way of love with us, how much more must it be so with our God, who is love itself. Could we but for one moment get a glimpse into the mighty depths of His love, our hearts would spring out to meet His will, and embrace it as our richest treasure; and we would abandon ourselves to it with an enthusiasm of gratitude and joy, that such a wondrous privilege could be ours.

A great many Christians actually seem to think that all their Father in heaven wants is a chance to make them miserable, and to take away all their blessings, and they imagine, poor souls, that if they hold on to things in their own will, they can hinder Him from doing this. I am ashamed to write the words, and yet we must face a fact which is making wretched hundreds of lives.

A Christian lady who had this feeling was once expressing to a friend how impossible she found it to say, "Thy will be done," and how afraid she should be to do it. She was the mother of one only little boy, who was the heir to a great fortune, and the idol of her heart. After she had stated her difficulties fully, her friend said, "Suppose your little Charley should come running to you tomorrow and say, 'Mother, I have made up my mind to let you have your own way with me from this time forward. I am always going to obey you, and I want you to do just whatever you think best with me. I know you love me, and I am going to trust myself to your love.' How would you feel toward him? Would you say to yourself, 'Ah, now I shall have a chance to make Charley miserable. I will take away all his pleasures, and fill his life with every hard and disagreeable thing I can find. I will compel him to do just the things that are the most difficult for him to do, and will give him all sorts of impossible commands'?" "Oh, no, no, no!" exclaimed the indignant mother. "You know I would not. You know I would hug him to my heart and cover him with kisses, and would hasten to fill his life with all that was sweetest and best." "And are you more tender and more loving than God?" asked her friend. "Ah, no," was the reply, "I see my mistake, and I will not be afraid of saying 'Thy will be done,' to my Heavenly Father, any more than I would want my Charley to be afraid of saying it to me."

Better and sweeter than health, or friends, or money, or fame, or ease, or prosperity, is the adorable will of our God. It gilds the darkest hours with a divine halo, and sheds brightest sunshine on the gloomiest paths. He always reigns who has made it his kingdom; and nothing can go amiss to him. Surely, then, it is nothing but a glorious privilege that is opening before you when I tell you that the first step you must take in order to enter into the life hid with Christ in God is that of entire consecration. I cannot have you look at it as a hard and stern demand. You must do it gladly, thankfully, enthusiastically. You must go in on what I call the privilege side of consecration; and I can assure you, from a blessed experience, that you will find it the happiest place you have ever entered yet.

Faith is the next thing. Faith is an absolutely necessary element in the reception of any gift; for let our friends give a thing to us ever so fully, it is not really ours until we believe it has been given and claim it as our own. Above all, this is true in gifts which are purely mental or spiritual. Love may be lavished upon us by another without stint or measure, but until we believe that we are loved, it never really becomes ours.

I suppose most Christians understand this principle in reference to the matter of their forgiveness. They know that the forgiveness of sins through Jesus might have been preached to them forever, but it would never have become theirs consciously until they believed this preaching, and claimed the forgiveness as their own. But when it comes to living the Christian life, they lose sight of this principle, and think that, having been saved by faith, they are now to live by works and efforts; and instead of continuing to receive, they are now to begin to do. This makes our declaration that the life hid with Christ in God is to be entered by faith, seem perfectly unintelligible to them. And yet it is plainly declared, that "as we have received Christ Jesus the Lord, so we are to walk in Him." We received Him by faith, and by faith alone; therefore we are to walk in Him by faith, and by faith alone. And the faith by which we enter into this hidden life is just the same as the faith by which we were translated out of the kingdom of darkness into the kingdom of God's dear Son, only it lays hold of a different thing. Then we believed that Jesus was our Savior from the guilt of sin, and according to our faith it was unto us. Now we must believe that He is our Savior from the power of sin, and according to our faith it shall be unto us. Then we trusted Him for our justification, and it became ours; now we must trust Him for our sanctification, and it shall become ours also. Then we took Him as a Savior in the future from the penalties of our sins; now we must take Him as a Savior in the present from the bondage of our sins. Then He was our Redeemer, now He is to be our Life. Then He lifted us out of the pit, now He is to seat us in heavenly places with Himself.

I mean all this of course experimentally and practically. Theologically and judicially I know that every believer has everything the minute he is converted. But experimentally nothing is his until by faith he claims it. "Every place that the sole of your foot shall tread upon, that have I given unto you." God "hath blessed us with all spiritual blessings in heavenly places in Christ," but until we set the foot of faith upon them they do not practically become ours. "According to our faith," is always the limit and the rule.

But this faith of which I am speaking must be a present faith. No faith that is exercised in the future tense amounts to anything. A man may believe forever that his sins will be forgiven at some future time, and he will never find peace. He has to come to the now belief, and say by faith, "My sins are now forgiven," before he can live the new life. And, similarly, no faith which looks for a future deliverance from the power of sin will ever lead a soul into the life we are describing. The enemy delights in this future faith, for he knows it is powerless to accomplish any practical results. But he trembles and flees when the soul of the believer dares to claim a present deliverance, and to reckon itself now to be free from his power.

To sum up, then: in order to enter into this blessed interior life of rest and triumph, you have two steps to take: first, entire abandonment; and second, absolute faith. No matter what may be the complications of your peculiar experience, no matter what your difficulties or your surroundings or your associations, these two steps, definitely taken and unwaveringly persevered in, will certainly bring you out sooner or later into the green pastures and still waters of this Higher Christian Life. You may be sure of this. And if you will let every other consideration go, and simply devote your attention to these two points, and be very clear and definite about them, your progress will be rapid and your soul will reach its desired haven far sooner than now you can think possible.

Shall I repeat the steps, that there may be no mistake? You are a child of God, and long to please Him. You love your precious Savior, and are sick and weary of the sin that grieves Him. You long to be delivered from its power. Everything you have hitherto tried has failed to deliver you, and now in your despair you are asking if it can indeed be, as these happy people say, that the Lord is able and willing to deliver you. Surely you know in your very soul that He is; that to save you out of the hand of all your enemies is in fact just the very thing He came to do. Then trust Him. Commit your case to Him in an absolute abandonment, and believe that He undertakes it; and at once, knowing what He is and what He has said, claim that He does even now fully save. Just as you believed at first that He delivered you from the guilt of sin because He said so, believe now that He delivers you from the power of sin because He says so. Let your faith now lay hold of a new power in Christ. You have trusted Him as your dying Savior, now trust Him as your living Savior. Just as much as He came to deliver you from future punishment, did He also come to deliver you from present bondage. Just as truly as He came to bear your sins for you, has He come to live His life in you. You are as utterly powerless in the one case as in the other. You could as easily have got yourself rid of your own sins, as you could now accomplish for yourself practical righteousness. Christ, and Christ only, must do both for you, and your part in both cases is simply to give the thing to Him to do, and then believe that He does it.

A lady, now very eminent in this life of trust, when she was seeking in great darkness and perplexity to enter in, said to the friend who was trying to help her, "You all say, 'Abandon yourself, and trust, abandon yourself, and trust,' but I do not know how. I wish you would just do it out loud, so that I may see how you do it."

Shall I do it out loud for you?

"Lord Jesus, I believe that Thou art able and willing to deliver me from all the care, and unrest and bondage of my Christian life. I believe thou didst die to set me free, not only in the future, but now and here. I believe thou art stronger than Satan, and that thou canst keep me, even me, in my extreme of weakness, from falling into his snares or yielding obedience to his commands. And, Lord, I am going to trust thee to keep me. I have tried keeping myself, and have failed, and failed most grievously. I am absolutely helpless; so now I will trust thee. I will give myself to thee; I keep back no reserves. Body, soul, and spirit, I present myself to thee, a worthless lump of clay, to be made into anything thy love and thy wisdom shall choose. And now, I am thine. I believe thou dost accept that which I present to thee; I believe that this poor, weak, foolish heart has been taken possession of by thee, and thou hast even at this very moment begun to work in me to will and to do of thy good pleasure. I trust thee utterly, and I trust thee now!"

Are you afraid to take this step? Does it seem too sudden, too much like a leap in the dark? Do you not know that the steps of faith always "fall on the seeming void, but find the rock beneath"? A man, having to descend a well by a rope, found, to his horror, when he was a great way down, that it was too short. He had reached the end, and yet was, he estimated, about thirty feet from the bottom of the well. He knew not what to do. He had not the strength or skill to climb up the rope, and to let go was to be dashed to pieces. His arms began to fail, and at last he decided that as he could not hold on much longer, he might as well let go and meet his fate at once. He resigned himself to destruction, and loosened his grasp. He fell! To the bottom of the well it was—just three inches!

If ever your feet are to touch the "rock beneath," you must let go of every holding-place and drop into God; for there is no other way. And to do it now may save you months and even years of strain and weariness.

In all the old castles of England there used to be a place called the keep. It was always the strongest and best protected place in the castle, and in it were hidden all who were weak and helpless and unable to defend themselves in times of danger. Had you been a timid, helpless woman in such a castle during a time of siege, would it have seemed to you a leap in the dark to have hidden yourself there? Would you have been afraid to do it? And shall we be afraid to hide ourselves in the keeping power of our Divine Keeper, who neither slumbers nor sleeps, and who has promised to preserve our going out and our coming in, from this time forth and even forever more?

V

Difficulties Concerning Consecration

IT IS VERY IMPORTANT that Christians should not be ignorant of the devices of the enemy; for he stands ready to oppose every onward step of the soul's progress. And especially is he busy when he sees a believer awakened to a hunger and thirst after righteousness, and seeking to reach out to apprehend all the fullness that is in the Lord Jesus Christ for him.

One of the first difficulties he throws in the way of such a one is concerning consecration. The seeker after holiness is told that he must consecrate himself; and he endeavors to do so. But at once he meets with a difficulty. He has done it, as he thinks, and yet does not feel differently from before; nothing seems changed, as he has been led to expect it would be, and he is completely baffled, and asks the question almost despairingly, "How am I to know when I am consecrated?"

The one grand temptation which has met such a soul at this juncture is the temptation which never fails to assert itself on every possible occasion, and generally with marked success, and that is in reference to feeling. The soul cannot believe it is consecrated until it feels that it is; and because it does not feel that God has taken it in hand, it cannot believe that He has. As usual, it puts feeling first and faith second. Now, God's invariable rule is faith first and feeling second, in everything; and it is striving against the inevitable when we seek to make it different.

The way to meet this temptation, then, in reference to consecration, is simply to take God's side in the matter, and to put faith before feeling. Give yourself to the Lord definitely and fully, according to your present light, asking the Holy Spirit to show you all that is contrary to God, either in your heart or life. If He shows you anything, give it to the Lord immediately, and say in reference to it, "Thy will be done." If He shows you nothing, then you must believe that there is nothing, and must conclude that you have given Him all. Then you must believe that He takes you. You positively must not wait to feel either that you have given yourself or that He has taken you. You must simply believe it, and reckon it to be the case.

If you were to give an estate to a friend, you would have to give it, and he would have to receive it by faith. An estate is not a thing that can be picked up and handed over to another; the gift of it and its reception are altogether a mental transaction and therefore one of faith. Now, if you should give an estate one day to a friend, and then should go away and wonder whether you really had given it, and whether he had actually taken it and considered it his own, and should feel it necessary to go the next day and renew the gift; and if on the third day you should still feel a similar uncertainty about it, and should again go and renew the gift, and on the fourth day go through a like process, and so on, day after day for months and years, what would your friend think, and what at last would be the condition of your own mind in reference to it? Your friend certainly would begin to doubt whether you ever had intended to give it to him at all; and you yourself would be in such hopeless perplexity about it, that you would not know whether the estate was yours, or his, or whose it was.

Now, is not this very much the way in which you have been acting toward God in this matter of consecration? You have given yourself to Him over and over daily, perhaps for months, but you have invariably come away from your seasons of consecration wondering whether you really have given yourself after all, and whether He has taken you; and because you have not felt any differently, you have concluded at last, after many painful tossings, that the thing has not been done. Do you know, dear believer, that this sort of perplexity will last forever, unless you cut it short by faith? You must come to the point of reckoning the matter to be an accomplished and settled thing, and leaving it there, before you can possibly expect any change of feeling what ever.

The very law of offerings to the Lord settles this as a primary fact, that everything which is given to Him becomes by that very act something holy, set apart from all other things, and cannot without sacrilege be put to any other uses. "Notwithstanding, no devoted thing that a man shall devote unto the Lord of all that he hath, both of man and beast, and of the field of his possession, shall be sold or redeemed: every devoted thing is most holy unto the Lord." Having once given it to the Lord, the devoted thing henceforth was reckoned by all Israel as being the Lord's, and no one dared to stretch forth a hand to retake it. The giver might have made his offering very grudgingly and half-heartedly, but having made it, the matter was taken out of his hands altogether, and the devoted thing by God's own law became "most holy unto the Lord."

It was not the intention of the giver that made it holy, but the holiness of the receiver. "The altar sanctifies the gift." And an offering once laid upon the altar, from that moment belonged to the Lord. I can imagine an offerer who had deposited a gift, beginning to search his heart as to his sincerity and honesty in doing it, and coming back to the priest to say that he was afraid after all he had not given it right, or had not been perfectly sincere in giving it. I feel sure that the priest would have silenced him at once with saying, "As to how you gave your offering, or what were your motives in giving it, I do not know. The facts are that you did give it, and that it is the Lord's, for every devoted thing is most holy unto Him. It is too late to recall the transaction now." And not only the priest but all Israel would have been aghast at the man who, having once given his offering, should have reached out his hand to take it back. And yet, day after day, earnest-hearted Christians, who would have shuddered at such an act of sacrilege on the part of a Jew, are guilty in their own experience of a similar act, by giving themselves to the Lord in solemn consecration, and then through unbelief taking back that which they have given.

Because God is not visibly present to the eye, it is difficult to feel that a transaction with

Him is real. I suppose if, when we made our acts of consecration, we could actually see Him present with us, we should feel it to be a very real thing, and would realize that we had given our word to Him and could not dare to take it back, no matter how much we might wish to do so. Such a transaction would have to us the binding power that a spoken promise to an earthly friend always has to a man of honor. And what we need is to see that God's presence is a certain fact always, and that every act of our soul is done right before Him, and that a word spoken in prayer is as really spoken to Him, as if our eyes could see Him and our hands could touch Him. Then we shall cease to have such vague conceptions of our relations with Him, and shall feel the binding force of every word we say in His presence.

I know some will say here, "Ah, yes; but if He would only speak to me, and say that He took me when I gave myself to Him, I would have no trouble then in believing it." No, of course you would not; but He does not generally say this until the soul has first proved its loyalty by believing what He has already said. It is he that believeth who has the witness, not he that doubteth. And by His very command to us to present ourselves to Him a living sacrifice, He has pledged Himself to receive us. I cannot conceive of an honorable man asking another to give him a thing which, after all, he was doubtful about taking; still less can I conceive of a loving parent acting so toward a darling child. "My son, give me thy heart," is a sure warrant for knowing that the moment the heart is given, it will be taken by the One who has commanded the gift. We may, nay we must, feel the utmost confidence then that when we surrender ourselves to the Lord, according to His own command, He does then and there receive us, and from that moment we are His. A real transaction has taken place, which cannot be violated without dishonor on our part, and which we know will not be violated by Him.

In Deuteronomy 26:17, 18, 19, we see God's way of working under these circumstances:—

"Thou hast avouched the Lord this day to be thy God, and to walk in His ways and to keep His statutes, and His commandments, and His judgments, and to hearken unto His voice; and the Lord hath avouched thee this day to be His peculiar people, as He hath promised thee, and that thou shouldst keep all His commandments;...and that thou mayest be an holy people unto the Lord, as He hath spoken."

When we avouch the Lord to be our God, and that we will walk in His ways and keep His commandments, He avouches us to be His, and that we shall keep all His commandments.

And from that moment He takes possession of us. This has always been His principle of working, and it continues to be so. "Every devoted thing is most holy to the Lord." This seems to me so plain as scarcely to admit of a question.

But if the soul still feels in doubt or difficulty, let me refer you to a New Testament declaration which approaches the subject from a different side, but which settles it, I think, quite as definitely. It is in 1 John 5:14, 15, and reads: "And this is the confidence that we have in Him, that if we ask anything according to His will, He heareth us; and if we know that He hear us, whatsoever we ask, we know that we have the petitions that we desired of Him." Is it according to His will that you should be entirely consecrated to Him? There can be, of course, but one answer to this, for He has commanded it. Is it not also according to His will that He should work in you to will and to do of His good pleasure? This question also can have but one answer, for He has declared it to be His purpose. You know, then, that these things are according to His will, therefore on God's own word you are obliged to know that He hears you; and knowing this much, you are compelled to go further and know that you have the petitions that you have desired of Him. That you have, I say, not will have, or may have, but have now in actual possession.

It is thus that we "obtain promises" by faith. It is thus that we have "access by faith" into the grace that is given us in our Lord Jesus Christ. It is thus, and thus only, that we come to know our hearts are "purified by faith," and are enabled to live by faith, to stand by faith, to walk by faith.

I desire to make this subject so plain and practical that no one need have any further difficulty about it, and therefore I will repeat again just what must be the acts of your soul in order to bring you out of this difficulty about consecration.

I suppose that you have trusted the Lord Jesus for the forgiveness of your sins, and know something of what it is to belong to the family of God, and to be made an heir of God through faith in Christ. And now you feel springing up in your soul the longing to be conformed to the image of your Lord. In order for this, you know there must be an entire surrender of yourself to Him, that He may work in you all the good pleasure of His will; and you have tried over and over to do it, but hitherto without any apparent success.

At this point it is that I desire to help you. What you must do now is to come once more to Him in a surrender of your whole self to His will, as complete as you know how to make it. You must ask Him to reveal to you by His

Spirit any hidden rebellion; and if He reveals nothing, then you must believe that there is nothing, and that the surrender is complete. This must, then, be considered a settled matter. You have abandoned yourself to the Lord, and from henceforth you do not in any sense belong to yourself; you must never even so much as listen to a suggestion to the contrary. If the temptation comes to wonder whether you really have completely surrendered yourself, meet it with an assertion that you have. Do not even argue the matter. Repel any such idea instantly and with decision. You meant it then, you mean it now, you have really done it. Your emotions may clamor against the surrender, but your will must hold firm. It is your purpose God looks at, not your feelings about that purpose, and your purpose, or will, is therefore the only thing you need attend to.

The surrender, then, having been made, never to be questioned or recalled, the next point is to believe that God takes that which you have surrendered, and to reckon that it is His. Not that it will be at some future time, but is now; and that He has begun to work in you to will, and to do, of His good pleasure. And here you must rest. There is nothing more for you to do, for you are the Lord's now, absolutely and entirely in His hands, and He has undertaken the whole care and management and forming of you; and will, according to His Word, "work in you that which is well-pleasing in His sight through Jesus Christ." But you must hold steadily here. If you begin to question your surrender, or God's acceptance of it, then your wavering faith will produce a wavering experience, and He cannot work. But while you trust He works, and the result of His working always is to change you into the image of Christ, from glory to glory, by His mighty Spirit.

Do you, then, now at this moment surrender yourself wholly to Him? You answer, Yes. Then, my dear friend, begin at once to reckon that you are His; that He has taken you, and that He is working in you to will and to do of His good pleasure. And keep on reckoning this. You will find it a great help to put your reckoning into words, and to say over and over to yourself and to your God, "Lord, I am thine; I do yield myself up to thee entirely, and I believe that thou dost take me. I leave myself with thee. Work in me all the good pleasure of thy will, and I will only lie still in thy hands, and trust thee."

Make this a daily definite act of your will, and many times a day recur to it, as being your continual attitude before Him. Confess it to yourself. Confess it to your God. Confess it to your friends. Avouch the Lord to be your God continually and unwaveringly, and declare your purpose of walking in His ways and keeping His statutes; and you will find in practical experience that He has avouched you to be His peculiar people and that you shall keep all His commandments, and that you will be "an holy people unto the Lord, as He hath spoken."

A few simple rules may be found helpful here. I would advise the use of them in daily times of devotion, making them the definite test and attitude of the soul, until the light shines clearly on this matter.

I. Express in definite words your faith in Christ as your Savior; and acknowledge definitely that you believe He has reconciled you to God; according to 2 Corinthians 5:18, 19.

II. Definitely acknowledge God as your Father, and yourself as His redeemed and forgiven child; according to Galatians 5:6.

III. Definitely surrender yourself to be all the Lord's, body, soul, and spirit; and to obey Him in everything where His will is made known; according to Romans 12:12.

IV. Believe and continue to believe, against all seemings, that God takes possession of that which you thus abandon to Him, and that He will henceforth work in you to will and to do of His good pleasure, unless you consciously frustrate His grace; according to 2 Corinthians 6:17, 18, and Philippians 2:13.

V. Pay no attention to your feelings as a test of your relations with God, but simply attend to the state of your will and of your faith. And count all these steps you are now taking as settled, though the enemy may make it seem otherwise. Hebrews 10:22, 23.

VI. Never, under any circumstances, give way for one single moment to doubt or discouragement. Remember, that all discouragement is from the devil, and refuse to admit it; according to John 14:1, 27.

VII. Cultivate the habit of expressing your faith in definite words, and repeat often, "I am all the Lord's and He is working in me now to will and to do of His good pleasure;" according to Hebrews 13:21.

VI

Difficulties Concerning Faith

THE NEXT STEP after consecration, in the soul's progress out of the wilderness of Christian experience, into the land that floweth with milk and honey, is that of faith. And here, as in the first step, the enemy is very skillful in making difficulties and interposing obstacles.

The child of God, having had his eyes opened to see the fullness there is in Jesus for him, and having been made to long to appropriate that fullness to himself, is met with the assertion on the part of every teacher to whom he applies, that this fullness is only to be received by faith. But the subject of faith is involved in such a hopeless mystery in his mind, that this assertion, instead of throwing light upon the way of entrance, only seems to make it more difficult and involved than ever.

"Of course it is to be by faith," he says, "for I know that everything in the Christian life is by faith. But then, that is just what makes it so hard, for I have no faith, and I do not even know what it is, nor how to get it." And, baffled at the very outset by this insuperable difficulty, he is plunged into darkness, and almost despair.

This trouble all arises from the fact that the subject of faith is very generally misunderstood; for in reality faith is the plainest and most simple thing in the world, and the most easy of attainment.

Your idea of faith, I suppose, has been something like this. You have looked upon it as in some way a sort of thing, either a religious exercise of soul, or an inward gracious disposition of heart; something tangible, in fact, which, when you have got, you can look at and rejoice over, and use as a passport to God's favor, or a coin with which to purchase His gifts. And you have been praying for faith, expecting all the while to get something like this, and never having received any such thing, you are insisting upon it that you have no faith. Now faith, in fact, is not in the least this sort of thing. It is nothing at all tangible. It is simply believing God, and, like sight, it is nothing apart from its object. You might as well shut your eyes and look inside to see whether you have sight, as to look inside to discover whether you have faith. You see something, and thus know that you have sight; you believe something, and thus know that you have faith. For, as sight is only seeing, so faith is only believing. And as the only necessary thing about seeing is that you see the thing as it is, so the only necessary thing about believing is that you believe the thing as it is. The virtue does not lie in your believing, but in the thing you believe. If you believe the truth you are saved; if you believe a lie you are lost. The believing in both cases is the same; the things believed in are exactly opposite, and it is this which makes the mighty difference. Your salvation comes, not because your faith saves you, but because it links you on to the Savior who saves; and your believing is really nothing but the link.

I do beg of you to recognize, then, the extreme simplicity of faith; that it is nothing more nor less than just believing God when He says He either has done something for us, or will do it; and then trusting Him to do it. It is so simple that it is hard to explain. If anyone asks me what it means to trust another to do a piece of work for me, I can only answer that it means letting that other one do it, and feeling it perfectly unnecessary for me to do it myself. Everyone of us has trusted very important pieces of work to others in this way, and has felt perfect rest in thus trusting, because of the confidence we have had in those who have undertaken to do it. How constantly do mothers trust their most precious infants to the care of nurses, and feel no shadow of anxiety? How continually we are all of us trusting our health and our lives, without a thought of fear, to cooks and coachmen, engine drivers, railway conductors, and all sorts of paid servants, who have us completely at their mercy, and could plunge us into misery or death in a moment, if they chose to do so, or even if they failed in the necessary carefulness? All this we do, and make no fuss about it. Upon the slightest acquaintance, often, we thus put our trust in people, requiring only the general knowledge of human nature, and the common rules of human intercourse; and we never feel as if we were doing anything in the least remarkable.

You have done all this yourself, dear reader, and are doing it continually. You would not be able to live in this world and go through the customary routine of life a single day, if you could not trust your fellow men. And it never enters into your head to say you cannot.

But yet you do not hesitate to say, continually, that you cannot trust your God!

I wish you would just now try to imagine yourself acting in your human relations as you do in your spiritual relations. Suppose you should begin tomorrow with the notion in your head that you could not trust anybody, because you had no faith. When you sat down to breakfast you would say, "I cannot eat anything on this table, for I have no faith, and I cannot believe the cook has not put poison in the coffee, or that the butcher has not sent home diseased meat." So you would go starving away. Then when you went out to your daily avocations, you would say, "I cannot ride in the railway train, for I have no faith, and therefore I cannot trust the engineer, nor the conductor, nor the builders of the carriages, nor the managers of the road." So you would be compelled to walk everywhere, and grow unutterably weary in the effort, besides being actually unable to reach many of the places you could have reached in the train. Then, when your friends met you with any statements, or your business agent with any accounts, you would say, "I am very sorry that I cannot believe you, but I have no faith, and never can believe anybody." If you opened a newspaper you would be forced to lay it down again, saying, "I really cannot believe a word this paper says, for I have no faith; I do not believe there is any such person as the queen, for I never saw her; nor any such country as Ireland, for I was never there. And I have no faith, so of course I cannot believe anything that I have not actually felt and touched myself. It is a great trial, but I cannot help it, for I have no faith."

Just picture such a day as this, and see how disastrous it would be to yourself, and what utter folly it would appear to anyone who should watch you through the whole of it. Realize how your friends would feel insulted, and how your servants would refuse to serve you another day. And then ask yourself the question, if this want of faith in your fellow men would be so dreadful, and such utter folly, what must it be when you tell God that you have no power to trust Him nor to believe His Word; that "it is a great trial, but you cannot help it, for you have no faith"?

Is it possible that you can trust your fellow men and cannot trust your God? That you can receive the "witness of men," and cannot receive the "witness of God"? That you can believe man's records, and cannot believe God's record? That you can commit your dearest earthly interests to your weak, failing fellow creatures without a fear, and are afraid to commit your spiritual interests to the blessed Savior who shed His blood for the very purpose of saving you, and who is declared to be "able to save you to the uttermost"?

Surely, surely, dear believer, you, whose very name of believer implies that you can believe, will never again dare to excuse yourself on the plea of having no faith. For when you say this, you mean of course that you have no faith in God, since you are not asked to have faith in yourself, and you would be in a very wrong condition of soul if you had. Let me beg of you then, when you think or say these things, always to complete the sentence and say, "I have no faith in God, I cannot believe God"; and this I am sure will soon become so dreadful to you, that you will not dare to continue it.

But you say, I cannot believe without the Holy Spirit. Very well, will you conclude that your want of faith is because of the failure of the blessed Spirit to do His work? For if it is, then surely you are not to blame, and need feel no condemnation; and all exhortations to you to believe are useless.

But, no! Do you not see that, in taking up this position, that you have no faith and cannot believe, you are not only "making God a liar," but you are also manifesting an utter want of confidence in the Holy Spirit? For He is always ready to help our infirmities. We never have to wait for Him, He is always waiting for us. And I for my part have such absolute confidence in the blessed Holy Ghost, and in His being always ready to do his work, that I dare to say to everyone of you, that you can believe now, at this very moment, and that if you do not, it is not the Spirit's fault, but your own.

Put your will then over on to the believing side. Say, "Lord I will believe, I do believe," and continue to say it. Insist upon believing, in the face of every suggestion of doubt with which you may be tempted. Out of your very unbelief, throw yourself headlong on to the word and promises of God, and dare to abandon yourself to the keeping and saving power of the Lord Jesus. If you have ever trusted a precious interest in the hands of any earthly friend, I conjure you, trust yourself now and all your spiritual interests in the hands of your Heavenly Friend, and never, never, NEVER allow yourself to doubt again.

And remember, there are two things which are more utterly incompatible than even oil and water, and these two are trust and worry. Would you call it trust, if you should give something into the hands of a friend to attend to for you, and then should spend your nights and days in anxious thought and worry as to whether it would be rightly and successfully done? And can you call it trust, when you have given the saving and keeping of your soul into the hands of the Lord, if day after day and night after night you are spending hours of anxious thought and questionings about the matter? When a believer really trusts anything, he ceases to worry about that thing which he has trusted. And when he worries, it is a plain proof that he does not trust. Tested by this rule how little real trust there is in the Church of Christ! No wonder our Lord asked the pathetic question, "When the Son of Man cometh shall he find faith on the earth?" He will find plenty of activity, a great deal of earnestness, and doubtless many consecrated hearts; but shall he find faith, the one thing He values more than all the rest? It is a solemn question, and I would that every Christian heart would ponder it well. But may the time past of our lives suffice us to have shared in the unbelief of the world; and let us every one, who know our blessed Lord and His unspeakable trustworthiness, set to our seal that He is true, by our generous abandonment of trust in Him.

I remember, very early in my Christian life, having every tender and loyal impulse within me stirred to its depths by an appeal I met with in a volume of old sermons to all who loved the Lord Jesus, that they should show to others how worthy He was of being trusted, by the steadfastness of their own faith in Him. And I remember my soul cried out with an eager longing that I might be called to walk in paths so dark, that an utter abandonment of trust might be my blessed and glorious privilege.

"Ye have not passed this way heretofore," it may be; but today it is your happy privilege to prove, as never before, your loyal confidence in the Lord by starting out with Him on a life and walk of faith, lived moment by moment in absolute and childlike trust in Him.

You have trusted Him in a few things, and He has not failed you. Trust Him now for everything, and see if He does not do for you exceeding abundantly above all that you could ever have asked or thought; not according to your power or capacity, but according to His own mighty power, that will work in you all the good pleasure of His most blessed will.

You find no difficulty in trusting the Lord with the management of the universe and all the outward creation, and can your case be any more complex or difficult than these, that you need to be anxious or troubled about his management of it. Away with such unworthy doubtings! Take your stand on the power and trustworthiness of your God, and see how quickly all difficulties will vanish before a steadfast determination to believe. Trust in the dark, trust in the light, trust at night, and trust in the morning, and you will find that the faith, which may begin by a mighty effort, will end sooner or later by becoming the easy and natural habit of the soul.

All things are possible to God, and "all things are possible to him that believeth." Faith has, in times past, "subdued kingdoms, wrought righteousness, obtained promises, stopped the mouths of lions, quenched the violence of fire, escaped the edge of the sword, waxed valiant in fight, turned to flight the armies of the aliens"; and faith can do it again. For our Lord Himself says unto us, "If ye have faith as a grain of mustard seed, ye shall say unto this mountain, Remove hence to yonder place, and it shall remove; and nothing shall be impossible unto you."

If you are a child of God at all, you must have at least as much faith as a grain of mustard seed, and therefore you dare not say again that you cannot trust because you have no faith. Say rather, "I can trust my Lord, and I will trust Him, and not all the powers of earth or hell shall be able to make me doubt my wonderful, glorious, faithful Redeemer!"

In that greatest event of this century, the emancipation of our slaves, there is a wonderful illustration of the way of faith. The slaves received their freedom by faith, just as we must receive ours. The good news was carried to them that the government had proclaimed their freedom. As a matter of fact they were free the moment the Proclamation was issued, but as a matter of experience they did not come into actual possession of their freedom until they had heard the good news and had believed it. The fact had to come first, but the believing was necessary before the fact became available, and the feeling would follow last of all. This is the divine order always, and the order of common sense as well.

I. The fact.

II. The faith.

III. The feeling.

But man reverses this order and says, I. The feeling. II. The faith. III. The fact.

Had the slaves followed man's order in regard to their emancipation, and refused to believe in it until they had first felt it, they might have remained in slavery a long while. I have heard of one instance where this was the case. In a little out-of-the-way Southern town a Northern lady found, about two or three years after the war was over, some slaves who had not yet taken possession of their freedom. An assertion of hers, that the North had set them free, aroused the attention of an old colored auntie, who interrupted her with the eager question,—

"O missus, is we free?"

"Of course you are," replied the lady.

"O missus, is you sure?" urged the woman, with intensest eagerness.

"Certainly, I am sure," answered the lady. "Why, is it possible you did not know it?"

"Well," said the woman, "we heered tell as how we was free, and we asked master, and he 'lowed we wasn't, and so we was afraid to go.

And then we heered tell again, and we went to the cunnel, and he 'lowed we'd better stay with ole massa. And so we's just been off and on. Sometimes we'd hope we was free, and then again we'd think we wasn't. But now, missus, if you is sure we is free, won't you tell me all about it?"

Seeing that this was a case of real need, the lady took the pains to explain the whole thing to the poor woman; all about the war, and the Northern army, and Abraham Lincoln, and his Proclamation of Emancipation, and the present freedom.

The poor slave listened with the most intense eagerness. She heard the good news. She believed it. And when the story was ended, she walked out of the room with an air of the utmost independence, saying as she went,— "I's free! I's ain't agoing to stay with ol massa any longer!"

She had at last received her freedom, and she had received it by faith. The government had declared her to be free long before, but this had not availed her, because she had never yet believed in this declaration. The good news had not profited her, not being "mixed with faith" in the one who heard it. But now she believed, and believing, she dared to reckon herself to be free. And this, not because of any change in herself or her surroundings, not because of any feelings of emotions of her own heart, but because she had confidence in the word of another, who had come to her proclaiming the good news of her freedom.

Need I make the application? In a hundred different messages God has declared to us our freedom, and over and over He urges us to reckon ourselves free. Let your faith then lay hold of His Proclamation, and assert it to be true. Declare to yourself, to your friends, and in the secret of your soul to God, that you are free. Refuse to listen for a moment to the lying assertions of your old master, that you are still his slave. Let nothing discourage you, no inward feelings nor outward signs. Hold on to your reckoning in the face of all opposition, and I can promise you, on the authority of our Lord, that according to your faith it shall be unto you.

Of all the worships we can bring our God, none is so sweet to Him as this utter self-abandoning trust, and none brings Him so much glory. Therefore in every dark hour remember that "though now for a season, if need be, ye are in heaviness through manifold temptations," it is in order that "the trial of your faith, being much more precious than of gold that perisheth, though it be tried with fire, might be found unto praise, and honor, and glory, at the appearing of Jesus Christ."

VII

Difficulties
Concerning the Will

WHEN THE CHILD OF GOD has, by the way of entire abandonment and absolute trust, stepped out of himself into Christ, and has begun to know something of the blessedness of the life hid with Christ in God, there is one form of difficulty which is very likely to start up in his path. After the first emotions of peace and rest have somewhat subsided, or if, as is sometimes the case, they have never seemed to come at all, he begins to feel such an utter unreality in the things he has been passing through, that he seems to himself like a hypocrite, when he says or even thinks they are real. It seems to him that his belief does not go below the surface, that it is a mere lip-belief, and therefore of no account, and that his surrender is not a surrender of the heart, and therefore cannot be acceptable to God. He is afraid to say he is altogether the Lord's, for fear he will be telling an untruth, and yet he cannot bring himself to say he is not, because he longs for it so intensely. The difficulty is real and very disheartening.

But there is nothing here which will not be very easily overcome, when the Christian once thoroughly understands the principles of the new life, and has learned how to live in it. The common thought is that this life hid with Christ in God is to be lived in the emotions, and consequently all the attention of the soul is directed toward them, and as they are satisfactory or otherwise, the soul rests or is troubled. Now the truth is that this life is not to be lived in the emotions at all, but in the will, and therefore the varying states of emotion do not in the least disturb or affect the reality of the life, if only the will is kept steadfastly abiding in its center, God's will.

To make this plain, I must enlarge a little. Fenelon says somewhere, that "pure religion resides in the will alone." By this he means that as the will is the governing power in the man's nature, if the will is set straight, all the rest of the nature must come into harmony. By the will I do not mean the wish of the man, nor even his purpose, but the choice, the deciding power, the king, to which all that is in the man must yield obedience. It is the man, in short, the "Ego," that which we feel to be ourselves.

It is sometimes thought that the emotions are the governing power in our nature. But, as a matter of practical experience, I think we all of us know that there is something within us, behind our emotions, and behind our wishes,—an independent self,—that after all decides everything and controls everything. Our emotions belong to us, and are suffered and enjoyed by us, but they are not ourselves; and if God is to take possession of us, it must be into this central will or personality that He shall enter. If, then, He is reigning there by the power of His Spirit, all the rest of our nature must come under His sway; and as the will is, so is the man.

The practical bearing of this truth upon the difficulty I am considering is very great. For the decisions of our will are often so directly opposed to the decisions of our emotions, that, if we are in the habit of considering our emotions as the test, we shall be very apt to feel like hypocrites in declaring those things to be real which our will alone has decided. But the moment we see that the will is king, we shall utterly disregard anything that clamors against it, and shall claim as real its decisions, let the emotions rebel as they may.

I am aware that this is a difficult subject to deal with, but it is so exceedingly practical in its bearing upon the life of faith, that I beg of you, dear reader, not to turn from it until you have mastered it.

Perhaps an illustration will help you. A young man of great intelligence, seeking to enter into this new life, was utterly discouraged at finding himself the slave to an inveterate habit of doubting. To his emotions nothing seemed true, nothing seemed real; and the more he struggled the more unreal did it all become. He was told this secret concerning the will, that if he would only put his will over on to the believing side; if he would choose to believe; if, in short, he would, in the Ego of his nature, say, "I will believe! I do believe!" he need not trouble about his emotions, for they would find themselves compelled, sooner or later, to come into harmony. "What!" he said, "do you mean to tell me that I can choose to believe in that way, when nothing seems true to me; and will that kind of believing be real?" "Yes," was the answer, "your part is only this,— to put your will over on God's side in this matter of believing; and when you do this, God immediately takes possession of it, and works in you to will of His good pleasure, and you will soon find that He has brought all the rest of your nature into subjection to Him- self." "Well," was the answer, "I can do this. I cannot control my emotions, but I can con- trol my will, and the new life begins to look possible to me, if it is only my will that needs to be set straight in the matter. I can give my will to God, and I do!"

From that moment, disregarding all the pitiful clamoring of his emotions, which continually accused him of being a wretched hypocrite, this young man held on steadily to the decision of his will, answering every accusation with the continued assertion that he chose to believe, he meant to believe, he did believe; until at the end of a few days he found himself triumphant, with every emotion and every thought brought into captivity to the mighty power of the blessed Spirit of God, who had taken possession of the will thus put into His hands. He had held fast the profession of his faith without wavering, although it had seemed to him that, as to real faith itself, he had none to hold fast. At times it had drained all the will power he possessed to his lips, to say that he believed, so contrary was it to all the evidence of his senses or of his emotions. But he had caught the idea that his will was, after all, himself, and that if he kept that on God's side, he was doing all he could do, and that God alone could change his emotions or control his being. The result has been one of the grandest Christian lives I know of, in its marvelous simplicity, directness, and power over sin.

The secret lies just here. That our will, which is the spring of all our actions, is in our natural state under the control of self, and self has been working it in us to our utter ruin and misery. Now God says, "Yield yourselves up unto Me, as those that are alive from the dead, and I will work in you to will and to do of my good pleasure." And the moment we yield ourselves, He of course takes possession of us, and does work in us "that which is well pleasing in His sight through Jesus Christ," giving us the mind that was in Christ, and transforming us into His image (see Romans 12:1, 2).

Let us take another illustration. A lady, who had entered into this life hid with Christ, was confronted by a great prospective trial. Every emotion she had within her rose up in rebellion against it, and had she considered her emotions to be her king, she would have been in utter despair. But she had learned this secret of the will, and knowing that, at the bottom, she herself did really choose the will of God for her portion, she did not pay the slightest attention to her emotions, but persisted in meeting every thought concerning the trial, with the words, repeated over and over, "Thy will be done! Thy will be done!" asserting in the face of all her rebelling feelings, that she did submit her will to God's, that she chose to submit, and that His will should be and was her delight! The result was, that in an incredibly short space of time every thought was brought into captivity; and she began to find even her very emotions rejoicing in the will of God.

Again, there was a lady who had a besetting sin, which in her emotions she dearly loved, but which in her will she hated. Having believed herself to be necessarily under the control of her emotions, she had therefore thought she was unable to conquer it, unless her emotions should first be changed. But she learned this secret concerning the will, and going to her knees she said, "Lord, Thou seest that with one part of my nature I love this sin, but in my real central self I hate it. And now I put my will over on thy side in the matter. I will not do it any more. Do thou deliver me." Immediately God took possession of the will thus surrendered to Himself, and began to work in her, so that His will in the matter gained the mastery over her emotions, and she found herself delivered, not by the power of an outward commandment, but by the inward power of the Spirit of God working in her that which was well pleasing in His sight.

And now, dear Christian, let me show you how to apply this principle to your difficulties. Cease to consider your emotions, for they are only the servants; and regard simply your will, which is the real king in your being. Is that given up to God? Is that put into His hands? Does your will decide to believe? Does your will choose to obey? If this is the case, then you are in the Lord's hands, and you decide to believe, and you choose to obey; for your will is yourself. And the thing is done. The transaction with God is as real, where only your will acts, as when every emotion coincides. It does not seem as real to you; but in God's sight it is as real. And when you have got hold of this secret, and have discovered that you need not attend to your emotions, but simply to the state of your will, all the Scripture commands, to yield yourself to God, to present yourself a living sacrifice to Him, to abide in Christ, to walk in the light, to die to self, become possible to you; for you are conscious that, in all these, your will can act, and can take God's side: whereas, if it had been your emotions that must do it, you would sink down in despair, knowing them to be utterly uncontrollable.

When, then, this feeling of unreality or hypocrisy comes, do not be troubled by it. It is only in your emotions, and is not worth a moment's thought. Only see to it that your will is in God's hands; that your inward self is abandoned to His working; that your choice, your decision, is on His side; and there leave it. Your surging emotions, like a tossing vessel, which, by degrees, yield to the steady pull of the cable, finding themselves attached to the mighty power of God by the choice of your will, must inevitably come into captivity, and give in their allegiance to Him; and you will verify the truth of the saying that, "If any man will do His will, he shall know of the doctrine."

The will is like a wise mother in a nursery; the feelings are like a set of clamoring, crying children. The mother decides upon a certain course of action, which she believes to be right and best. The children clamor against it, and declare it shall not be. But the mother, knowing that she is mistress and not they, pursues her course calmly, unmoved by their clamors, and takes no notice of them except in trying to soothe and quiet them. The result is that the children are sooner or later compelled to yield, and fall in with the decision of the mother. Thus order and harmony are preserved. But if that mother should for a moment let in the thought that the children were the mistresses instead of herself, confusion would reign unchecked. Such instances have been known in family life! And in how many souls at this very moment is there nothing but confusion, simply because the feelings are allowed to govern, instead of the will!

Remember, then, that the real thing in your experience is what your will decides, and not the verdict of your emotions; and that you are far more in danger of hypocrisy and untruth in yielding to the assertions of your feelings, than in holding fast to the decision of your will. So that, if your will is on God's side, you are no hypocrite at this moment in claiming as your own the blessed reality of belonging altogether to Him, even though your emotions may all declare the contrary.

I am convinced that, throughout the Bible, the expressions concerning the "heart" do not mean the emotions, that which we now understand by the word "heart"; but they mean the will, the personality of the man, the man's own central self; and that the object of God's dealings with man is that this "I" may be yielded up to Him, and this central life abandoned to His entire control. It is not the feelings of the man God wants, but the man himself.

Have you given Him yourself, dear reader? Have you abandoned your will to His working? Do you consent to surrender the very center of your being into His hands? Then, let the outposts of your nature clamor as they may, it is your right to say, even now, with the apostle, "I am crucified with Christ; nevertheless, I live; yet not I, but Christ liveth in me: and the life which I now live in the flesh, I live by the faith of the Son of God, who loved me, and gave Himself for me."

After this had been enclosed to the printer, the following remarkable practical illustration of its teaching was presented by Pastor Theodore Monod, of Paris. It is the experience of a Presbyterian minister, which this pastor had carefully kept for many years:—

Newburgh, Sept. 26, 1842.

DEAR BROTHER,—I take a few moments of that time which I have devoted to the Lord, in writing a short epistle to you, His servant. It is sweet to feel we are wholly the Lord's, that He has received us and called us His. This is religion,—a relinquishment of the principle of self-ownership, and the adoption in full of the abiding sentiment, "I am not my own, I am bought with a price." Since I last saw you, I have been pressing forward, and yet there has been nothing remarkable in my experience of which I can speak; indeed I do not know that it is best to look for remarkable things; but strive to be holy, as God is holy, pressing right on toward the mark of the prize.

I do not feel myself qualified to instruct you; I can only tell you the way in which I was led. The Lord deals differently with different souls, and we ought not to attempt to copy the experience of others, yet there are certain things which must be attended to by every one who is seeking after a clean heart.

There must be a personal consecration of all to God, a covenant made with God, that we will be wholly and forever His. This I made intellectually without any change in my feeling, with a heart full of hardness and darkness, unbelief and sin and insensibility.

I covenanted to be the Lord's, and laid all upon the altar, a living sacrifice, to the best of my ability. And after I rose from my knees, I was conscious of no change in my feeling. I was painfully conscious that there was no change. But yet I was sure that I did, with all the sincerity and honesty of purpose of which I was capable, make an entire and eternal consecration of myself to God. I did not then consider the work done by any means, but I engaged to abide in a state of entire devotion to God, a living perpetual sacrifice. And now came the effort to do this.

I knew that I must believe that God did accept me, and had come in to dwell in my heart. I was conscious I did not believe this, and yet I desired to do so.

I read with much prayer John's First Epistle, and endeavored to assure my heart of God's love to me as an individual. I was sensible that my heart was full of evil. I seemed to have no power to overcome pride, or to repel evil thoughts, which I abhorred. But Christ was manifested to destroy the works of the devil, and it was clear that the sin in my heart was the work of the devil. I was enabled, therefore, to believe that God was working in me, to will and to do, while I was working out my own salvation with fear and trembling.

I was convinced of unbelief, that it was voluntary and criminal. I clearly saw that unbelief was an awful sin, it made the faithful God a liar. The Lord brought before me my besetting sins which had dominion over me, especially preaching myself instead of Christ, and indulging self-complacent thoughts after preaching. I was enabled to make myself of no reputation, and to seek the honor which cometh from God only. Satan struggled hard to beat me back from the Rock of Ages but thanks to God I finally hit upon the method of living by the moment, and then I found rest.

I trusted in the blood of Jesus already shed, as a sufficient atonement for all my past sins, and the future I committed wholly to the Lord, agreeing to do His will under all circumstances as He should make it known, and I saw that all I had to do was to look to Jesus for a present supply of grace, and to trust Him to cleanse my heart and keep me from sin at the present moment.

I felt shut up to a momentary dependence upon the grace of Christ. I would not permit the adversary to trouble me about the past or future, for I each moment looked for the supply for that moment. I agreed that I would be a child of Abraham, and walk by naked faith in the Word of God, and not by inward feelings and emotions: I would seek to be a Bible Christian. Since that time, the Lord has given me a steady victory over sins which before enslaved me. I delight in the Lord, and in His Word. I delight in my work as a minister: my fellowship is with the Father and with His Son Jesus Christ. I am a babe in Christ; I know my progress has been small compared with that made by many. My feelings vary, but when I have feelings, I praise God, and I trust in His Word; and when I am empty and my feelings are gone, I do the same. I have covenanted to walk by faith and not by feelings.

The Lord, I think, is beginning to revive His work among my people. "Praise the Lord." May the Lord fill you with all His fullness and give you all the mind of Christ. Oh, be faithful! Walk before God and be perfect. Preach the Word. Be instant in season and out of season. The Lord loves you. He works with you. Rest your soul fully upon that promise, "Lo, I am with you always, even unto the end of the world."

Your fellow soldier,
William Hill

There may be some who will object to this teaching, that it ignores the work of the blessed Holy Spirit. But I must refer such to the introductory of this book, in which I have fully explained myself. I am not writing upon that side of the subject; I am considering man's part in the matter, and not the part of the Spirit. I realize intensely that all a man can do or try to do would be utterly useless, if the Holy Spirit did not work in that man continually. And it is only because I believe in the Spirit as a mighty power, ever present and always ready to do his work, that I can write as I do. But, like the wind that bloweth where it listeth, and thou hearest the sound thereof, but canst not tell whence it cometh, and whither it goeth, the operations of the Spirit are beyond our control, and also beyond our comprehension.

The results we know, and the steps on our part which lead to those results, but we know nothing more. And yet, like a workman in a great manufactory, who does not question the commands of his employer, and is not afraid to undertake apparent impossibilities, because he knows there is a mighty unseen power, called steam, behind his machinery, which can accomplish it all, so we dare to urge upon men that they shall simply and courageously set themselves to do that which they are commanded to do, because we know that the mighty Spirit will never fail to supply at each moment the necessary power for that moment's act. And we boldly claim that we who thus write can say from our very hearts, as earnestly and as solemnly as any other Christians, We believe in the Holy Ghost.

VIII

Difficulties Concerning Guidance

YOU HAVE NOW BEGUN, dear reader, the life of faith. You have given yourself to the Lord to be His wholly and altogether, and He has taken you and has begun to mould and fashion you into a vessel unto His honor. Your one most earnest desire is to be very pliable in His hands, and to follow Him whithersoever He may lead you, and you are trusting Him to work in you to will and to do of His good pleasure. But you find a great difficulty here. You have not learned yet to know the voice of the Good Shepherd, and are therefore in great doubt and perplexity as to what really is His will concerning you.

Perhaps there are certain paths into which God seems to be calling you, of which your friends utterly disapprove. And these friends, it may be, are older than yourself in the Christian life, and seem to you also to be much further advanced. You can scarcely bear to differ from them or distress them; and you feel also very diffident of yielding to any seeming impressions of duty of which they do not approve. And yet you cannot get rid of these impressions, and you are plunged into great doubt and uneasiness.

There is a way out of all these difficulties to the fully surrendered soul. I would repeat, fully surrendered, because if there is any reserve of will upon any point, it becomes almost impossible to find out the mind of God in reference to that point; and therefore the first thing is to be sure that you really do purpose to obey the Lord in every respect. If however this is the case, and your soul only needs to know the will of God in order to consent to it, then you surely cannot doubt His willingness to make His will known, and to guide you in the right paths. There are many very clear promises in reference to this. Take, for instance, John 10:3, 4: "He calleth His own sheep by name, and leadeth them out. And when He putteth forth His own sheep He goeth before them, and the sheep follow Him, for they know His voice." Or, John 14:26: "But the Comforter, which is the Holy Ghost, whom the Father will send in my name, He shall teach you all things, and bring all things to your remembrance, whatsoever I have said unto you." Or, James 1:5, 6: "If any of you lack wisdom, let Him ask of God, that giveth to all men liberally, and upbraideth not; and it shall be given him." With such passages as these, and many more like them, we must believe that Divine guidance is promised to us, and our faith must confidently look for and expect it. This is essential; for in James 1:6, 7, we are told, "Let him ask in faith nothing wavering. For he that wavereth is like a wave of the sea, driven with the wind and tossed. For let not such a man think that he shall receive anything of the Lord."

Settle this point then first of all, that Divine guidance has been promised, and that you are sure to have it, if you ask for it; and let no suggestion of doubt turn you from this.

Next, you must remember that our God has all knowledge and all wisdom, and that therefore it is very possible He may guide you into paths wherein He knows great blessings are awaiting you, but which to the shortsighted human eyes around you seem sure to result in confusion and loss. You must recognize the fact that God's thoughts are not as man's thoughts, nor His ways as man's ways; and that He who knows the end of things from the beginning alone can judge of what the results of any course of action may be. You must therefore realize that His very love for you may perhaps lead you to run counter to the loving wishes of even your dearest friends. You must learn from Luke 14:26-33, and similar passages, that in order, not to be saved only, but to be a disciple or follower of your Lord, you may perhaps be called upon to forsake all that you have, and to turn your backs on even father or mother, or brother or sister, or husband or wife, or it may be your own life also. Unless the possibility of this is clearly recognized, the soul would be very likely to get into difficulty, because it often happens that the child of God who enters upon this life of obedience is sooner or later led into paths which meet with the disapproval of those he best loves; and unless he is prepared for this, and can trust the Lord through it all, he will scarcely know what to do.

All this, it will of course be understood, is perfectly in harmony with those duties of honor and love which we owe to one another in the various relations of life. The nearer we are to Christ, the more shall we be enabled to exemplify the meekness and gentleness of our Lord, and the more tender will be our consideration for those who are our natural guardians and counselors. The Master's guidance will always manifest itself by the Master's Spirit, and where, in obedience to Him, we are led to act contrary to the advice or wishes of our friends, we shall prove that this is our motive, by the love and patience which will mark our conduct.

But this point having been settled, we come now to the question as to how God's guidance is to come to us, and how we shall be able to know His voice.

There are four especial ways in which God speaks: by the voice of Scripture, the voice of the inward impressions of the Holy Spirit, the voice of our own higher judgment, and the voice of providential circumstances.

Where these four harmonize, it is safe to say that God speaks. For I lay it down as a foundation principle, which no one can gainsay, that of course His voice will always be in harmony with itself, no matter in how many different ways He may speak. The voices may be many, the message can be but one. If God tells me in one voice to do or to leave undone anything, He cannot possibly tell me the opposite in another voice. If there is a contradiction in the voices, the speaker cannot be the same. Therefore, my rule for distinguishing the voice of God would be to bring it to the test of this harmony.

If I have an impression, therefore, I must see if it is in accordance with Scripture, and whether it commends itself to my own higher judgment, and also whether, as we Quakers say, "way opens" for its carrying out. If either one of these tests fail, it is not safe to proceed; but I must wait in quiet trust until the Lord shows me the point of harmony, which He surely will, sooner or later, if it is His voice that has spoken.

For we must not overlook the fact that there are other voices that speak to the soul. There is the loud and clamoring voice of self, that is always seeking to be heard. And there are the voices, too, of evil and deceiving spirits, who lie in wait to entrap every traveler entering these higher regions of the spiritual life. In the same epistle which tells us that we are seated in "heavenly places in Christ" (Ephesians 2:6), we are also told that we shall have to fight there with spiritual enemies (Ephesians 6:12). These spiritual enemies, whoever or whatever they may be, must necessarily communicate with us by means of our spiritual faculties, and their voices, therefore, will be, as the voice of God is, an inward impression made upon our spirits.

Therefore, just as the Holy Spirit may tell us, by impressions, what is the will of God concerning us, so also will these spiritual enemies tell us, by impressions, what is their will concerning us, though not of course giving it their name. It is very plain, therefore, that we must have some test or standard by which to try these inward impressions, in order that we may know whose voice it is that is speaking. And that test will always be the harmony to which I have referred. Sometimes, under a mistaken idea of exalting the Divine Spirit, earnest and honest Christians have ignored and even violated the teachings of Scripture, have disregarded the plain pointings of Providence, and have outraged their own higher judgment. God, who sees the sincerity of their hearts, can and does pity and forgive, but the consequences as to this life are often very sad.

Our first test, therefore, of the Divine authority of any voice which may seem to speak to us, must be its harmony in moral character with the mind and will of God, as revealed to us in the Gospel of Christ. Whatever is contrary to this cannot be Divine, because God cannot contradict Himself.

Until we have found and obeyed God's will in reference to any subject, as it is revealed in the Bible, we cannot expect a separate direct personal revelation. A great many fatal mistakes are made in this matter of guidance, by the overlooking of this simple rule. Where our Father has written out for us plain directions about anything, He will not, of course, make an especial revelation to us concerning it. No man, for instance, needs or could expect any direct revelation to tell him not to steal, because God has already in the Scriptures plainly declared His will about it. This seems such an obvious thing that I would not speak of it, but that I have frequently met with Christians who have altogether overlooked it, and have gone off into fanaticism as the result. For the Scriptures are far more explicit even about details than most people think. And there are not many important affairs in life for which a clear direction may not be found in God's book. Take the matter of dress, and we have 1 Peter 3:3, 4, and 1 Timothy 2:9, 10. Take the matter of conversation, and we have Ephesians 4:29, and 5:4. Take the matter of avenging injuries and standing up for your rights, and we have Romans 12:19, 20, 21, and Matthew 5:38-48, and 1 Peter 2:19-21. Take the matter of forgiving one another, and we have Ephesians 4:32 and Mark 11:25, 26. Take the matter of conformity to the world, and we have Romans 12:2, and 1 John 2:15-17, and James 4:4. Take the matter of anxieties of all kind, and we have Matthew 6:25-34, and Philippians 4:6, 7.

I only give these as examples to show how very full and practical the Bible guidance is. If, therefore, you find yourself in perplexity, first of all search and see whether the Bible speaks on the point in question, asking God to make plain to you by the power of His Spirit, through the Scripture, what is His mind. And whatever shall seem to you to be plainly taught there, that you must obey.

When we read and meditate upon this record of God's mind and will, with our understandings thus illuminated by the inspiring Spirit, our obedience will be as truly an obedience to a present, living word, as though it were afresh spoken to us today by our Lord from Heaven. The Bible is not only an ancient message from God sent to us many ages ago, but it is a present message sent to us now each time we read it. "The words that I speak unto you, they are spirit, and they are life," and obedience to these words now is a living obedience to a present and personal command.

But it is essential in this connection to remember that the Bible is a book of principles, and not a book of disjointed aphorisms. Isolated texts may often be made to sanction things, to which the principles of Scripture are totally opposed. I heard not long ago of a Christian woman in a Western meeting, who, having had the text, "For we walk by faith, and not by sight," brought very vividly before her mind, felt a strong impression that it was a command to be literally obeyed in the outward; and, blindfolding her eyes, insisted on walking up and down the aisle of the meeting-house, as an illustration of the walk of faith. She very soon stumbled and fell against the stove, burning herself seriously, and then wondered at the mysterious dispensation. The principles of Scripture, and her own sanctified common-sense, if applied to this case, would have saved her from the delusion.

The second test, therefore, to which our impressions must be brought, is that of our own higher judgment, or common sense.

It is as true now as in the days when Solomon wrote, that a "man of understanding shall attain unto wise counsels"; and his exhortation still continues binding upon us: "Wisdom is the principal thing, therefore get wisdom; and with all thy getting, get understanding."

As far as I can see, the Scriptures everywhere make it an essential thing for the children of God to use all the faculties which have been given them, in their journey through this world. They are to use their outward faculties for their outward walk, and their inward faculties for their inward walk. And they might as well expect to be "kept" from dashing their feet against a stone in the outward, if they walk blindfold, as to be "kept" from spiritual stumbling, if they put aside their judgment and common sense in their interior life.

I asked a Christian of "sound mind" lately how she distinguished between the voice of false spirits and the guidance of the Holy Spirit, and she replied promptly, "I rap them over the head, and see if they have any common sense."

Some, however, may say here, "But I thought we were not to depend on our human understanding in Divine things." I answer to this, that we are not to depend on our unenlightened human understanding, but upon our human judgment and common sense, enlightened by the Spirit of God. That is, God will speak to us through the faculties He has Himself given us, and not independently of them. That is, just as we are to use our eyes when we walk, no matter how full of faith we may be, so also we are to use our mental faculties in our inward life.

The third and last test to which our impressions must be brought is that of providential circumstances. If a "leading" is of God, the way will always open for it. Our Lord assures us of this when He says in John 10:4, "And when He putteth forth His own sheep he goeth before them, and the sheep follow Him, for they know his voice." Notice here the expression "goeth before," and "follow." He goes before to open a way, and we are to follow in the way thus opened. It is never a sign of a Divine leading when the Christian insists on opening his own way, and riding roughshod over all opposing things. If the Lord "goes before" us, He will open all doors for us, and we shall not need ourselves to hammer them down.

The fourth point I would make is this: that, just as our impressions must be tested, as I have shown, by the other three voices, so must these other voices be tested by our inward impressions; and if we feel a "stop in our minds" about anything, we must wait until that is removed before acting. A Christian who had advanced with unusual rapidity in the Divine life gave me as her secret this simple receipt: "I always mind the checks." We must not ignore the voice of our inward impressions, nor ride roughshod over them, any more than we must the other three voices of which I have spoken.

These four voices, then, will always be found to agree in any truly Divine leading, i.e., the voice of our impressions, the voice of the Scripture, the voice of our own sanctified judgment, and the voice of providential circumstances; and where these four do not all agree at first, we must wait until they do.

A divine sense of "oughtness," derived from the harmony of all God's various voices, is the only safe foundation for any action.

And now I have guarded the points of danger, do permit me to let myself out for a little to the blessedness and joy of this direct communication of God's will to us. It seems to me to be the grandest of privileges. In the first place, that God should love me enough to care about the details of my life is perfectly wonderful. And then that He should be willing to tell me all about it, and to let me know just now to live and walk so as to perfectly please Him, seems almost too good to be true. We never care about the little details of people's lives unless we love them. It is a matter of indifference to us with the majority of people we meet, as to what they do or how they spend their time; but as soon as we begin to love anyone, we begin at once to care. That God cares, therefore, is just a precious proof of His love; and it is most blessed to have Him speak to us about everything in our lives, about our duties, about our pleasures, about our friendships, about our occupations, about all that we do, or think, or say. You must know this in your own experience, dear reader, if you would come into the full joy and privilege of this life hid with Christ in God, for it is one of His most precious gifts!

God's promise is that He will work in us to will as well as to do of His good pleasure. This, of course, means that He will take possession of our will, and work it for us, and that His suggestions will come to us, not so much commands from the outside, as desires springing up within. They will originate in our will; we shall feel as though we wanted to do so and so, not as though we must. And this makes it a service of perfect liberty; for it is always easy to do what we desire to do, let the accompanying circumstances be as difficult as they may.

Every mother knows that she could secure perfect and easy obedience in her child, if she could only get into that child's will and work it for him, making him want himself to do the things she willed he should. And this is what our Father does for His children in the new dispensation; He writes His laws on our hearts and on our minds, and we love them, and are drawn to our obedience by our affections and judgment, not driven by our fears.

The way in which the Holy Spirit, therefore, usually works in His direct guidance is to impress upon the mind a wish or desire to do or leave undone certain things.

The soul when engaged, perhaps, in prayer, feels a sudden suggestion made to its inmost consciousness in reference to a certain point of duty. "I would like to do this or the other," it thinks, "I wish I could." Or perhaps the suggestion may come as question, "I wonder whether I had not better do so and so?" Or it may be only at first in the way of a conviction that such is the right and best thing to be done.

At once the matter should be committed to the Lord, with an instant consent of the will to obey Him; and if the suggestion is in accordance with the Scriptures, and a sanctified judgment, and with providential circumstances, an immediate obedience is the safest and easiest course. At the moment when the

Spirit speaks, it is always easy to obey; if the soul hesitates and begins to reason, it becomes more and more difficult continually. As a general rule, the first convictions are the right ones in a fully surrendered heart; for God is faithful in His dealings with us, and will cause His voice to be heard before any other voices. Such convictions, therefore, should never be met by reasoning. Prayer and trust are the only safe attitudes of the soul; and even these should be but momentary, as it were, lest the time for action should pass and the blessing be missed.

If, however, the suggestion does not seem quite clear enough to act upon, and doubt and perplexity ensue, especially if it is something about which one's friends hold a different opinion, then we shall need to wait for further light. The Scripture rule is, "Whatsoever is not of faith is sin"; which means plainly that we must never act in doubt. A clear conviction of right is the only safe guide. But we must wait in faith, and in an attitude of entire surrender, saying, "Yes," continually to the will of our Lord, whatever it may be. I believe the lack of a will thus surrendered lies at the root of many of our difficulties; and next to this lies the want of faith in any real Divine guidance. God's children are amazingly skeptical here. They read the promises and they feel the need, but somehow they cannot seem to believe the guidance will be given to them; as if God should want us to obey His voice, but did not know how to make us hear and understand Him. It is, therefore, very possible for God to speak, but for the soul not to hear, because it does not believe He is speaking. No earthly parent or master could possibly guide his children or servants, if they should refuse to believe he was speaking, and should not accept his voice as being really the expression of his will.

God, who at sundry times and in
manners many,

Spake to the fathers and is speaking
still,

Eager to see if ever or if any

Souls will obey and hearken to His
will.

Every moment of our lives our Father is seeking to reveal Himself to us. "I that speak unto thee am He. I that speak in thy heart, I that speak in thy outward circumstances, I that speak in thy losses, I that speak in thy gains, I that speak in thy sorrows or in thy joys, I that speak everywhere and in everything, am He."

We must, therefore, have perfect confidence that the Lord's voice is speaking to us to teach and lead us, and that He will give us the wisdom needed for our right guidance; and when we have asked for light, we must accept our strongest conviction of "oughtness" as being the guidance we have sought.

A few rules will help us here.

I. We must believe that God will guide us.

II. We must surrender our own will to His guidance.

III. We must hearken for the Divine voice.

IV. We must wait for the divine harmony.

V. When we are sure of the guidance, we must obey without question.

God only is the creature's home;
    Though rough and strait the rod,
    Yet nothing less can satisfy
    The love that longs, for God.

How little of that road, my soul!
    How little hast thou gone!
Take heart, and let the thought of God
    Allure thee further on.

The perfect way is hard to flesh;
    It is not hard to love;

If thou wert sick for want of God,
    How swiftly wouldst thou move.

Dole not thy duties out to God,
    But let thy hand be free;
Look long at Jesus, His sweet love,
    How was it dealt to thee?

And only this perfection needs
    A heart kept calm all day,
To catch the words the Spirit there,
    From hour to hour may say.

Then keep thy conscience sensitive,
    No inward token miss:
And go where grace entices thee—
    Perfection lies in this.

Be docile to thine unseen Guide,
    Love Him as He loves thee;
Time and obedience are enough,
    And thou a saint shalt be.

Difficulties Concerning Doubts

A GREAT MANY CHRISTIANS are slaves to the habit of doubting. No drunkard was ever more utterly bound by the chains of his fatal habit than they are by theirs. Every step of their whole Christian life is taken against the fearful odds of an army of doubts that are forever lying in wait to assail them at each favorable moment. Their lives are made wretched, their usefulness is effectually hindered, and their communion with God is continually broken by their doubts. And although the entrance of the soul upon the life of faith, of which this book treats, does in many cases take it altogether out of the region where these doubts live and flourish, yet even here it sometimes happens that the old tyrant will rise up and reassert his sway, and will cause the feet to stumble and the heart to fail, even when he cannot succeed in utterly turning the believer back into the dreary wilderness again.

We all of us remember, doubtless, the childish fascination, and yet horror, of that story of Christian's imprisonment in Doubting Castle by the wicked giant Despair, and our exultant sympathy in his escape through those massive gates and from that cruel tyrant. Little did we suspect then that we should ever find ourselves taken prisoner by the same giant, and imprisoned in the same castle. And yet I fear to every member of the Church of Christ there has been at least one such experience. Turn to the account again, if it is not fresh in your minds, and see if you do not see pictured there experiences of your own that have been very grievous to bear at the time, and very sorrowful to look back upon afterward.

It seems strange that people, whose very name of Believers implies that their one chiefest characteristic is that they believe, should have to confess to such experiences. And yet it is such a universal habit that I feel if the majority of the Church were to be named over again, the only fitting and descriptive name that could be given them would be that of Doubters. In fact, most Christians have settled down under their doubts, as to a sort of inevitable malady, from which they suffer acutely, but to which they must try to be resigned as a part of the necessary discipline of this earthly life. And they lament over their doubts as a man might lament over his rheumatism, making themselves out as an "interesting case" of especial and peculiar trial, which requires the tenderest sympathy and the utmost consideration.

And this is too often true of believers, who are earnestly longing to enter upon the life and walk of faith, and who have made perhaps many steps toward it. They have got rid, it may be, of the old doubts that once tormented them, as to whether their sins are really forgiven, and whether they shall, after all, get safe to Heaven; but they have not got rid of doubting. They have simply shifted the habit to a higher platform. They are saying, perhaps, "Yes, I believe my sins are forgiven, and I am a child of God through faith in Jesus Christ. I dare not doubt this any more. But then—" And this "but then" includes an interminable array of doubts concerning every declaration and every promise our Father has made to His children. One after another they fight with them and refuse to believe them, until they can have some more reliable proof of their being true, than the simple word of their God. And then they wonder why they are permitted to walk in such darkness, and look upon themselves almost in the light of martyrs, and groan under the peculiar spiritual conflicts they are compelled to endure.

Spiritual conflicts! Far better would they be named did we call them spiritual rebellions! Our fight is to be a fight of faith, and the moment we doubt, our fight ceases and our rebellion begins.

I desire to put forth, if possible, one vigorous protest against this whole thing. Just as well might I join in with the lament of a drunkard and unite with him in prayer for grace to endure the discipline of his fatal indulgence, as to give way for one instant to the weak complaints of these enslaved souls, and try to console them under their slavery. To one and to the other I would dare to do nothing else but proclaim the perfect deliverance the Lord Jesus Christ has in store or them, and beseech, entreat, command them, with all the force of my whole nature, to avail themselves of it and be free. Not for one moment would I listen to their despairing excuses. You ought to be free, you can be free, you MUST be free!

Will you undertake to tell me that it is an inevitable necessity for God to be doubted by His children? Is it an inevitable necessity for your children to doubt you? Would you tolerate their doubts a single hour? Would you pity your son and condole with him, and feel that he was an interesting case, if he should come to you and say, "Father, I cannot believe your word, I cannot trust your love"?

I remember once seeing the indignation of a mother I knew, stirred to its very depths by a little doubting on the part of one of her children. She had brought two little girls to my house to leave them while she did some errands. One of them, with the happy confidence of childhood, abandoned herself to all the pleasures she could find in my nursery, and sang and played until her mother's return. The other one, with the wretched caution and mistrust of maturity, sat down alone in a corner to wonder whether her mother would remember to come back for her, and to fear she would be forgotten, and to imagine her mother would be glad of the chance to get rid of her anyhow, because she was such a naughty girl, and ended with working herself up into a perfect frenzy of despair. The look on that mother's face, when upon her return the weeping little girl told what was the matter with her, I shall not easily forget. Grief, wounded love, indignation, and pity, all strove together for mastery. But indignation gained the day, and I doubt if that little girl was ever so vigorously dealt with before. A hundred times in my life since has that scene come up before me with deepest teaching, and has compelled me, peremptorily, to refuse admittance to the doubts about my Heavenly Father's love, and care, and remembrance of me, that have clamored at the door of my heart for entrance.

I am convinced that to many people doubting is a real luxury, and to deny themselves from indulging in it would be to exercise the hardest piece of self-denial they have ever known. It is a luxury that, like the indulgence in all other luxuries, brings very sorrowful results; and, perhaps, looking at the sadness and misery it has brought into your own Christian experience, you may be tempted to say, "Alas! This is no luxury to me, but only a fearful trial." But pause for a moment. Try giving it up, and you will soon find out whether it is a luxury or not. Do not your doubts come trooping to your door as a company of sympathizing friends, who appreciate your hard case, and have come to condole with you? And is it no luxury to sit down with them and entertain them, and listen to their arguments, and join in with their condolences? Would it be no self-denial to turn resolutely from them, and refuse to hear a word they have to say? If you do not know, try it and see.

Have you never tasted the luxury of indulging in hard thoughts against those who have, as you think, injured you? Have you never known what a positive fascination it is to brood over their unkindnesses, and to pry into their malice, and to imagine all sorts of wrong and uncomfortable things about them? It has made you wretched, of course, but it has been a fascinating sort of wretchedness that you could not easily give up.

And just like this is the luxury of doubting. Things have gone wrong with you in your experience. Dispensations have been mysterious, temptations have been peculiar, your case has seemed different from that of any one's around you. What more natural than to conclude that for some reason God has forsaken you, and does not love you, and is indifferent to your welfare? And how irresistible is the conviction that you are too wicked for Him to care for, or too difficult for Him to manage.

You do not mean to blame Him, or accuse Him of injustice, for you feel that His indifference and rejection of you are fully deserved because of your unworthiness. And this very subterfuge leaves you at liberty to indulge in your doubts under the guise of a just and true appreciation of your own shortcomings. But all the while you are as really indulging in hard and wrong thoughts of your Lord as ever you did of a human enemy; for He says He came not to save the righteous, but sinners; and your very sinfulness and unworthiness is your chiefest claim upon His love and His care.

As well might the poor little lamb that has wandered from the flock and got lost in the wilderness say, "The shepherd does not love me, nor care for me, nor remember me, because I am lost. He only loves and cares for the lambs that never wander." As well might the ill man say, "The doctor will not come to see me, nor give me any medicines, because I am ill. He only cares for and visits well people." Jesus says, "They that are whole need not a physician, but they that are sick." And again He says, "What man of you, having an hundred sheep, if he lose one of them, doth not leave the ninety and nine in the wilderness, and go after that which is lost, until he find it?" Any thoughts of Him, therefore, which are different from what He says of Himself, are hard thoughts; and to indulge in them is far worse than to indulge in hard thoughts of any earthly friend or foe. From the beginning to the end of your Christian life it is always sinful to indulge in doubts. Doubts are all from the devil, and are always untrue. And the only way to meet them is by a direct and emphatic denial.

And this brings me to the practical part of the whole subject, as to how to get deliverance from this fatal habit. My answer would be that the deliverance from this can be by no other means than the deliverance from any other sin. It is to be found in the Lord and in Him only. You must hand your doubting over to Him, as you have learned to hand your other temptations. You must do just what you do with your temper, or your pride. You must give it up to the Lord. I believe myself the only effectual remedy is to take a pledge against it as you would urge a drunkard to do against drink, trusting in the Lord alone to keep you steadfast.

Like any other sin, the stronghold is in the will and the will to doubt must be surrendered exactly as you surrender the will to yield to any other temptation. God always takes possession of a surrendered will. And if we come to the point of saying that we will not doubt, and surrender this central fortress of our nature to Him, His blessed Spirit will begin at once to work in us all the good pleasure of His will, and we shall find ourselves kept from doubting by His mighty and overcoming power.

The trouble is that in this matter of doubting the soul does not always make a full surrender, but is apt to reserve to itself a little secret liberty to doubt, looking upon it as being sometimes a necessity. "I do not want to doubt any more," we will say, or, "I hope I shall not"; but it is hard to come to the point of saying, "I will not doubt again." But no surrender is effectual until it reaches the point of saying, "I will not." The liberty to doubt must be given up forever. And the soul must consent to a continuous life of inevitable trust. It is often necessary, I think, to make a definite transaction of this surrender of doubting, and to come to a point about it. I believe it is quite as necessary in the case of a doubter as in the case of a drunkard. It will not do to give it up by degrees. The total abstinence principle is the only effectual one here.

Then, the surrender once made, the soul must rest absolutely upon the Lord for deliverance in each time of temptation. It must lift up the shield of faith the moment the assault comes. It must hand the very first suggestion of doubt over to the Lord, and must tell the enemy to settle the matter with Him. It must refuse to listen to the doubt a single moment. Let it come ever so plausibly, or under whatever guise of humility, the soul must simply say, "I dare not doubt; I must trust. The Lord is good, and HE DOES love me. Jesus saves me; He saves me now." Those three little words, repeated over and over,—"Jesus saves me, Jesus saves me,"—will put to flight the greatest army of doubts that ever assaulted any soul. I have tried it times without number, and have never known it to fail. Do not stop to argue the matter out with your doubts, nor try to prove that they are wrong. Pay no attention to them whatever; treat them with the utmost contempt. Shut your door in their faces, and emphatically deny every word they say to you. Bring up some "It is written," and hurl it after them. Look right at Jesus, and tell Him you trust Him, and you mean to trust Him. Let the doubts clamor as they may, they cannot hurt you if you will not let them in.

I know it will look to you sometimes as though you were shutting the door against your best friends, and your heart will long after your doubts more than ever the Israelites longed after the flesh-pots of Egypt. But deny yourself; take up your cross in this matter, and unmercifully refuse ever to listen to a single word.

This very day a perfect army of doubts stood awaiting my awaking, and clamored at my door for admittance. Nothing seemed real, nothing seemed true; and least of all did it seem possible that I—miserable, wretched—could be the object of the Lord's love, or care, or notice. If I only had been at liberty to let these doubts in, and invite them to take seats and make themselves at home, what a luxury I should have felt it to be! But years ago I made a pledge against doubting; and I would as soon think of violating my pledge against intoxicating liquor as to violate this one. I DARED not admit the first doubt. I therefore lifted up my shield of faith the moment I was conscious of these suggestions, and handing the whole army over to my Lord to conquer, I began to say, over and over, "The Lord does love me. He is my present and my perfect Savior; Jesus saves me, Jesus saves me now!" The victory was complete. The enemy had come in like a flood, but the Lord lifted up a standard against him, and he was routed and put to flight; and my soul is singing the song of Moses and the children of Israel, saying, "I will sing unto the Lord, for He hath triumphed gloriously: the horse and his rider hath He thrown into the sea. The Lord is my strength and my song, and He is become my salvation. The Lord is a man of war; the Lord is His name."

It will help you to resist the assaults of this temptation to doubt, to see clearly that doubting is sin. It is certainly a direct disobedience to our Lord, who commands us, "Let not your heart be troubled, neither let it be afraid." And all through the Bible everywhere the commands to trust are imperative, and admit of no exceptions. Time and room would fail me to refer to one-hundredth part of these, but no one can read the Psalms without being convinced that the man who trusts without a question is the only man who pleases God and is accepted of Him. The "provocation" of Israel was that they did not trust; "anger also came up against Israel, because they believed not in God, and trusted not in His salvation" (Psalms 78:17-22). And in contrast, we read in Isaiah concerning those who trust, "Thou wilt keep him in perfect peace whose mind is stayed on Thee, because he trusteth in Thee." Nothing grieves or wounds our hearts like doubting on the part of a friend, and nothing, I am convinced, grieves the heart of God more than doubting from us.

One of my children, who is now with the Lord, said to me one evening as I was tucking her up in bed, "Well, mother, I have had my first doubt." "Oh, Ray," I said, "what was it?" "Why," she replied, "Satan came to me and told me not to believe the Bible, for it was not a word of it true." "And what did thee say to him?" I asked. "Oh," she replied, triumphantly, "I just said to him, Satan, I will believe it. So there!" I was delighted with the child's spiritual intelligence in knowing so well how to meet doubts, and encouraged her with all my heart, explaining to her how all doubts and discouragements are from the enemy, and how he is always a liar and must not be listened to for a moment. The next night, I had forgotten all about it, however, and was surprised and startled when she said, as I was tucking her in bed, "Well, mother, Satan has been at it again." "Oh, Ray darling!" I exclaimed in dismay, "what did he say this time?" "Well," she replied, "he just told me that I was such a naughty little girl that Jesus could not love me, and I was foolish to think He did." "And what did thee say this time?" I asked. "Oh!" she replied, "I just looked at him cross and said, Satan, shut thy mouth!" And then she added, with a smile, "He can't make me unhappy one bit." A grander battle no soul ever fought than this little child had done, and no greater victory was ever won!

Dear, doubting soul, go and do likewise; and a similar victory shall be thine. As you lay down this book, take up your pen and write out your determination never to doubt again. Make it a real transaction between your soul and the Lord. Give up your liberty to doubt forever. Put your will in this matter over on the Lord's side, and trust Him to keep you from falling. Tell him all about your utter weakness and your long-encouraged habits of doubt, and how helpless you are before your enemy, and commit the whole battle to Him. Tell Him you will not doubt again; and then henceforward keep your face steadfastly looking unto Jesus, away from yourself and away from your doubts, holding fast the profession of your faith without wavering, because He is faithful who has promised. And as surely as you do thus hold the beginning of your confidence steadfast unto the end, just so surely shall you find yourself in this matter made more than conqueror, through Him who loves you.

X

Difficulties
Concerning Temptation

CERTAIN VERY GREAT MISTAKES are made concerning this matter of temptation, in the practical
working out of this life of faith.

First of all, people seem to expect that, after the soul
has entered into its rest in God, temptations will cease;
and to think that the promised deliverance is not only
to be from yielding to temptation, but even also from
being tempted. Consequently, when they find the
Canaanite still in the land, and see the cities great and
walled up to Heaven, they are utterly discouraged, and
think they must have gone wrong in some way, and
that this cannot be the true land after all.

Then, next they make the mistake of looking upon
temptation as sin, and of blaming themselves for what
in reality is the fault of the enemy only. This brings
them into condemnation and discouragement; and

discouragement, if continued in, always ends at last in actual sin. The enemy makes an easy prey of a discouraged soul; so that we fall often from the very fear of having fallen.

To meet the first of these difficulties it is only necessary to refer to the Scripture declarations, that the Christian life is to be throughout a warfare; and that, especially when seated in heavenly places in Christ Jesus, we are to wrestle against spiritual enemies there, whose power and skill to tempt us must doubtless be far superior to any we have ever heretofore encountered. As a fact, temptations generally increase in strength tenfold after we have entered into the interior life, rather than decrease; and no amount or sort of them must ever for a moment lead us to suppose we have not really found the true abiding place. Strong temptations are generally a sign of great grace, rather than of little grace. When the children of Israel had first left Egypt, the Lord did not lead them through the country of the Philistines, although that was the nearest way; for God said, "lest peradventure the people repent when they see war, and they return to Egypt." But afterward, when they learned better how to trust Him, He permitted their enemies to attack them. Then also in their wilderness journey they met with but few enemies and fought but few battles, compared to those in the land, where they found seven great nations and thirty-one kings to be conquered, besides walled cities to be taken, and giants to be overcome.

They could not have fought with the Canaanites, or the Hittites, and the Amorites, and the Perizzites, and the Hivites, and the Jebusites, until they had gone into the land where these enemies were. And the very power of your temptations, dear Christian, therefore, may perhaps be one of the strongest proofs that you really are in the land you have been seeking to enter, because they are temptations peculiar to that land. You must never allow your temptations to cause you to question the fact of your having entered the promised "heavenly places."

The second mistake is not quite so easy to deal with. It seems hardly worthwhile to say that temptation is not sin, and yet most of the distress about it arises from not understanding this fact. The very suggestion of wrong seems to bring pollution with it, and the evil agency not being recognized, the poor tempted soul begins to feel as if it must be very bad indeed, and very far off from God to have had such thoughts and suggestions. It is as though a burglar should break into a man's house to steal, and, when the master of the house began to resist him and to drive him out, should turn round and accuse the owner of being himself the thief. It is the enemy's grand ruse for entrapping us. He comes and whispers suggestions of evil to us, doubts, blasphemies, jealousies, envyings, and pride; and then turns round and says, "Oh, how wicked you must be to think of such things! It is very plain that you are not trusting the Lord; for if you were, it would have been impossible for these things to have entered your heart." This reasoning sounds so very plausible that the soul often accepts it as true, and at once comes under condemnation, and is filled with discouragement; then it is easy for it to be led on into actual sin. One of the most fatal things in the life of faith is discouragement. One of the most helpful is cheerfulness. A very wise man once said that in overcoming temptations, cheerfulness was the first thing, cheerfulness the second, and cheerfulness the third. We must expect to conquer. That is why the Lord said so often to Joshua, "Be strong and of a good courage"; "Be not afraid, neither be thou dismayed"; "Only be thou strong and very courageous." And it is also the reason He says to us, "Let not your heart be troubled neither let it be afraid." The power of temptation is in the fainting of our own hearts. The enemy knows this well, and always begins his assaults by discouraging us, if it can in any way be accomplished.

Sometimes this discouragement arises from what we think is a righteous grief and disgust at ourselves that such things could be any temptation to us; but which is really a mortification arising from the fact that we have been indulging in a secret self-congratulation that our tastes were too pure, or our separation from the world was too complete for such things to tempt us. We have expected something from ourselves, and have been sorely disappointed not to find that something there, and are discouraged in consequence. This mortification and discouragement are really a far worse condition than the temptation itself, though they present an appearance of true humility, for they are nothing but the results of wounded self-love. True humility can bear to see its own utter weakness and foolishness revealed, because it never expected anything from itself, and knows that its only hope and expectation must be in God. Therefore, instead of discouraging the soul from trusting, it drives it to a deeper and more utter trust. But the counterfeit humility which springs from self, plunges the soul into the depths of a faithless discouragement, and drives it into the very sin at which it is so distressed.

I remember once hearing an allegory that illustrated this to me wonderfully. Satan called together a council of his servants to consult how they might make a good man sin. One evil spirit started up and said, "I will make him sin." "How will you do it?" asked Satan. "I will set before him the pleasures of sin," was the reply; "I will tell him of its delights and the rich rewards it brings." "Ah," said Satan, "that will not do; he has tried, it, and knows better than that." Then another spirit started up and said, "I will make him sin." "What will you do?" asked Satan. "I will tell him of the pains and sorrows of virtue. I will show him that virtue has no delights, and brings no rewards." "Ah, no!" exclaimed Satan, "that will not do at all; for he has tried it, and knows that 'wisdom's ways are ways of pleasantness and all her paths are peace.'" "Well," said another imp, starting up, "I will undertake to make him sin." "And what will you do?" asked Satan, again. "I will discourage his soul," was the short reply. "Ah, that will do," cried Satan,—"that will do! We shall conquer him now." And they did.

An old writer says, "All discouragement is from the devil"; and I wish every Christian would just take this as a pocket piece, and never forget it. We must fly from discouragement as we would from sin.

But this is impossible if we fail to recognize the true agency in temptation. For if the temptations are our own fault, we cannot help being discouraged. But they are not. The Bible says, "Blessed is the man that endureth temptation"; and we are exhorted to "count it all joy when we fall into divers temptations." Temptation, therefore, cannot be sin; and the truth is, it is no more a sin to hear these whispers and suggestions of evil in our souls, than it is for us to hear the swearing or wicked talk of bad men as we pass along the street. The sin only comes in either case by our stopping and joining in with them. If, when the wicked suggestions come, we turn from them at once, as we would from wicked talk, and pay no more attention to them, we do not sin. But if we carry them on in our minds, and roll them under our tongues, and dwell on them with a half-consent of our will to them as true, then we sin. We may be enticed by evil a thousand times a day without sin, and we cannot help these enticings. But if the enemy can succeed in making us think that his enticings are our sin, he has accomplished half the battle, and can hardly fail to gain a complete victory.

A dear lady once came to me under great darkness, simply from not understanding this. She had been living very happily in the life of faith for some time, and had been so free from temptation as almost to begin to think she would never be tempted any more. But suddenly a very peculiar form of temptation had assailed her, which had horrified her. She found that the moment she began to pray, dreadful thoughts of all kinds would rush into her mind. She had lived a very sheltered, innocent life, and these thoughts seemed so awful to her, that she felt she must be one of the most wicked of sinners to be capable of having them. She began by thinking she could not possibly have entered into the rest of faith, and ended by concluding that she had never even been born again. Her soul was in an agony of distress. I told her that these dreadful thoughts were altogether the suggestions of the enemy, who came to her the moment she kneeled in prayer, and poured them into her mind, and that she herself was not to blame for them at all; that she could not help them any more than she could help hearing if a wicked man should pour out his blasphemies in her presence. And I urged her to recognize and treat them as from the enemy; not to blame herself or be discouraged, but to turn at once to Jesus and commit them to Him. I showed her how great an advantage the enemy had gained by making her think these thoughts were originated by herself, and plunging her into condemnation and discouragement on account of them. And I assured her she would find a speedy victory if she would pay no attention to them; but, ignoring their presence, would simply turn her back on them and look to the Lord.

She grasped the truth, and the next time these thoughts came she said to the enemy, "I have found you out now. It is you who are suggesting these dreadful thoughts to me, and I hate them, and will have nothing to do with them. The Lord is my Savior; take them to Him, and settle them in His presence." Immediately the baffled enemy, finding himself discovered, fled in confusion, and her soul was perfectly delivered.

Another thing also. The enemy knows that if a Christian recognizes a suggestion of evil as coming from him, he will recoil from it far more quickly than if it seems to be the suggestion of his own mind. If Satan prefaced each temptation with the words, "I am Satan, your relentless enemy; I have come to make you sin," I suppose we would hardly feel any desire at all to yield to his suggestions. He has to hide himself in order to make his baits attractive. And our victory will be far more easily gained if we are not ignorant of his devices, but recognize him at his very first approach.

We also make another great mistake about temptations in thinking that all time spent in combating them is lost. Hours pass, and we seem to have made no progress, because we have been so beset with temptations. But it often happens that we have been serving God far more truly during these hours, than in our times of comparative freedom from temptation. Temptation is really more the devil's wrath against God, than against us. He cannot touch our Savior, but he can wound our Savior by conquering us, and our ruin is important to him only as it accomplishes this. We are, therefore, really fighting our Lord's battles when we are fighting temptation, and hours are often worth days to us under these circumstances. We read, "Blessed is the man that endureth temptation"; and I am sure this means enduring the continuance of it and its frequent recurrence. Nothing so cultivates the grace of patience as the endurance of temptation, and nothing so drives the soul to an utter dependence upon the Lord Jesus as its continuance. And finally, nothing brings more praise and honor and glory to our dearest Lord Himself than the trial of our faith which comes through manifold temptations. We are told that it is more precious than gold, though it be tried with fire, and that we, who patiently endure the trial, shall receive for our reward "the crown of life which the Lord hath promised to them that love Him."

We cannot wonder, therefore, any longer at the exhortation with which the Holy Ghost opens the Book of James: "Count it all joy when ye fall into divers temptations, knowing this, that the trying of your faith worketh patience.

But let patience have her perfect work, that ye may be perfect and entire, wanting nothing."

Temptation is plainly to be the blessed instrument used by God to complete our perfection, and thus the enemy's own weapons are turned against himself, and we see how it is that all things, even temptations, can work together for good to them that love God.

As to the way of victory over temptations, it seems hardly necessary to say to those whom I am at this time especially addressing, that it is to be by faith. For this is, of course, the foundation upon which the whole interior life rests. Our one great motto is throughout, "We are nothing, Christ is all." And always and everywhere we have started out to stand, and walk, and overcome, and live by faith. We have discovered our own utter helplessness, and know that we cannot do anything for ourselves. Our only way, therefore, is to hand the temptation over to our Lord, and trust Him to conquer it for us. But when we put it into His hands we must leave it there. It must be as real a committing of ourselves to Him for victory, as it was at first a committing of ourselves to Him for salvation. He must do all for us in the one case, as completely as in the other. It was faith only then, and it must be faith only now.

And the victories which the Lord works in conquering the temptations of those who thus trust Him are nothing short of miracles, as thousands can testify.

But into this part of the subject I cannot go at present, as my object has been rather to present temptation in its true light, than to develop the way of victory over it. I want to deliver conscientious, faithful souls from the bondage into which they are sure to be brought, if they fail to understand the true nature and use of temptation, and confound it with sin. I want that they should not be ignorant of the fact that temptations are, after all, an invaluable part of our soul's development; and that, whatever may be their original source, they are used by God to work out in us many blessed graces of character which would otherwise be lacking. Wherever temptation is, there is God also, superintending and controlling its power. "Where wert thou, Lord I while I was being tempted?" cried the saint of the desert. "Close beside thee, my son, all the while," was the tender reply.

Temptations try us; and we are worth nothing if we are not tried. They develop our spiritual strength and courage and knowledge; and our development is the one thing God cries for. How shallow would all our spirituality be if it were not for temptations. "Blessed is the man that endureth temptation: for when he is tried he shall receive the crown of life, which the Lord hath promised to them that love Him." This "crown of life" will be worth all that it has cost of trial and endurance to obtain it; and without these it could not be attained.

An invalid lady procured once the cocoon of a very beautiful butterfly with unusually magnificent wings hoping to have the pleasure of seeing it emerge from its cocoon in her sick-chamber. She watched it eagerly as spring drew on, and finally was delighted to see the butterfly beginning to emerge. But it seemed to have great difficulty. It pushed, and strained, and struggled, and seemed to make so little headway, that she concluded it must need some help, and with a pair of delicate scissors she finally clipped the tight cord that seemed to bind in the opening of the cocoon. Immediately the cocoon opened wide, and the butterfly escaped without any further struggle. She congratulated herself on the success of her experiment, but found in a moment that something was the matter with the butterfly. It was all out of the cocoon it is true, but its great wings were lifeless and colorless, and dragged after it as a useless burden. For a few days it lived a miserable sickly life, and then died, without having once lifted its powerless wings. The lady was sorely disappointed and could not understand it. But when she related the circumstance to a naturalist, he told her that it had all been her own fault. That it required just that pushing and struggling to send the life fluid into the veins of the wings, and that her mistaken kindness in shortening the struggle, had left the wings lifeless and colorless.

Just so do our spiritual wings need the struggle and effort of our conflict with temptation and trial; and to grant us an escape from it would be to weaken the power of our soul to "mount up with wings as eagles," and would deprive us of the "crown of life" which is promised to those who endure.

XI

Difficulties Concerning Failures

THE VERY TITLE of this may perhaps startle some. "Failures," they will say; "we thought there were no failures in this life of faith!"

To this I would answer that there ought not to be, and need not be; but, as a fact, there sometimes are. And we have got to deal with facts, and not with theories. No teacher of this interior life ever says that it becomes impossible to sin; they only insist that sin ceases to be a necessity, and that a possibility of uniform victory is opened before us. And there are very few who do not confess that, as to their own actual experience, they have at times been overcome by momentary temptation.

Of course, in speaking of sin here, I mean conscious, known sin. I do not touch on the subject of sins of ignorance, or what is called the inevitable sin of our nature, which are all covered by the atonement, and do not disturb our fellowship with God. I have no desire nor ability to treat of the doctrines concerning sin; these I will leave with the theologians to discuss and settle, while I speak only of the believer's experience in the matter. And I wish it to be fully understood that in all I shall say, I have reference simply to that which comes within the range of our consciousness.

Misunderstanding, then, on this point of known or conscious sin, opens the way for great dangers in the Higher Christian Life. When a believer, who has, as he trusts, entered upon the highway of holiness, finds himself surprised into sin, he is tempted either to be utterly discouraged, and to give everything up as lost; or else, in order to preserve the doctrine untouched, he feels it necessary to cover his sin up, calling it infirmity, and refusing to be honest and aboveboard about it. Either of these courses is equally fatal to any real growth and progress in the life of holiness. The only way is to face the sad fact at once, call the thing by its right name, and discover, if possible, the reason and the remedy. This life of union with God requires the utmost honesty with Him and with ourselves. The communion which the sin itself would only momentarily disturb is sure to be lost by any dishonest dealing with it. A sudden failure is no reason for being discouraged and giving up all as lost. Neither is the integrity of our doctrine touched by it. We are not preaching a state, but a walk. The highway of holiness is not a place, but a way. Sanctification is not a thing to be picked up at a certain stage of our experience, and forever after possessed, but it is a life to be lived day by day, and hour by hour. We may for a moment turn aside from a path, but the path is not obliterated by our wandering, and can be instantly regained. And in this life and walk of faith, there may be momentary failures, which, although very sad and greatly to be deplored, need not, if rightly met, disturb the attitude of the soul as to entire consecration and perfect trust, nor interrupt, for more than the passing moment, its happy communion with its Lord.

The great point is an instant return to God. Our sin is no reason for ceasing to trust, but only an unanswerable argument why we must trust more fully than ever. From whatever cause we have been betrayed into failure, it is very certain that there is no remedy to be found for it in discouragement. As well might a child who is learning to walk, lie down in despair when he has fallen, and refuse to take another step; as a believer, who is seeking to learn how to live and walk by faith, give up in despair because of having fallen into sin. The only way in both cases is to get right up and try again. When the children of Israel had met with that disastrous defeat, soon after their entrance into the land, before the little city of Ai, they were all so utterly discouraged that we read:

"Wherefore the hearts of the people melted, and became as water. And Joshua rent his clothes, and fell to the earth upon his face before the ark of the Lord until the eventide, he and the elders of Israel, and put dust upon their heads. And Joshua said, Alas! O Lord God, wherefore hast Thou at all brought this people over Jordan to deliver us into the hands of the Amorites to destroy us? Would to God we had been content, and dwelt on the other side Jordan! O Lord, what shall I say, when Israel turneth their backs before their enemies? For the Canaanites and all the inhabitants of the land shall hear of it, and shall environ us round and cut off our name from the earth: and what wilt Thou do unto Thy great name?"

What a wail of despair this was! And how exactly it is repeated by many a child of God in the present day, whose heart, because of a defeat, melts and becomes as water, and who cries out, "Would to God we had been content and dwelt on the other side Jordan!" and predicts for itself further failures and even utter discomfiture before its enemies. No doubt

Joshua thought then, as we are apt to think now, that discouragement and despair were the only proper and safe condition after such a failure. But God thought otherwise. "And the Lord said unto Joshua, Get thee up; wherefore liest thou upon thy face?"

The proper thing to do was not to abandon themselves thus to utter discouragement, humble as it might look, but at once to face the evil and get rid of it, and afresh and immediately to "sanctify themselves." "Up, sanctify the people," is always God's command. "Lie down and be discouraged," is always the enemy's temptation. Our feeling is that it is presumptuous, and even almost impertinent, to go at once to the Lord, after having sinned against Him. It seems as if we ought to suffer the consequences of our sin first for a little while, and endure the accusings of our conscience. And we can hardly believe that the Lord can be willing at once to receive us back into loving fellowship with Himself.

A little girl once expressed the feeling to me, with a child's outspoken candor. She had asked whether the Lord Jesus always forgave us for our sins as soon as we asked Him, and I had said, "Yes, of course He does." "Just as soon" she repeated, doubtingly. "Yes," I replied, "the very minute we ask, He forgives us." "Well," she said deliberately, "I cannot believe that.

I should think He would make us feel sorry for two or three days first. And then I should think He would make us ask Him a great many times, and in a very pretty way too, not just in common talk. And I believe that is the way He does, and you need not try to make me think He forgives me right at once, no matter what the Bible says." She only said what most Christians think, and, what is worse, what most Christians act on, making their discouragement and their very remorse separate them infinitely further off from God than their sin would have done. Yet it is so totally contrary to the way we like our children to act toward us, that I wonder how we ever could have conceived such an idea of God. How a mother grieves when a naughty child goes off alone in despairing remorse, and doubts her willingness to forgive; and how, on the other hand, her whole heart goes out in welcoming love to the darling who runs to her at once and begs her forgiveness! Surely our God knew this yearning love when He said to us, "Return, ye backsliding children, and I will heal your backslidings."

The fact is that the same moment which brings the consciousness of having sinned ought to bring also the consciousness of being forgiven. This is especially essential to an unwavering walk in the highway of holiness, for no separation from God can be tolerated here for an instant.

We can only walk in this path by looking continually unto Jesus, moment by moment; and if our eyes are taken off of Him to look upon our own sin and our own weakness, we shall leave the path at once. The believer, therefore, who has, as he trusts, entered upon this highway, if he finds himself overcome by sin, must flee with it instantly to the Lord. He must act on 1 John 1:9: "If we confess our sins, He is faithful and just to forgive us our sins, and to cleanse us from all unrighteousness." He must not hide his sin and seek to salve it over with excuses, or to push it out of his memory by the lapse of time. But he must do as the children of Israel did, rise up "early in the morning," and "run" to the place where the evil thing is hidden, and take it out of its hiding place, and lay it "out before the Lord." He must confess his sin. And then he must stone it with stones, and burn it with fire, and utterly put it away from him, and raise over it a great heap of stones, that it may be forever hidden from his sight. And he must believe, then and there, that God is, according to His Word, faithful and just to forgive him his sin, and that He does do it; and further, that He also cleanses him from all unrighteousness. He must claim an immediate forgiveness and an immediate cleansing by faith, and must go on trusting harder and more absolutely than ever.

As soon as Israel's sin had been brought to light and put away, at once God's word came again in a message of glorious encouragement, "Fear not, neither be thou dismayed... See, I have given into thy hand the king of Ai, and his people, and his city, and his land." Our courage must rise higher than ever, and we must abandon ourselves more completely to the Lord that His mighty power may more perfectly work in us all the good pleasure of His will. Moreover, we must forget our sin as soon as it is thus confessed and forgiven. We must not dwell on it, and examine it, and indulge in a luxury of distress and remorse. We must not put it on a pedestal, and then walk around it and view it on every side, and so magnify it into a mountain that hides our God from our eyes. We must follow the example of Paul, and "forgetting those things which are behind, and reaching forth unto those things which are before," we must "press toward the mark for the prize of the high calling of God in Christ Jesus."

I would like to bring up two contrastive illustrations of these things. One was an earnest Christian man, an active worker in the Church, who had been living for several months in the enjoyment of full salvation. He was suddenly overcome by a temptation to treat a brother unkindly. Not having supposed it possible that he could ever sin again, he was at once plunged into the deepest discouragement, and concluded he had been altogether mistaken, and had never entered into the life of full trust at all. Day by day his discouragement increased, until it became despair, and he concluded he had never even been born again, and gave himself up for lost. He spent three years of utter misery, going further and further away from God, and being gradually drawn off into one sin after another, until his life was a curse to himself and to all around him. His health failed under the terrible burden, and fears were entertained for his reason.

At the end of three years he met a Christian lady, who understood the truth about sin that I have been trying to explain. In a few moments' conversation she found out his trouble, and at once said, "You sinned in that act, there is no doubt about it, and I do not want you to try and excuse it. But have you never confessed it to the Lord and asked Him to forgive you?" "Confessed it!" he exclaimed, "why it seems to me I have done nothing but confess it, and entreat God to forgive me night and day for all these three dreadful years." "And you have never believed He did forgive you?" asked the lady. "No," said the poor man, "how could I, for I never felt as if He did?" "But suppose He had said He forgave you, would not that have done as well as for you to feel it?" "Oh, yes," replied the man, "if God said it, of course I would believe it." "Very well, He does say so," was the lady's answer, and she turned to the verse we have taken above (1 John 1:9) and read it aloud. "Now," she continued, "you have been all these three years confessing and confessing your sin, and all the while God's record has been declaring that He was faithful and just to forgive it and to cleanse you, and yet you have never once believed it. You have been 'making God a liar' all this while by refusing to believe His record."

The poor man saw the whole thing, and was dumb with amazement and consternation; and when the lady proposed they should kneel down, and that he should confess his past unbelief and sin, and should claim, then and there, a present forgiveness and a present cleansing, he obeyed like one in a maze. But the result was glorious. In a few moments the light broke in, and he burst out into praise at the wonderful deliverance. In three minutes his soul was enabled to traverse back by faith the whole long weary journey that he had been three years in making, and he found himself once more resting in Jesus, and rejoicing in the fullness of His salvation.

The other illustration was the case of a Christian lady who had been living in the land of promise about two weeks, and who had had a very bright and victorious experience. Suddenly, at the end of that time, she was overcome by a violent burst of anger. For a moment a flood of discouragement swept over her soul. The enemy said, "There, now, that shows it was all a mistake. Of course you have been deceived about the whole thing, and have never entered into the life of full trust at all. And now you may as well give up altogether, for you never can consecrate yourself any more entirely, nor trust any more fully, than you did this time; so it is very plain this life of holiness is not for you!" These thoughts flashed through her mind in a moment, but she was well taught in the ways of God, and she said at once, "Yes, I have sinned, and it is very sad. But the Bible says that if we confess our sins, God is faithful and just to forgive us our sins and to cleanse us from all unrighteousness, and I believe He will do it."

She did not delay a moment, but while still boiling over with anger, she ran, she could not walk, into a room where she could be alone, and kneeling down beside the bed, she said, "Lord, I confess my sin. I have sinned, I am even at this very moment sinning. I hate it, but I cannot get rid of it. I confess it with shame and confusion of face to Thee. And now I believe that, according to Thy word, Thou dost forgive and Thou dost cleanse." She said it out loud, for the inward turmoil was too great for it to be said inside. As the words "Thou dost forgive and Thou dost cleanse" passed her lips, the deliverance came. The Lord said, "Peace, be still," and there was a great calm. A flood of light and joy burst on her soul, the enemy fled, and she was more than conqueror through Him that loved her. The whole thing, the sin and the recovery from it, had occupied not five minutes, and her feet trod on more firmly than ever in the blessed highway of holiness. Thus the valley of Achor became to her a door of hope, and she sang afresh and with deeper meaning her song of deliverance, "I will sing unto the Lord, for He hath triumphed gloriously."

The truth is the only remedy, after all in every emergency, is to trust in the Lord. And if this is all we ought to do, and all we can do, is it not better to do it at once? I have often been brought up short by the question, "Well, what can I do but trust?" And I have realized at once the folly of seeking for deliverance in any other way, by saying to myself, "I shall have to come to simple trusting in the end, and why not come to it at once now in the beginning?" It is a life and walk of faith we have entered upon, and if we fail in it our only recovery must lie in an increase of faith, not in a lessening of it.

Let every failure, then, if any occur, drive you instantly to the Lord, with a more complete abandonment and a more perfect trust; and you will find that, sad as they are, they will not take you out of the land of rest, nor permanently interrupt your sweet communion with Him.

And now, having shown the way of deliverance from failure, I want to say a little as to the causes of failure in this life of full salvation. The causes do not lie in the strength of the temptation nor in our own weakness, nor, above all, in any lack in the power or willingness of our Savior to save us. The promise to Israel was positive, "There shall not any man be able to stand before thee all the days of thy life." And the promise to us is equally positive. "God is faithful, who will not suffer you to be tempted above that ye are able; but will with the temptation also make a way of escape that ye may be able to bear it."

The men of Ai were "but few," and yet the people who had conquered the mighty Jericho "fled before the men of Ai." It was not the strength of their enemy, neither had God failed them. The cause of their defeat lay somewhere else, and the Lord Himself declares it, "Israel hath sinned, and they have also transgressed my covenant which I commanded them; for they have even taken of the accursed thing, and have also stolen and dissembled also, and they have put it even among their own stuff. Therefore the children of Israel could not stand before their enemies, but turned their backs upon their enemies." It was a hidden evil that conquered them. Deep down under the earth, in an obscure tent in that vast army, was hidden something against which God had a controversy, and this little hidden thing made the whole army helpless before their enemies. "There is an accursed thing in the midst of thee, O Israel; thou canst not stand before thine enemies until ye take away the accursed thing from among you."

The teaching here is simply this, that anything allowed in the heart which is contrary to the will of God, let it seem ever so insignificant, or be ever so deeply hidden, will cause us to fall before our enemies. Any root of bitterness cherished toward another, any self-seeking and harsh judgments indulged in, any slackness in obeying the voice of the Lord, any doubtful habits or surroundings, any one of these things will effectually cripple and paralyze our spiritual life. We may have hidden the evil in the most remote corner of our hearts, and may have covered it over from our sight, refusing even to recognize its existence, of which, however, we cannot help being all the time secretly aware. We may steadily ignore it, and persist in declarations of consecration and full trust, we may be more earnest than ever in our religious duties, and have the eyes of our understanding opened more and more to the truth and the beauty of the life and walk of faith. We may seem to ourselves and to others to have reached an almost impregnable position of victory, and yet we may find ourselves suffering bitter defeats. We may wonder, and question, and despair, and pray; nothing will do any good until the accursed thing is dug up from its hiding place, brought out to the light, and laid before God. And the moment a believer who is walking in this interior life meets with a defeat, he must at once seek for the cause not in the strength of that particular enemy, but in something behind, some hidden want of consecration lying at the very center of his being. Just as a headache is not the disease itself, but only a symptom of a disease situated in some other part of the body, so the sin in such a Christian is only the symptom of an evil hidden probably in a very different part of his being.

Sometimes the evil may be hidden even in that, which at a cursory glance, would look like good. Beneath apparent zeal for the truth may be hidden a judging spirit, or a subtle leaning to our own understanding. Beneath apparent Christian faithfulness may be hidden an absence of Christian love. Beneath an apparently rightful care for our affairs may be hidden a great want of trust in God. I believe our blessed Guide, the indwelling Holy Spirit, is always secretly discovering these things to us by continual little twinges and pangs of conscience, so that we are left without excuse. But it is very easy to disregard His gentle voice, and insist upon it to ourselves that all is right; and thus the fatal evil will continue hidden in our midst causing defeat in most unexpected quarters.

A capital illustration of this occurred to me once in my housekeeping. I had moved into a new house and, in looking over it to see if it was all ready for occupancy, I noticed in the cellar a very clean-looking cider-cask headed up at both ends. I debated with myself whether I should have it taken out of the cellar and opened to see what was in it, but concluded, as it seemed empty and looked nice, to leave it undisturbed, especially as it would have been quite a piece of work to get it up the stairs. I did not feel quite easy, but reasoned away my scruples and left it. Every spring and fall, when house-cleaning time came on, I would remember that cask, with a little twinge of my housewifely conscience, feeling that I could not quite rest in the thought of a perfectly cleaned house, while it remained unopened, for how did I know but under its fair exterior it contained some hidden evil. Still I managed to quiet my scruples on the subject, thinking always of the trouble it would involve to investigate it; and for two or three years the innocent-looking cask stood quietly in my cellar.

Then, most unaccountably, moths began to fill my house. I used every possible precaution against them, and made every effort to eradicate them, but in vain. They increased rapidly and threatened to ruin everything I had. I suspected my carpets as being the cause, and subjected them to a thorough cleaning. I suspected my furniture, and had it newly upholstered. I suspected all sorts of impossible things. At last the thought of the cask flashed on me. At once I had it brought up out of the cellar and the head knocked in, and I think it is safe to say that thousands of moths poured out. The previous occupant of the house must have headed it up with something in it which bred moths, and this was the cause of all my trouble.

Now I believe that, in the same way, some innocent-looking habit or indulgence, some apparently unimportant and safe thing, about which we yet have now and then little twinges of conscience, something which is not brought out fairly into the light, and investigated under the searching eye of God, lies at the root of most of the failure in this higher life. All is not given up. Some secret corner is kept locked against the entrance of the Lord. And therefore we cannot stand before our enemies, but find ourselves smitten down in their presence.

In order to prevent failure, or to discover its cause if we have failed, it is necessary that we should keep continually before us this prayer, "Search me, O God, and know my heart; try me and know my thoughts; and see if there be any evil way in me, and lead me in the way everlasting."

There may be something very deceptive in our sufferings over our failures. We may seem to ourselves to be wholly occupied with the glory of God, and yet in our inmost souls it may be self alone that occasions all our trouble. Our self-love is touched in a tender spot by the discovery that we are not so saintly as we thought we were; and this chagrin is often a greater sin than the original fault itself.

The only safe way to treat our failures is neither to justify nor condemn ourselves on account of them, but to lay them quietly and in simplicity before the Lord, looking at them in peace and in the spirit of love.

All the old mystic writers tell us that our progress is aided far more by a simple, peaceful turning to God, than by all our chagrin and remorse over our lapses from Him. Only be faithful, they say, in turning quietly to Him alone, the moment you perceive what you have done, and His presence will deliver you from the snares which have entrapped you. To look at self plunges you deeper into the slough, for this very slough is after all nothing but self; while the gentlest look toward God will calm and deliver your heart.

Finally, let us never forget for one moment, no matter how often we may fail, that the Lord Jesus is able, according to the declaration concerning Him, to deliver us out of the hands of our enemies, that we may "serve Him without fear, in holiness and righteousness before Him all the days of our life."

Let us then pray, every one of us, day and night, "Lord, keep us from sinning, and make us living witnesses of Thy mighty power to save to the uttermost"; and let us never be satisfied until we are so pliable in His hands, and have learned so to trust Him, that He will be able to "make us perfect, in every good work to do His will, working in us that which is well-pleasing in His sight, through Jesus Christ; to whom be glory for ever and ever. Amen."

XII

Is God in Everything?

ONE OF THE GREATEST OBSTACLES to living unwaveringly this life of entire surrender is the difficulty of seeing God in everything. People say, "I can easily submit to things which come from God; but I cannot submit to man, and most of my trials and crosses come through human instrumentality." Or they say, "It is all well enough to talk of trusting; but when I commit a matter to God, man is sure to come in and disarrange it all; and while I have no difficulty in trusting God, I do see serious difficulties in the way of trusting men."

This is no imaginary trouble, but it is of vital importance, and if it cannot be met, it does really make the life of faith an impossible and visionary theory. For nearly everything in life comes to us through human instrumentalities, and most of our trials are the result of somebody's failure, or ignorance, or carelessness, or sin. We know God cannot be the author of these things, and yet unless He is the agent in the matter, how can we say to Him about it, "Thy will be done"?

Besides, what good is there in trusting our affairs to God, if, after all, man is to be allowed to come in and disarrange them; and how is it possible to live by faith, if human agencies, in whom it would be wrong and foolish to trust, are to have a predominant influence in molding our lives?

Moreover, things in which we can see God's hand always have a sweetness in them which consoles while it wounds. But the trials inflicted by man are full of bitterness.

What is needed, then, is to see God in everything, and to receive everything directly from His hands, with no intervention of second causes. And it is just to this that we must be brought, before we can know an abiding experience of entire abandonment and perfect trust. Our abandonment must be to God, not to man, and our trust must be in Him, not in any arm of flesh, or we shall fail at the first trial.

The question here confronts us at once, "But is God in everything, and have we any warrant from the Scripture for receiving everything from His hands, without regarding the second causes which may have been instrumental in bringing it about?" I answer to this, unhesitatingly, Yes. To the children of God everything comes directly from their Father's hand, no matter who or what may have been the apparent agents. There are no "second causes" for them.

The whole teaching of the Bible asserts and implies this. "Not a sparrow falls to the ground without our Father." The very hairs of our head are all numbered. We are not to be careful about anything, because our Father cares for us. We are not to avenge ourselves, because our Father has charged Himself with our defense. We are not to fear, for the Lord is on our side. No one can be against us, because He is for us. We shall not want, for He is our Shepherd. When we pass through the rivers they shall not overflow us, and when we walk through the fire we shall not be burned, because He will be with us. He shuts the mouths of lions, that they cannot hurt us. "He delivereth and rescueth." "He changeth the times and the seasons; He removeth kings and setteth up kings." A man's heart is in His hand, and, "as the river of water, He turneth it whithersoever He will." He ruleth over all the kingdoms of the heathen; and in His hand there is power and might, "so that none is able to withstand" Him. "He ruleth the raging of the sea; when the waves thereof arise, He stilleth them." He "bringeth the counsel of the heathen to nought; He maketh the devices of the people of none effect." "Whatsoever the Lord pleaseth, that does He in heaven, and in earth, in the seas, and all deep places."

"If thou seest the oppression of the poor, and violent perverting of judgment and justice in a province, marvel not at the matter; for He that is higher than the highest regardeth; and there be higher than they."

"Lo, these are a part of His ways; but how little a portion is heard of Him? But the thunder of His power who can understand?" "Hast thou not known, hast thou not heard, that the everlasting God, the Lord, the Creator of the ends of the earth, fainteth not, neither is weary? There is no searching of His understanding."

And this "God is our refuge and strength, a very present help in trouble. Therefore will not we fear, though the earth be removed, and though the mountains be carried into the midst of the sea; though the waters thereof roar and be troubled; though the mountains shake with the swelling thereof." "I will say of the Lord, He is my refuge and my fortress, my God, in Him will I trust. Surely He shall deliver thee from the snare of the fowler, and from the noisome pestilence. He shall cover thee with His feathers, and under His wings shalt thou trust. His truth shall be thy shield and buckler. Thou shalt not be afraid for the terror by night, nor for the arrow that flieth by day, nor for the pestilence that walketh in darkness, nor for the destruction that wasteth at noonday. A thousand shall fall at thy side, and ten thousand at thy right hand; but it shall not come nigh thee." "Because thou hast made the Lord, which is my refuge, even the Most High, thy habitation, there shall no evil befall thee, neither shall any plague come nigh thy dwelling. For He shall give His angels charge over thee, to keep thee in all thy ways."

To my own mind, these Scriptures, and many others like them, settle forever the question as to the power of second causes in the life of the children of God. They are all under the control of our Father, and nothing can touch us except with His knowledge and by His permission. It may be the sin of man that originates the action, and therefore the thing itself cannot be said to be the will of God but by the time it reaches us, it has become God's will for us, and must be accepted as directly from His hands. No man or company of men, no power in earth or heaven, can touch that soul which is abiding in Christ, without first passing through Him, and receiving the seal of His permission. If God be for us, it matters not who may be against us; nothing can disturb or harm us, except He shall see that it is best for us, and shall stand aside to let it pass.

An earthly parent's care for his helpless child is a feeble illustration of this. If the child is in its father's arms, nothing can touch it without that father's consent, unless he is too weak to prevent it. And even if this should be the case, he suffers the harm first in his own person, before he allows it to reach his child. And if an earthly parent would thus care for his little helpless one, how much more will our Heavenly Father, whose love is infinitely greater, and whose strength and wisdom can never be baffled! I am afraid there are some, even of God's own children, who scarcely think that He is equal to themselves in tenderness, and love, and thoughtful care; and who in their secret thoughts, charge Him with a neglect and indifference of which they would feel themselves incapable. The truth really is that His care is infinitely superior to any possibilities of human care; and that He who counts the very hairs of our head, and suffers not a sparrow to fall without Him, takes note of the minutest matters that can affect the lives of His children, and regulates them all according to His own sweet will, let their origin be what they may.

The instances of this are numberless. Take Joseph. What could have seemed more apparently on the face of it to be the result of sin, and utterly contrary to the will of God, than his being sold into slavery? And yet Joseph, in speaking of it, said, "As for you, ye thought evil against me: but God meant it unto good." "Now, therefore, be not grieved nor angry with yourselves, that ye sold me hither, for God did send me before you to preserve life." To the eye of sense it was surely Joseph's wicked brethren who had sent him into Egypt; and yet Joseph, looking at it with the eye of faith, could say, "God sent me." It had been undoubtedly a grievous sin in his brethren, but, by the time it had reached Joseph, it had become God's will for him, and was in truth, though at first it did not look so, the greatest blessing of his whole life. And thus we see how the Lord can make even the wrath of man to praise Him, and how all things, even the sins of others, shall work together for good to them that love Him.

I learned this lesson practically and experimentally long years before I knew the scriptural truth concerning it. I was attending a prayer meeting held for the promotion of scriptural holiness, when a strange lady rose to speak, and I looked at her, wondering who she could be, little thinking she was to bring a message to my soul which would teach me such a grand lesson. She said she had had great difficulty in living the life of faith, on account of the second causes that seemed to her to control nearly everything that concerned her.

Her perplexity became so great that at last she began to ask God to teach her the truth about it, whether He really was in everything or not. After praying this for a few days, she had what she described as a vision. She thought she was in a perfectly dark place, and that there advanced toward her from a distance a body of light, which gradually surrounded and enveloped her and everything around her. As it approached, a voice seemed to say, "This is the presence of God; this is the presence of God." While surrounded with this presence, all the great and awful things in life seemed to pass before her,—fighting armies, wicked men, raging beasts, storms and pestilences, sin and suffering of every kind.

She shrank back at first in terror, but she soon saw that the presence of God so surrounded and enveloped each one of these, that not a lion could reach out its paw, nor a bullet fly through the air, except as His presence moved out of the way to permit it. And she saw that, let there be ever so thin a sheet, as it were, of this glorious presence between herself and the most terrible violence, not a hair of her head could be ruffled, nor anything touch her, unless the presence divided to let the evil through. Then all the small and annoying things of life passed before her, and equally she saw that these all were so enveloped in this presence of God that not a cross look, not a harsh word, nor petty trial of any kind, could reach her unless His presence moved out of the way to let them through.

Her difficulty vanished. Her question was answered forever. God was in everything; and to her henceforth there were no second causes. She saw that her life came to her day by day and hour by hour directly from His hand, let the agencies which should seem to control it be what they might. And never again had she found any difficulty in an abiding consent to His will and an unwavering trust in His care.

If we look at the seen things, we shall not be able to understand the secret of this. But the children of God are called to look, "not at the things which are seen: for the things which are seen are temporal, but the things which are not seen are eternal." Could we but see with our bodily eyes His unseen forces surrounding us on every side, we would walk through this world in an impregnable fortress, which nothing could ever overthrow or penetrate, for "the angel of the Lord encampeth round about them that fear Him, and delivereth them."

We have a striking illustration of this in the history of Elisha. The king of Syria was warring against Israel, but his evil designs were continually frustrated by the prophet; and at last he sent his army to the prophet's own city for the express purpose of taking him captive. We read, "He sent thither horses and chariots and a great host; and they came by night and compassed the city about." This was the seen thing. And the servant of the prophet, whose eyes had not yet been opened to see the unseen things, was alarmed. And we read, "And when the servant of the man of God was risen early and gone forth, behold a host compassed the city, both with horses and chariots. And his servant said unto him, Alas, my master, how shall we do?" But his master could see the unseen things, and he replied, "Fear not; for they that be with us are more than they that be with them." And then he prayed, saying, "Lord, I pray thee, open his eyes that he may see. And the Lord opened the eyes of the young man, and he saw; and behold, the mountain was full of horses and chariots of fire round about Elisha."

The presence of God is the fortress of His people. Nothing can withstand it. At His presence the wicked perish; the earth trembles; the hills melt like wax; the cities are broken down; "the heavens also dropped, and Sinai itself was moved at the presence of God." And in the secret of this presence He has promised to hide His people from the pride of man, and from the strife of tongues. "My presence shall go with thee," He says, "and I will give thee rest."

I wish it were only possible to make every Christian see this truth as plainly as I see it; for I am convinced it is the only clue to a completely restful life. Nothing else will enable a soul to live only in the present moment, as we are commanded to do, and to take no thought for the morrow. Nothing else will take all the risks and "supposes" out of a Christian's heart, and enable him to say, "Surely goodness and mercy shall follow me all the days of my life." Abiding in God's presence, we run no risks; and such a soul can triumphantly say,—

"I know not what it is to doubt,
    My heart is always gay;
I run no risks, for, come what will,
    God always has His way."

I once heard of a colored woman who earned a precarious living by daily labor, but who was a joyous, triumphant Christian. "Ah! Nancy," said a gloomy Christian lady to her one day, who almost disapproved of her constant cheerfulness, and yet envied it,—"ah! Nancy, it is all well enough to be happy now; but I should think the thoughts of your future would sober you. Only suppose, for instance, that you should have a spell of sickness and be unable to work; or suppose your present employers should move away, and no one else should give you anything to do; or suppose—" "Stop!" cried Nancy, "I never supposes. De Lord is my shepherd, and I knows I shall not want. And, honey," she added to her gloomy friend, "it's all dem supposes as is makin' you so misable. You'd better give dem all up, and just trust de Lord."

There is one text that will take all the "suppose" out of a believer's life, if only it is received and acted out in a childlike faith; it is in Hebrews 3:5, 6: "Be content, therefore, with such things as ye have; for He hath said I will never leave thee, nor forsake thee"; so that we may boldly say, "THE LORD IS MY HELPER, AND I WILL NOT FEAR WHAT MAN SHALL DO UNTO ME." What if dangers of all sorts shall threaten you from every side, and the malice or foolishness or ignorance of men shall combine to do you harm? You may face every possible contingency with these triumphant words, "The Lord is my helper, and I will not fear what man shall do unto me." If the Lord is your helper, how can you fear what man may do unto you? There is no man in this world, nor company of men, that can touch you, unless your God, in whom you trust, shall please to let them. "He will not suffer thy foot to be moved: He that keepeth thee will not slumber. Behold, He that keepeth Israel shall neither slumber nor sleep. The Lord is thy keeper; the Lord is thy shade upon thy right hand. The sun shall not smite thee by day nor the moon by night. The Lord shall preserve thee from all evil: He shall preserve thy soul. The Lord shall preserve thy going out, and thy coming in, from this time forth, and even for evermore."

Nothing else but this seeing God in everything will make us loving and patient with those who annoy and trouble us. They will be to us then only the instruments for accomplishing His tender and wise purposes toward us, and we shall even find ourselves at last inwardly thanking them for the blessings they bring us.

Nothing else will completely put an end to all murmuring or rebelling thoughts. Christians often feel a liberty to murmur against man, when they would not dare to murmur against God. But this way of receiving things would make it impossible ever to murmur. If our Father permits a trial to come, it must be because that trial is the sweetest and best thing that could happen to us, and we must accept it with thanks from His dear hand. The trial itself may be hard to flesh and blood, and I do not mean that we can like or enjoy the suffering of it. But we can and must love the will of God in the trial, for His will is always sweet, whether it be in joy or in sorrow.

Our trials may be our chariots. We long for some victory over sin and self, and we ask God to grant it to us. His answer comes in the form of a trial which He means shall be the chariot to bear us to the longed-for triumph. We may either let it roll over us and crush us as a juggernaut car, or we may mount into it and ride triumphantly onward. Joseph's chariots, which bore him on to the place of his exaltation, were the trials of being sold into slavery, and being cast unjustly into prison. Our chariots may be much more insignificant things than these; they may be nothing but irritating people or uncomfortable circumstances. But whatever they are, God means them to be our cars of triumph, which shall bear us onward to the victories we have prayed for. If we are impatient in our dispositions and long to be made patient, our chariot will probably be a trying person to live in the house with us, whose ways or words will rasp our very souls. If we accept the trial as from God, and bow our necks to the yoke, we shall find it just the discipline that will most effectually produce in us the very grace of patience for which we have asked.

God does not order the wrong thing, but He uses it for our blessing; just as He used the cruelty of Joseph's wicked brethren, and the false accusations of Pharaoh's wife. In short, this way of seeing our Father in everything makes life one long thanksgiving, and gives a rest of heart, and more than that, a gayety of spirit, that is unspeakable. Someone says, "God's will on earth is always joy, always tranquility." And since He must have His own way concerning His children, into what wonderful green pastures of inward rest, and beside what blessedly still waters of inward refreshment, is the soul led that learns this secret.

If the will of God is our will, and if He always has His way, then we always have our way also, and we reign in a perpetual kingdom. He who sides with God cannot fail to win in every encounter; and whether the result shall be joy or sorrow, failure or success, death or life, we may, under all circumstances, join in the apostle's shout of victory, "Thanks be unto God, which always causeth us to triumph in Christ!"

XIII

Bondage or Freedom?

THERE ARE TWO KINDS of Christian experience, one of which is an experience of bondage, and the other an experience of freedom. In bondage, the soul is controlled by a stern sense of duty and obeys the law of God either from fear of punishment or from expectation of wages. In the experience of freedom, the controlling power is an inward life principle that works out, by the force of its own motions or instincts, the will of the divine Life-giver without fear of punishment or hope of reward. In the first the Christian is a servant and works for hire. In the second he is a son and works for love.

This contrast in the experience of Christians should not be. To "walk in freedom" is plainly their only right and normal condition. But as we have to deal with what is, rather than with what ought to be, we cannot shut our eyes to the sad condition of bondage in which so many of God's children spend a large part of their

Christian lives. The reason and the remedy for this are not difficult to find. The reason is legality and the remedy is Christ.

Nowhere do we find those two forms or stages of Christian life more fully developed and contrasted than in the Epistle to the Galatians. The occasion of its being written was that some Jewish brethren came among the churches in Galatia. They tried to draw them away from the liberty of the Gospel by presenting certain forms and ceremonies as necessary to their salvation. Peter allowed himself to unite with these teachers. Therefore Paul reproves, not only the Galatians, but also Peter himself.

Neither Peter nor the Galatians committed any moral sin. They did, however, commit a spiritual sin. They got into a wrong attitude toward God a legal attitude. They began, as Christians generally do, in the right attitude. That is, they entered by the "hearing of faith" into the spiritual life. But when it came to a question of how they were to live in this life, they changed their ground. They sought to substitute works for faith. Having "begun in the Spirit," they were now seeking to be "made perfect by the flesh." They descended in their Christian living from the plane of life to the plane of law.

An illustration will help us to understand this. There are two men who do not steal. Outwardly their actions are equally honest, but inwardly there is a vital difference. One man had a dishonest nature that wants to steal, and is prevented from doing so only by the fear of a penalty. The other possesses an honest nature that hates thieving and could not be induced to steal even by the hope of a reward. The one is honest in the spirit. The other is honest only in the flesh. No words are needed to identify which sort the Christian life is meant to be.

We are, however, continually tempted to forget that it is not what men do that is important, but what they are. In Christ Jesus neither following or not following legal observances matters. 2 Corinthians 5:17 tells us, "Therefore if any man be in Christ, he is a new creature: old things are passed away; behold, all things are become new." God is more concerned about our really being "new creatures" than about anything else. He knows that if we are right in our inward being, we will certainly do right in our outward actions. We may, in fact, sometimes even do right without being right at all. It is very evident that no doing of this kind has any vitality in it, nor is of any real account. The essential thing is character. Doing is valuable only as it is an indication of being.

Paul was grieved with the Galatian Christians because they seemed to have lost sight of this vital truth—that the inward life, the "new creature," was the only thing that mattered. They began on this plane, but fell from grace to a lower plane. Romans 7:6 tells us, "But now we are delivered from the law...we should serve in newness of spirit, and not in the oldness of the letter." "Christ is become of no effect unto you, whosoever of you are justified by the law; ye are fallen from grace" (Galatians 5:4).

This passage is the only one in which the expression "fallen from grace" is used in the New Testament. It means that the Galatians made the mistake of thinking that something else other than Christ was necessary for their right Christian living. The Jewish brethren who had come among them had taught them that Christ alone was not enough, and obedience to the ceremonial law must be added.

They, therefore, believed that some ceremonies of the Jewish ritual were necessary for salvation, and had tried to urge the "Gentiles to live as do the Jews" (Galatians 2:14). Modern Christians are greatly surprised at them and wonder how they could have been so legal. But are not some modern Christians tempted in a different way to follow legality? They added the ceremonial law. We add resolutions, or Christian work, or church-going, or religious ceremonies of one sort or another. Therefore, what is the difference between us and them? It does not make much difference what you add, the wrong thing is to add anything at all.

We condemn outward deeds and outward ceremonies as bringing salvation. But I fear there are many like the Galatian Christians who frustrate the grace of God by legalism.

The following contrasts may help some to understand the difference between these two beliefs, and may enable them to discover where the secret of their own experience of legal bondage lies:

The Law	The Gospel
Demands holiness.	*Gives* holiness.
Says, *Do.*	*Says*, Done.
Extorts the unwilling service of a slave.	*Wins* the loving service of a son.
Makes blessings the results of *obedience.*	Makes obedience the result of *blessings.*
Says, *If.*	Says, *Therefore.*
Was given to restrain man's old nature. Salvation was *wages.*	Was given to bring freedom to man's new nature. Salvation is a *gift.* Christ set us free.

Paul tells us that the law is our "school-master" (Galatians 3:25), not our savior. He emphasizes the fact that it is our schoolmaster only for the purpose of bringing us to Christ, for after faith in Christ is come, he declares we are no longer to be under a schoolmaster. He uses the contrast between a servant and a son as an illustration of his meaning in Galatians 4:7. "Wherefore," he says, "thou art no more a servant, but a son." Galatians 5:11 begs us, because of this, to "Stand fast in the liberty wherewith Christ hath made us free, and be not entangled again with the yoke of bondage."

It is as if a woman was paid for her work in weekly wages as a servant in a house. She was under the law of her master, whom she tried to please, but toward whom her service was one only of duty. Finally, however, the master offers her his love, and lifts her up from the place of a servant to be his bride and to share his fortunes. At once the whole spirit of her service is changed. She may perhaps continue to do the same things that she did before, but she does them now from a different motive. The old sense of duty is lost in the new sense of love. The cold word "master" is transformed into the loving word "husband." "And it shall be at that day, saith the Lord, that thou shalt call me Ishi (my husband), and shalt call me no more Baali (my lord)" (Hosea 2:16).

But imagine this bride beginning after a while to look back upon her former low position and begin to feel unworthy of union with her husband. Who can doubt that very soon the old sense of working for wages would drive out the new sense of working for love, and in spirit the old name of "my master" would again take the place of the new name of "my husband?"

We are amazed at such thinking. But isn't this just what happens to many Christians now? The slavery of duty takes the place of the service of love. God is looked upon as the stern taskmaster who demands our obedience, instead of the loving Father who wins it.

We all know that nothing so destroys the sweetness of any relationship as when this legal spirit creeps in. The moment a husband and wife stop serving each other out of a heart of love and union, and begin to serve from a sense of duty alone, the sweetness of the union is lost. The marriage tie then becomes a bondage, and things that were a joy before are turned into crosses. Many Christians think that taking up the cross means doing something we ought to do, but dislike to do. Such service is thought to have merit. We all know very well that we would not endure it a moment toward ourselves. What wife could endure her husband using language toward her that Christians are continually using toward the Lord? If he would say, for instance, every morning as he went to work, "I am going to work for you today, but I want you to know that it is a very great cross and I hardly know how to bear it." Or what husband would like such language from his wife? No wonder Paul was alarmed when he found there was danger of a legal spirit such as this creeping into the Church of Christ.

Legal Christians do not deny Christ. They only seek to add something to Christ. Their idea is Christ and something besides. Perhaps it is Christ and good works, or Christ and earnest feelings, or Christ and clear doctrines, or Christ and certain religious performances. All these are good in themselves, and good as the results or fruits of salvation. However, to add anything to Christ, no matter how good it may be is to deny His completeness and to exalt self.

A religion of bondage always exalts self. It is what I do—*my* efforts, *my* wrestlings, *my* faithfulness. But a religion of liberty leaves self nothing to glory in; it is all Christ, and what He does, and what He is, and how wonderfully He saves. The child does not boast of itself, but of his father and mother. Our souls can "make (their) boast in the Lord" (Psalm 34:2) when, in this life of liberty, we have learned to know that He and He alone is the sufficient supply for our every need.

We are the children of God. Therefore, we are His heirs. Our possessions come to us, not by working for them, but by inheritance from our Father. Ah, dear friends, how little some of you act like the "heirs of God" (Romans 8:17)! How poverty-stricken you are, and how hard you work for the little you do possess! You may think that good has come from your own effort, which does seem to have a "(show) of wisdom in will worship, and humility, and neglecting of the body" (Colossians 2:2, 3). But I am convinced that any good results have come in spite of, and not because of, your legal working.

I had a friend once whose Christian life was a life of bondage. She worked for her salvation harder than any slave ever worked to purchase his freedom. She never felt as if the day could go right for herself or any of her family, unless she started it with a season of wrestling, and agonizing, and conflict. "Winding up her machine," I called it. One day we were talking about it, and she was telling me of the difficulty and bondage of her Christian life. She wondered what the Bible meant when it said Christ's yoke was easy and His burden light (Matthew 11:30). I told her that I thought she must have gotten things wrong somehow, that the Bible did not suggest that any such wrestling and agonizing are necessary.

"What would you think," I asked, "of children who had to wrestle and agonize with their parents every morning for their necessary food and clothing, or of sheep that had to wrestle with their shepherd, before they could secure the necessary care?"

"Of course I see that would be all wrong," she said. "But then why do I have such good times after I have gone through these conflicts?"

This puzzled me for a moment, but then I asked, "What finally brings about those good times?"

"Why, finally," she replied, "I come to the point of trusting the Lord."

"Suppose you came to that point in the beginning?" I asked.

"Oh," she replied, with sudden illumination, "I never until this minute thought that I might!"

Christ says that except we "become as little children we cannot enter into the Kingdom of heaven" (see Matthew 18:3). But it is impossible to get the child-spirit until the servant-spirit has disappeared. Notice, I do not say the spirit of service, but the servant-spirit. Every good child is filled with the spirit of service, but shouldn't have the servant-spirit. The child serves from love. The servant works for wages.

If a child of loving parents would get the idea that its parents would not give him food and clothing unless he earned them in some way, all the sweetness of the relationship between parent and child would be destroyed. I knew a little girl who did get this idea, and who went around the neighborhood asking at the doors for work so that she might earn a little money to buy herself some clothes. It nearly broke the hearts of her parents when they discovered it. Legal Christians grieve the heart of their Heavenly Father, far more than they know, by letting the servant-spirit creep into their relationship with Him. As soon as we begin to "work for our living" in spiritual things, we have stepped out of the son's place into the servant's, and have fallen from grace.

One servant, of whom we read in the twenty-fifth of Matthew, thought his lord was a hard master. The spirit of bondage makes us think the same now. How many Christians there are who have bowed their necks to the yoke of Christ as to a "yoke of bondage." They have read His declaration that His yoke is easy, as though it were a fairy tale, and gone on their way, never dreaming that it was meant to be actually realized as fact! When some children of God find themselves experiencing freedom, they at once begin to think there must be something wrong in their experience because they no longer find anything to be a "cross" to them. A wife might as well think that there must be something wrong in her love for her husband, when she finds all her services for him are a pleasure instead of a trial!

Sometimes I think that the whole secret of the Christian life that I have been trying to describe is revealed in the child relationship. Nothing more is needed than just to believe that God is as good a Father as the best ideal earthly father. The relationship of a Christian to Him is just the same as that of a child to its parent in this world. Children do not need to carry money with them for their support. If the father has plenty, that satisfies them. This is a great deal better than if it were in the child's own possession since it might get lost. In the same way, it is not necessary for Christians to have all their spiritual possessions in their own keeping. It is far better that their riches should be stored up for them in Christ, and that when they want anything they should receive it directly from His hands. Christ is "made unto us wisdom, and righteousness, and sanctification, and redemption" (1 Corinthians 1:30). Apart from Him, we have nothing.

When people are comparative strangers to one another, they cannot receive gifts from each other comfortably. But when they are united in spirit with a bond of true love between them, no matter how great the gifts, they can be accepted without embarrassment or obligation. This principle holds true in the spiritual life. When Christians are living apart from God, they cannot be brought to accept any great gifts from Him. They feel as if they are too unworthy and do not deserve such gifts. Even when He puts the blessing into their hands, their false humility prevents them from seeing it, and they go on their way without it.

But when Christians get near enough to the Lord to feel the true spirit of adoption, they are ready to accept with delight all the blessings He has in store for them. They never think anything is too much to receive. For then they discover that He is only eager, as parents are, to pour out every good gift upon His children. All things are theirs because they are Christ's, and Christ is God's.

Sometimes a great mystery is made out of the life hid with Christ in God, as though it were a strange mystical thing that ordinary people could not understand. But this contrast between bondage and freedom makes it very plain. It is only to find out that we really are sons, not servants (see Galatians 4:7), that we can enter into the blessed privileges of this relationship. All can understand what it is to be a little child. There is no mystery about that. God did not use the description of Father and children without knowing all that this relationship implies. Those who know Him as their Father know the whole secret. They are their Father's heirs and may enter now into possession of all that is necessary for their present needs. They will therefore be very simple in their prayers. "Lord," they will say, "I am your child, and I need such and such." "My child," He answers, "all things are yours in Christ. Come and take just what you need."

Where the executors of an estate are honorable men, the heirs are not obliged to "wrestle" for their inheritance. The executors are appointed to help them possess it. I sometimes think Christians look upon our Lord as someone appointed to keep them out of their possessions, instead of the one who has come to bring them in. They know little how such an implication grieves and dishonors Him.

It is because legal Christians do not know the truth of their relationship to God, as children to a father, and do not recognize His fatherly heart toward them, that they are in bondage. When they do recognize it, the spirit of bondage becomes impossible to them.

Our freedom must come, therefore, from an understanding of the mind and thoughts of God toward us.

What are the facts of the case? If He has called us to the servants' place, rather than the Christians', whose lives are lives of weary bondage, we are right. But if He has called us to be children and heirs, if we are His friends, His brethren, His bride, how sadly and grievously wrong we are in being entangled under any yoke of bondage whatever, no matter how pious a yoke it may seem to be!

The thought of bondage is utterly abhorrent to any of earth's true relationships, and surely it must be more repugnant to a heavenly relationship. It will not hinder the final entrance of the poor enslaved soul into its heavenly rest, but it will put it into the sad condition of those who are described in 1 Corinthians 3:1-5. "(Their) work shall be burned, (and they) shall suffer loss; (yet they themselves) shall be saved; yet so as by fire."

"Against such there is no law" (Galatians 5:2, 3) is the divine sentence concerning all who live and walk in the Spirit. You will find it most blessedly true in your own experience, if you will lay aside all self-effort and self-dependence of every kind and will consent to let Christ live in you, work in you, and be your indwelling life. The man who lives by the power of an inward righteous nature is not under bondage to the outward law of righteousness. But, he who is restrained by the outward law alone, without the inward restraint of a righteous nature, is a slave to the law. The one fulfills the law in his soul, and is therefore free. The other rebels against the law in his soul, and is therefore bound. I truly wish that every child of God knew the deliverance from bondage which I have tried to present!

XIV

Growth

WHEN THE BELIEVER has been brought to the point of entire surrender and perfect trust, and finds himself dwelling and walking in a life of happy communion and perfect peace, the question naturally arises, "Is this the end?" I answer emphatically "No, it is only the beginning."

And yet this is so little understood that one of the greatest objections made against the advocates of this life of faith is that they do not believe in growth in grace. They are supposed to teach that the soul arrives at a state of perfection beyond which there is no advance, and that all the exhortations in the Scripture which point toward growth and development are rendered void by this teaching.

As exactly the opposite of this is true, I have thought it important next to consider this subject carefully, that I may, if possible, fully answer such objections, and may also show what is the scriptural place to grow in, and how the soul is to grow.

The text which is most frequently quoted is 2 Peter 3:18, "But grow in grace, and in the knowledge of our Lord and Saviour Jesus Christ." Now this text exactly expresses what we believe to be God's will for us, and what also we believe He has made it possible for us to experience. We accept, in their very fullest meaning, all the commands and promises concerning our being no more children, and our growing up into Christ in all things, until we come unto a perfect man, unto the measure of the stature of the fullness of Christ. We rejoice that we need not continue always to be babes, needing milk; but that we may, by reason of use and development become such as have need of strong meat, skillful in the word of righteousness, and able to discern both good and evil. And none would grieve more than we at the thought of any finality in the Christian life beyond which there could be no advance.

But then we believe in a growing that does really produce maturity, and in a development that, as a fact, does bring forth ripe fruit. We expect to reach the aim set before us, and if we do not, we feel sure there must be some fault in our growing. No parent would be satisfied with the growth of his child, if, day after day, and year after year, it remained the same helpless babe it was in the first months of its life; and no farmer would feel comfortable under such growing of his grain as should stop short at the blade, and never produce the ear, nor the full corn in the ear. Growth, to be real, must be progressive, and the days and weeks and months must see a development and increase of maturity in the thing growing. But is this the case with a large part of that which is called growth in grace? Does not the very Christian who is the most strenuous in his longings and in his efforts after it too often find that at the end of the year he is not as far on in his Christian experience as at the beginning, and that his zeal, and his devotedness, and his separation from the world are not as whole-souled or complete as when his Christian life first began?

I was once urging upon a company of Christians the privileges and rest of an immediate and definite step into the land of promise, when a lady of great intelligence interrupted me, with what she evidently felt to be a complete rebuttal of all I had been saying, exclaiming, "Ah! but, my dear friend, I believe in growing in grace." "How long have you been growing?" I asked. "About twenty-five years," was her answer. "And how much more unworldly and devoted to the Lord are you now than when you began your Christian life?" I continued. "Alas!" was the answer, "I fear I am not nearly so much so"; and with this answer her eyes were opened to see that at all events her way of growing had not been successful, but quite the reverse.

The trouble with her, and every other such case, is simply this, they are trying to grow into grace, instead of in it. They are like a rosebush, which the gardener should plant in the hard, stony path, with a view to its growing into the flower bed, and which would of course dwindle and wither in consequence, instead of flourishing and maturing. The children of Israel wandering in the wilderness are a perfect picture of this sort of growing. They were traveling about for forty years, taking many weary steps, and finding but little rest from their wanderings, and yet, at the end of it all, were no nearer the promised land than they were at the beginning. When they started on their wanderings at Kadesh Barnea, they were at the borders of the land, and a few steps would have taken them into it.

When they ended their wanderings in the plains of Moab, they were also at its borders; only with this great difference, that now there was a river to cross, which at first there would not have been. All their wanderings and fightings in the wilderness had not put them in possession of one inch of the promised land. In order to get possession of this land, it was necessary first to be in it; and in order to grow in grace, it is necessary first to be planted in grace. But when once in the land, their conquest was very rapid; and when once planted in grace, the growth of the soul in one month will exceed that of years in any other soil. For grace is a most fruitful soil, and the plants that grow therein are plants of a marvelous growth. They are tended by a Divine Husbandman, and are warmed by the Sun of Righteousness, and watered by the dew from Heaven. Surely it is no wonder that they bring forth fruit, "some an hundred-fold, some sixty-fold, some thirty-fold."

But, it will be asked, what is meant by growing in grace? It is difficult to answer this question because so few people have any conception of what the grace of God really is. To say that it is free, unmerited favor, only expresses a little of its meaning. It is the wondrous, boundless love of God, poured out upon us without stint or measure, not according to our deserving, but according to His infinite heart of love, which passeth knowledge, so unfathomable are its heights and depths. I sometimes think we give a totally different meaning to the word "love" when it is associated with God, from that we so well understand in its human application. But if ever human love was tender and self-sacrificing and devoted; if ever it could bear and forbear; if ever it could suffer gladly for its loved ones; if ever it was willing to pour itself out in a lavish abandonment for the comfort or pleasure of its objects,—then infinitely more is Divine love tender and self-sacrificing and devoted, and glad to bear and forbear, and to suffer, and to lavish its best of gifts and blessings upon the objects of its love. Put together all the tenderest love you know of, dear reader, the deepest you have ever felt, and the strongest that has ever been poured out upon you, and heap upon it all the love of all the loving human hearts in the world, and then multiply it by infinity, and you will begin perhaps to have some faint glimpses of what the love of God in Christ Jesus is. And this is grace. And to be planted in grace is to live in the very heart of this love, to be enveloped by it, to be steeped in it, to revel in it, to know nothing else but love only and love always, to grow day by day in the knowledge of it, and in faith in it, to intrust everything to its care, and to have no shadow of a doubt but that it will surely order all things well.

To grow in grace is opposed to all self-dependence, to all self-effort, to all legality of every kind. It is to put our growing, as well as everything else, into the hands of the Lord, and leave it with Him. It is to be so satisfied with our Husbandman, and with His skill and wisdom, that not a question will cross our minds as to His modes of treatment or His plan of cultivation. It is to grow as the lilies grow, or as the babes grow, without a care and without anxiety; to grow by the power of an inward life principle that cannot help but grow; to grow because we live and therefore must grow; to grow because He who has planted us has planted a growing thing, and has made us to grow.

Surely this is what our Lord meant when He said "Consider the lilies, how they grow; they toil not, neither do they spin: and yet I say unto you, that even Solomon in all his glory was not arrayed like one of these." Or, when He says again, "Which of you by taking thought can add one cubit unto his stature?" There is no effort in the growing of a child or of a lily. They do not toil nor spin, they do not stretch nor strain, they do not make any effort of any kind to grow; they are not conscious even that they are growing; but by an inward life principle, and through the nurturing care of God's providence, and the fostering of caretaker or gardener, by the heat of the sun and the falling of the rain, they grow and grow.

And the result is sure. Even Solomon, our Lord says, in all his glory, was not arrayed like one of these. Solomon's array cost much toiling and spinning, and gold and silver in abundance, but the lily's array costs none of these. And though we may toil and spin to make for ourselves beautiful spiritual garments, and may strain and stretch in our efforts after spiritual growth, we shall accomplish nothing; for no man by taking thought can add one cubit to his stature; and no array of ours can ever equal the beautiful dress with which the great Husbandman clothes the plants that grow in His garden of grace and under His fostering care.

If I could but make each one of my readers realize how utterly helpless we are in this matter of growing, I am convinced a large part of the strain would be taken out of many lives at once. Imagine a child possessed of the monomania that he would not grow unless he made some personal effort after it, and who should insist upon a combination of rope and pulleys whereby to stretch himself up to the desired height. He might, it is true, spend his days and years in a weary strain, but after all there would be no change in the inexorable fact, "No man by taking thought can add one cubit unto his stature"; and his years of labor would be only wasted, if they did not really hinder the longed-for end.

Imagine a lily trying to clothe itself in beautiful colors and graceful lines, stretching its leaves and stems to make them grow, and seeking to manage the clouds and the sunshine, that its needs might be all judiciously supplied!

And yet in these two pictures we have, I conceive, only too true a picture of what many Christians are trying to do; who, knowing they ought to grow, and feeling within them an instinct that longs for growth, yet think to accomplish it by toiling, and spinning, and stretching, and straining, and pass their lives in such a round of self-effort as is a weariness to contemplate.

Grow, dear friends, but grow, I beseech you, in God's way, which is the only effectual way. See to it that you are planted in grace, and then let the Divine Husbandman cultivate you in His own way and by His own means. Put yourselves out in the sunshine of His presence, and let the dew of heaven come down upon you, and see what will come of it. Leaves and flowers and fruit must surely come in their season, for your Husbandman is a skillful one, and He never fails in His harvesting. Only see to it that you interpose no hindrance to the shining of the Sun of Righteousness or the falling of the dew from Heaven. A very thin covering may serve to keep off the heat or the moisture, and the plant may wither even in their midst; and the slightest barrier between your soul and Christ may cause you to dwindle and fade as a plant in a cellar or under a bushel. Keep the sky clear. Open wide every avenue of your being to receive the blessed influences our Divine Husbandman may bring to bear upon you. Bask in the sunshine of His love. Drink in of the waters of His goodness. Keep your face up-turned to Him. Look, and your soul shall live.

You need make no efforts to grow; but let your efforts instead be all concentrated on this, that you abide in the Vine. The Husbandman who has the care of the vine will care for its branches also, and will so prune and purge and water and tend them that they will grow and bring forth fruit, and their fruit shall remain; and, like the lily, they shall find themselves arrayed in apparel so glorious that that of Solomon will be as nothing to it.

What if you seem to yourselves to be planted at this moment in a desert soil where nothing can grow! Put yourself absolutely into the hands of the great Husbandman, and He will at once make that desert blossom as the rose, and will cause springs and fountains of water to start up out of its sandy wastes; for the promise is sure, that the man who trusts in the Lord "shall be as a tree planted by the waters, and that spreadeth out her roots by the river, and shall not see when heat cometh, but her leaf shall be green; and shall not be careful in the year of drought, neither shall cease from yielding fruit." It is the great prerogative of our Divine Husbandman that He is able to turn any soil, whatever it may be like, into the soil of grace, the moment we put our growing into His hands. He does not need to transplant us into a different field, but right where we are, with just the circumstances that surround us, He makes His sun to shine and His dew to fall upon us, and transforms the very things that were before our greatest hindrances into the chiefest and most blessed means of our growth. I care not what the circumstances may be, His wonder-working power can accomplish this. And we must trust Him with it all. Surely He is a Husbandman we can trust. And if He sends storms, or winds, or rains, or sunshine, all must be accepted at His hands with the most unwavering confidence that He who has undertaken to cultivate us, and to bring us to maturity, knows the very best way of accomplishing His end, and regulates the elements, which are all at His disposal, expressly with a view to our most rapid growth.

Let me entreat of you, then, to give up all your efforts after growing, and simply to let yourselves grow. Leave it all to the Husbandman, whose care it is, and who alone is able to manage it. No difficulties in your case can baffle Him. No dwarfing of your growth in years that are past, no apparent dryness of your inward springs of life, no crookedness or deformity in any of your past development, can in the least mar the perfect work that He will accomplish, if you will only put yourselves absolutely into His hands, and let Him have His own way with you. His own gracious promise to His backsliding children assures you of this. "I will heal their backslidings," He says: "I will love them freely, for mine anger is turned away from him. I will be as the dew unto Israel; he shall grow as the lily, and cast forth his roots as Lebanon. His branches shall spread, and his beauty shall be as the olive-tree, and his smell as Lebanon. They that dwell under His shadow shall return; they shall revive as the corn, and grow as the vine; the scent thereof shall be as the wine of Lebanon." And again He says, "Be not afraid, for the pastures of the wilderness do spring, for the tree beareth her fruit, the fig-tree and the vine do yield their strength. And the floors shall be full of wheat, and the fats shall overflow with wine and oil. And I will restore to you the years that the locust hath eaten; and ye shall eat in plenty and be satisfied, and praise the name of the Lord your God, who hath dealt wondrously with you; and my people shall never be ashamed."

Oh! that you could but know just what your Lord meant when He said, "Consider the lilies, how they grow; for they toil not, neither do they spin." Surely these words give us a picture of a life and of a growth far different from the ordinary life and growth of Christians; a life of rest, and a growth without effort; and yet a life and a growth crowned with glorious results. And to every soul that will thus become a lily in the garden of the Lord, and will grow as the lilies grow, the same glorious array will be surely given as is given them; and they will know the fulfillment of that wonderful mystical passage concerning their Beloved, that "He feedeth among the lilies."

This is the sort of growth in grace in which we who have entered into the life of full trust believe: a growth which brings the desired results, which blossoms out into flower and fruit, and becomes a tree planted by the rivers of water, that bringeth forth his fruit in his season; whose leaf also does not wither, and who prospers in whatsoever he doeth. And we rejoice to know that there are growing up now in the Lord's heritage many such plants, who, as the lilies behold the face of the sun and grow thereby, are, by beholding as in a glass the glory of the Lord, being changed into the same image from glory to glory, even as by the spirit of the Lord.

Should you ask such, how it is that they grow so rapidly and with such success, their answer would be that they are not concerned about their growing, and are hardly conscious that they do grow; that their Lord has told them to abide in Him, and has promised that if they do thus abide, they shall certainly bring forth much fruit; and that they are concerned only about the abiding, which is their part, and leave the cultivating and the growing and the training and pruning to their good Husband-man, who alone is able to manage these things or bring them about. You will find that such souls are not engaged in watching self, but in looking unto Jesus. They do not toil nor spin for their spiritual garments, but leave them-selves in the hands of the Lord to be arrayed as it may please Him. Self-effort and self-depen-dence are at an end with them. Their interest in self is gone, transferred over into the hands of another. Self has become really nothing, and Christ alone is all in all to such as these. And the blessed result is that not even Solo-mon, in all his glory, was arrayed like these shall be.

Let us look at this subject practically. We all know that growing is not a thing of effort, but is the result of an inward life, a principle of growth. All the stretching and pulling in the world could not make a dead oak grow. But a live oak grows without stretching. It is plain, therefore, that the essential thing is to get within you the growing life, and then you cannot help but grow. And this life is the life hid with Christ in God, the wonderful divine life of an indwelling Holy Ghost. Be filled with this, dear believer, and, whether you are conscious of it or not, you must grow, you cannot help growing. Do not trouble about your growing, but see to it that you have the growing life. Abide in the Vine. Let the life from Him flow through all your spiritual veins. Interpose no barrier to His mighty life-giving power, working in you all the good pleasure of His will. Yield yourself up utterly to His sweet control. Put your growing into His hands, as completely as you have put all your other affairs. Suffer Him to manage it as He will. Do not concern yourself about it, nor even think of it. Trust Him absolutely, and always. Accept each moment's dispensation as it comes to you, from His dear hands, as being the needed sunshine or dew for that moment's growth. Say a continual "Yes" to your Father's will.

Heretofore you have perhaps tried, as so many do, to be both the lily and the gardener, both the vineyard and the Husbandman. You have taken upon your shoulders the burdens and responsibilities that belong only to the Divine Husbandman, and which He alone is able to bear. Henceforth consent to take your rightful place and to be only what you really are. Say to yourself, If I am the garden only, and not the gardener, if I am the vine only, and not the Husbandman, it is surely essential to my right growth and well-being that I should keep the place and act the part of the garden, and should not usurp the gardener's place, nor try to act the gardener's part.

Do not seek then to choose your own soil, nor the laying out of your borders; do not plant your own seeds, nor dig about, nor prune, nor watch over your own vines. Be content with what the Divine Husbandman arranges for you, and with the care He gives. Let Him choose the sort of plants and fruits He sees best to cultivate, and grow a potato as gladly as a rose, if such be His will, and homely every-day virtues as willingly as exalted fervors. Be satisfied with the seasons He sends, with the sunshine and rain He gives, with the rapidity or slowness of your growth, in short, with all His dealings and processes, no matter how little we may comprehend them.

There is infinite repose in this. As the violet rests in its little nook, receiving contentedly its daily portion satisfied to let rains fall, and suns rise, and the earth to whirl, without one anxious pang, so must we repose in the present as God gives it to us, accepting contentedly our daily portion, and with no anxiety as to all that may be whirling around us, in His great creative and redemptive plan.

The wind that blows can never kill
The tree God plants;
It bloweth east, it bloweth west,
The tender leaves have little rest,
But any wind that blows is best.
The tree God plants
Strikes deeper root, grows higher still,
Spreads wider boughs, for God's good-will
Meets all its wants.

There is no frost hath power to blight
The tree God shields;
The roots are warm beneath soft snows,
And when spring comes it surely knows,
And every bud to blossom grows.
The tree God shields
Grows on apace by day and night,
Till, sweet to taste and fair to sight,
Its fruit it yields.

There is no storm hath power to blast
The tree God knows;
No thunder-bolt, nor beating rain,
Nor lightning flash, nor hurricane;
When they are spent it doth remain.

The tree God knows
Through every tempest standeth fast,
And, from its first day to its last,
Still fairer grows.

If in the soul's still garden-place
A seed God sows—
A little seed—it soon will grow,
And far and near all men will know
For heavenly land He bids it blow.
A seed God sows,
And up it springs by day and night;
Through life, through death, it groweth right,
Forever grows.

XV

Service

THERE IS, PERHAPS, NO PART of Christian experience where a greater change is known upon entering into the life hid with Christ in God, than in the matter of service. In all the lower forms of Christian life, service is apt to have more or less of bondage in it; that is, it is one purely as a matter of duty, and often as a trial and a cross. Certain things, which at the first may have been a joy and delight, become weary tasks, performed faithfully, perhaps, but with much secret disinclination, and many confessed or unconfessed wishes that they need not be done at all, or at least that they need not be done so often. The soul finds itself saying, instead of the "May I" of love, the "Must I" of duty. The yoke, which was at first easy, begins to gall, and the burden feels heavy instead of light.

One dear Christian expressed it once to me in this way. "When I was first converted," she said, "I was so full of joy and love that I was only too glad and thankful to be allowed to do anything for my Lord, and I eagerly entered every open door. But after a while, as my early joy faded away, and my love burned less fervently, I began to wish I had not been quite so eager; for I found myself involved in lines of service which were gradually becoming very distasteful and burdensome to me. I could not very well give them up, since I had begun them, without exciting great remark, and yet I longed to do so increasingly. I was expected to visit the sick, and pray beside their beds. I was expected to attend prayer meetings, and speak at them. I was expected to be always ready for every effort in Christian work, and the sense of these expectations bowed me down continually. At last it became so unspeakably burdensome to me to live the sort of Christian life I had entered upon, and was expected by all around me to live, that I felt as if any kind of manual labor would have been easier, and I would have preferred, infinitely, scrubbing all day on my hands and knees, to being compelled to go through the treadmill of my daily Christian work. I envied," she said, "the servants in the kitchen, and the women at the washtubs."

This may seem to some like a strong statement: but does it not present a vivid picture of some of your own experiences, dear Christian? Have you never gone to your work as a slave to his daily task, knowing it to be your duty, and that therefore you must do it, but rebounding like an India-rubber ball back into your real interests and pleasures the moment your work was over?

Of course you have known this was the wrong way to feel, and have been ashamed of it from the bottom of your heart, but still you have seen no way to help it. You have not loved your work, and, could you have done so with an easy conscience, you would have been glad to have given it up altogether.

Or, if this does not describe your case, perhaps another picture will. You do love your work in the abstract; but, in the doing of it, you find so many cares and responsibilities connected with it, so many misgivings and doubts as to your own capacity or fitness, that it becomes a very heavy burden, and you go to it bowed down and weary, before the labor has even begun. Then also you are continually distressing yourself about the results of your work, and greatly troubled if they are not just what you would like, and this of itself is a constant burden.

Now from all these forms of bondage the soul is entirely delivered that enters fully into the blessed life of faith. In the first place, service of any sort becomes delightful to it, because, having surrendered its will into the keeping of the Lord, He works in it to will and to do of His good pleasure, and the soul finds itself really wanting to do the things God wants it to do. It is always very pleasant to do the things we want to do, let them be ever so difficult of accomplishment, or involve ever so much of bodily weariness. If a man's will is really set on a thing, he regards with a sublime indifference the obstacles that lie in the way of his reaching it, and laughs to himself at the idea of any opposition or difficulties hindering him. How many men have gone gladly and thankfully to the ends of the world in search of worldly fortunes, or to fulfill worldly ambitions, and have scorned the thoughts of any cross connected with it! How many mothers have congratulated themselves and rejoiced over the honor done to their sons in being promoted to some place of power and usefulness in their country's service, although it has involved perhaps years of separation, and a life of hardship for their dear ones? And yet these same men and these very mothers would have felt and said that they were taking up crosses too heavy almost to be borne, had the service of Christ required the same sacrifice of home, and friends, and worldly ease. It is altogether the way we look at things, whether we think they are crosses or not. And I am ashamed to think that any Christian should ever put on a long face and shed tears over doing a thing for

Christ, which a worldly man would be only too glad to do for money.

What we need in the Christian life is to get believers to want to do God's will, as much as other people want to do their own will. And this is the idea of the Gospel. It is what God intended for us; and it is what He has promised. In describing the new covenant in Hebrews 8:6-13, He says it shall no more be the old covenant made on Sinai, that is, a law given from the outside, controlling a man by force, but it shall be a law written within constraining a man by love. "I will put my laws," He says, "in their mind, and write them in their hearts." This can mean nothing but that we shall love His law, for anything written on our hearts we must love. And putting it into our minds is surely the same as God working in us to "will and to do of His good pleasure," and means that we shall will what God wills, and shall obey His sweet commands, not because it is our duty to do so, but because we ourselves want to do what He wants us to do. Nothing could possibly be conceived more effectual than this. How often have we thought when dealing with our children, "Oh, if I could only get inside of them and make them want to do just what I want, how easy it would be to manage them then!" And how often practically in experience we have found that, to deal with cross-grained people, we must carefully avoid suggesting our wishes to them, but must in some way induce them to suggest them themselves, sure that then there will be no opposition to contend with. And we, who are by nature stiff-necked people, always rebel more or less against a law from outside of us, while we joyfully embrace the same law springing up within.

God's plan for us therefore is to get possession of the inside of a man, to take the control and management of his will, and to work it for him; and then obedience is easy and a delight, and service becomes perfect freedom, until the Christian is forced to exclaim, "This happy service! Who could dream earth had such liberty?"

What you need to do then, dear Christian, if you are in bondage, is to put your will over completely into the hands of your Lord, surrendering to Him the entire control of it. Say, "Yes, Lord, YES!" to everything; and trust Him so to work in you to will, as to bring your whole wishes and affections into conformity with His own sweet and lovable and most lovely will. I have seen this done over and over, in cases where it looked beforehand an utterly impossible thing. In one case, where a lady had been for years rebelling fearfully against a thing which she knew was right, but which she hated, I saw her, out of the depths of despair and without any feeling, give her will in that matter up into the hands of her Lord, and begin to say to Him, "Thy will be done; thy will be done!" And in one short hour that very thing began to look sweet and precious to her. It is wonderful what miracles God works in wills that are utterly surrendered to Him. He turns hard things into easy, and bitter things into sweet. It is not that He puts easy things in the place of the hard, but He actually changes the hard thing into an easy one. And this is salvation. It is grand. Do try it, you who are going about your daily Christian living as to a hard and weary task, and see if your Divine Master will not transform the very life you live now as a bondage, into the most delicious liberty!

Or again, if you do love His will in the abstract, but find the doing of it hard and burdensome, from this also there is deliverance in the wonderful life of faith. For in this life no burdens are carried, nor anxieties felt. The Lord is our burden-bearer, and upon Him we must lay off every care. He says, in effect, Be careful for nothing, but just make your requests known to Me, and I will attend to them all. Be careful for nothing, He says, not even your service. Above all, I should think, our service, because we know ourselves to be so utterly helpless in this, that even if we were careful, it would not amount to anything.

What have we to do with thinking whether we are fit or not! The Master-workman surely has a right to use any tool He pleases for His own work, and it is plainly not the business of the tool to decide whether it is the right one to be used or not. He knows; and if He chooses to use us, of course we must be fit. And in truth, if we only knew it, our chiefest fitness is in our utter helplessness. His strength can only be made perfect in our weakness. I can give you a convincing illustration of this.

I was once visiting an idiot asylum and looking at the children going through dumb-bell exercises. Now we all know that it is a very difficult thing for idiots to manage their movements. They have strength enough, generally, but no skill to use this strength, and as a consequence cannot do much. And in these dumb-bell exercises this deficiency was very apparent. They made all sorts of awkward movements. Now and then, by a happy chance, they would make a movement in harmony with the music and the teacher's directions, but for the most part all was out of harmony. One little girl, however, I noticed, who made perfect movements. Not a jar nor a break disturbed the harmony of her exercises. And the reason was, not that she had more strength than the others, but that she had no strength at all. She could not so much as close her hands over the dumb-bells, nor lift her arms, and the master had to stand behind her and do it all. She yielded up her members as instruments to him, and his strength was made perfect in her weakness. He knew how to go through those exercises, for he himself had planned them, and therefore when he did it, it was done right. She did nothing but yield herself up utterly into his hands, and he did it all. The yielding was her part, the responsibility was all his. It was not her skill that was needed to make harmonious movements, but only his. The question was not of her capacity, but of his. Her utter weakness was her greatest strength. And if this is a picture of our Christian life, it is no wonder that Paul could say, "Most gladly therefore will I rather glory in my infirmities, that the power of Christ may rest upon me." Who would not glory in being so utterly weak and helpless, that the Lord Jesus Christ should find no hindrance to the perfect working of His mighty power through us and in us?

Then, too, if the work is His, the responsibility is His, and we have no room left for worrying about it. Everything in reference to it is known to Him, and He can manage it all. Why not leave it all with Him then, and consent to be treated like a child and guided where to go. It is a fact that the most effectual workers

I know are those who do not feel the least care or anxiety about their work, but who commit it all to their dear Master, and, asking Him to guide them moment by moment in reference to it, trust Him implicitly for each moment's needed supplies of wisdom and of strength. To see such, you would almost think perhaps that they were too free from care, where such mighty interests are at stake. But when you have learned God's secret of trusting, and see the beauty and the power of that life which is yielded up to His working, you will cease to condemn, and will begin to wonder how any of God's workers can dare to carry burdens, or assume responsibilities which He alone is able to bear.

There are one or two other bonds of service from which this life of trust delivers us. We find out that we are not responsible for all the work in the world. The commands cease to be general, and become personal and individual. The Master does not map out a general course of action for us and leaves us to get along through it by our own wisdom and skill as best we may, but He leads us step by step, giving us each hour the special guidance needed for that hour. His blessed Spirit dwelling in us, brings to our remembrance at the time the necessary command; so that we do not need to take any thought ahead but simply to take each step as it is made known to us, following our Lord whithersoever He leads us. "The steps of a good man are ordered of the Lord" not his way only, but each separate step in that way. Many Christians make the mistake of expecting to receive God's commands all in a lump, as it were. They think because He tells them to give a tract to one person in a railway train, for instance, that He means them always to give tracts to everybody, and they burden themselves with an impossible command.

There was a young Christian once, who, because the Lord had sent her to speak a message to one soul whom she met in a walk, took it as a general command for always, and thought she must speak to every one she met about their souls. This was, of course, impossible, and as a consequence she was soon in hopeless bondage about it. She became absolutely afraid to go outside of her own door, and lived in perpetual condemnation. At last she disclosed her distress to a friend who was instructed in the ways of God with His servants, and this friend told her she was making a great mistake; that the Lord had His own especial work for each especial workman, and that the servants in a well-regulated household might as well each one take it upon himself to try and do the work of all the rest, as for the Lord's servants to think they were each one under obligation to do everything. He told her just to put herself under the Lord's personal guidance as to her work, and trust Him to point out to her each particular person to whom He would have her speak, assuring her that He never puts forth His own sheep without going before them, and making a way for them Himself. She followed this advice, and laid the burden of her work on the Lord, and the result was a happy pathway of daily guidance, in which she was led into much blessed work for her Master, but was able to do it all without a care or a burden, because He led her out and prepared the way before her.

Putting ourselves into God's hands in this way seems to me just like making the junction between the machinery and the steam engine. The power is not in the machinery, but in the steam; disconnected from the engine, the machinery is perfectly useless; but let the connection be made, and the machinery goes easily and without effort, because of the mighty power there is behind it. Thus the Christian life becomes an easy, natural life when it is the development of the divine working within. Most Christians live on a strain, because their wills are not fully in harmony with the will of God, the connection is not perfectly made at every point, and it requires an effort to move the machinery. But when once the connection is fully made, and the law of the Spirit of life in Christ Jesus can work in us with all its mighty power, we are then indeed made free from the law of sin and death, and shall know the glorious liberty of the children of God. We shall lead frictionless lives.

Another form of bondage as to service, from which the life of faith delivers the soul, is in reference to the after-reflections which always follow any Christian work. These self-reflections are of two sorts. Either the soul congratulates itself upon its success, and is lifted up; or it is distressed over its failure, and is utterly cast down. One of these is sure to come, and of the two I think the first is the more to be dreaded, although the last causes at the time the greater suffering. But in the life of trust, neither will trouble us; for, having committed ourselves and our work to the Lord, we will be satisfied to leave it to Him, and will not think about ourselves in the matter at all.

Years ago I came across this sentence in an old book: "Never indulge, at the close of an action, in any self-reflective acts of any kind, whether of self-congratulation or of self-despair. Forget the things that are behind, the moment they are past, leaving them with God." It has been of unspeakable value to me. When the temptation comes, as it always does, to indulge in these reflections, either of one sort or the other, I turn from them at once, and positively refuse to think about my work at all, leaving it with the Lord to overrule the mistakes, and to bless it as He chooses.

To sum it all up then, what is needed for happy and effectual service is simply to put your work into the Lord's hands, and leave it there. Do not take it to Him in prayer, saying, "Lord, guide me; Lord, give me wisdom; Lord, arrange for me," and then arise from your knees, and take the burden all back, and try to guide and arrange for yourself. Leave it with the Lord, and remember that what you trust to Him, you must not worry over nor feel anxious about. Trust and worry cannot go together. If your work is a burden, it is because you are not trusting it to Him. But if you do trust it to Him, you will surely find that the yoke He puts upon you is easy, and the burden He gives you to carry is light, and even in the midst of a life of ceaseless activity you shall find rest to your soul.

But some may say that this teaching would make us into mere puppets. I answer, No, it would simply make us into servants. It is required of a servant, not that he shall plan, or arrange, or decide, or supply the necessary material, but simply and only that he shall obey. It is for the Master to do all the rest. The servant is not responsible, either, for results. The Master alone knows what results he wished to have produced, and therefore he alone can judge of them. Intelligent service will, of course, include some degree of intelligent sympathy with the thoughts and plans of the Master, but after all there cannot be a full comprehension, and the responsibility cannot be transferred from the Master's shoulders to the servant's. And in our case, where our outlook is so limited and our ignorance so great, we can do very little more than be in harmony with the will of our Divine Master, without expecting to comprehend it very fully, and we must leave all the results with Him. What looks to us like failure on the seen side is often, on the unseen side, the most glorious success; and if we allow ourselves to lament and worry, we shall often be doing the foolish and useless thing of weeping where we ought to be singing and rejoicing.

Far better is it to refuse utterly to indulge in any self-reflective acts at all; to refuse, in fact, to think about self in any way, whether for good or evil. We are not our own property, nor our own business. We belong to God, and are His instruments and His business; and since He always attends to His own business, He will of course attend to us.

I heard once of a slave who was on board a vessel in a violent storm, and who was whistling contentedly while every one else was in an agony of terror. At last someone asked him if he was not afraid he would be drowned. He replied with a broad grin, "Well, missus, s'pose I is. I don't b'long to myself, and it will only be massa's loss any how."

Something of this spirit would deliver us from many of our perplexities and sufferings in service. And with a band of servants thus abandoned to our Master's use and to His care, what might He not accomplish? Truly one such would "chase a thousand, and two would put ten thousand to flight"; and nothing would be impossible to them. For it is nothing with the Lord "to help, whether with many or with them that have no power."

May God raise up such an army speedily!

And may you, my dear reader, enroll your name in this army today and, yielding yourself unto God as one who is alive from the dead, may every one of your members be also yielded unto Him as instruments of righteousness, to be used by Him as He pleases.

XVI

Practical Results in the Daily Walk and Conversation

IF ALL THAT HAS BEEN SAID concerning the life hid with Christ in God be true, its results in the practical daily walk and conversation ought to be very marked, and the people who have entered into the enjoyment of it ought to be, in very truth, a "peculiar people, zealous of good works."

My son at college once wrote to a friend to this effect: that Christians are God's witnesses necessarily, because the world will not read the Bible, but they will read our lives; and that upon the report these give will very much depend their belief in the Divine nature of the religion we profess. As we all know, this is an age of facts, and inquiries are being increasingly turned from theories to realities. If our religion is to make any headway now, it must be proved to be more than a theory, and we must present, to the investigation of the critical minds of our age, the grand facts of lives which have been actually and manifestly transformed by the mighty power of God working in us all the good pleasure of His will. Give us "forms of life," say the scientists, and we will be convinced. And when the Church is able to present to them in all its members, the form of a holy life, their last stronghold will be conquered.

I desire, therefore, before closing my book, to speak very solemnly of what I conceive to be the necessary fruits of a life of faith, such as I have been describing, and to press home to the hearts of every one of my readers their responsibility to walk worthy of the high calling wherewith they have been called.

And I would speak to some of you, at least, as personal friends, for I feel sure we have not gone this far together through this book without there having grown in your hearts, as there has in mine, a tender personal interest and longing for one another, that we may in everything show forth the praises of Him who has called us out of darkness into His marvelous light. As a friend, then, to friends, I am sure I may speak very plainly, and will be pardoned if I go into some particulars of life and character which are vital to all true Christian development.

The standard of practical holy living has been so low among Christians that any good degree of real devotedness of life and walk is looked upon with surprise, and even often with disapprobation, by a large portion of the Church. And, for the most part, the professed followers of the Lord Jesus Christ are so little like Him in character or in action, that to an outside observer there would not seem to be much harmony between them.

But we, who have heard the call of our God to a life of entire consecration and perfect trust, must do differently from all this. We must come out from the world and be separate, and must not be conformed to it in our characters nor in our purposes. We must no longer share in its spirit or its ways. Our conversation must be in Heaven, and we must seek those things that are above, where Christ sitteth on the right hand of God. We must walk through the world as Christ walked. We must have the mind that was in Him. As pilgrims and strangers, we must abstain from fleshly lusts that war against the soul. As good soldiers of Jesus Christ, we must disentangle ourselves from the affairs of this life as far as possible, that we may please Him who hath chosen us to be soldiers. We must abstain from all appearance of evil. We must be kind one to another, tenderhearted, forgiving one another, even as God, for Christ's sake, hath forgiven us. We must not resent injuries or unkindness, but must return good for evil, and turn the other cheek to the hand that smites us. We must take always the lowest place among our fellow men; and seek not our own honor, but the honor of others. We must be gentle, and meek, and yielding; not standing up for our own rights, but for the rights of others. All that we do must be done for the glory of God. And, to sum it all up, since He which hath called us is holy, so we must be holy in a manner of conversation; because it is written, "Be ye holy, for I am holy."

Now, dear friends, this is all exceedingly practical and means, surely, a life very different from the lives of most professors around us. It means that we do really and absolutely turn our backs on self, and on self's motives and self's aims. It means that we are a peculiar people, not only in the eyes of God, but in the eyes of the world around us; and that, wherever we go, it will be known from our Christ-like lives and conversation that we are followers of the Lord Jesus Christ; and are not of the world, even as He was not of the world. We shall no longer feel that our money is our own, but the Lord's, to be used in His service. We shall not feel at liberty to use our energies exclusively in the pursuit of worldly means, but, seeking first the kingdom of God and His righteousness, shall have all needful things added unto us. We shall find ourselves forbidden to seek the highest places, or to strain after worldly advantages. We shall not be permitted to be conformed to the world in our ways of thinking or of living. We shall feel no desire to indulge in the world's frivolous pursuits. We shall find our affections set upon heavenly things, rather than upon earthly things. Our days will be spent not in serving ourselves, but in serving our Lord; and all our rightful duties will be more perfectly performed than ever, because whatever we do will be done "not with eye-service as men-pleasers, but as the servants of Christ, doing the will of God from the heart."

Into all these things we shall undoubtedly be led by the blessed Spirit of God, if we give ourselves up to His guidance. But unless we have the right standard of Christian life set before us, we shall be hindered by our ignorance from recognizing His voice; and it is for this reason I desire to be very plain and definite in my statements.

I have noticed that wherever there has been a faithful following of the Lord in a consecrated soul, several things have inevitably followed, sooner or later.

Meekness and quietness of spirit become in time the characteristics of the daily life; a submissive acceptance of the will of God, as it comes in the hourly events of each day; pliability in the hands of God to do or to suffer all the good pleasure of His will; sweetness under provocation; calmness in the midst of turmoil and bustle; yieldingness to the wishes of others, and an insensibility to slights and affronts, absence of worry or anxiety deliverance from care and fear: all these, and many other similar graces are invariably found to be the natural outward development of that inward life which is hid with Christ in God. Then as to the habits of life: we always see such Christians sooner or later giving themselves up to some work for God and their fellow men, willing to spend and be spent in the Master's service. They become indifferent to outward show in the furniture of their houses and the style of their living, and make all personal adornment secondary to the things of God. The voice is dedicated to God, to talk and sing for Him. The purse is placed at His disposal. The pen is dedicated to write for Him, the lips to speak for Him, the hands and the feet to do His bidding. Year after year such Christians are seen to grow more unworldly, more heavenly minded, more transformed, more like Christ, until even their very faces express so much of the beautiful inward Divine life, that all who look at them cannot but take knowledge of them that they live with God, and are abiding in Him.

I feel sure that to each one of you have come at least some Divine intimations or foreshadowings of the life I here describe. Have you not begun to feel dimly conscious of the voice of God speaking to you in the depths of your soul about these things? Has it not been a pain and a distress to you of late to discover how much there is wrong in your life? Has not your soul been plunged into inward trouble and doubt about certain dispositions and ways in which you have been formerly accustomed to indulge? Have you not begun to feel uneasy with some of your habits of life, and to wish that you could do differently in these respects? Have not paths of devotedness and of service begun to open out before you, with the longing thought, "Oh, that I could walk in them"?

All these longings and doubts, and this inward distress, are the voice of the Good Shepherd in your heart seeking to call you out of all that is contrary to His will. Oh! let me entreat of you not to turn away from His gentle pleadings. You little know the secret paths into which He means to lead you by these very steps, nor the wonderful stores of blessedness that lie at their end, or you would spring forward with an eager joy to yield to every one of His requirements. The heights of Christian perfection can only be reached by faithfully following the Guide who is to lead you there, and He reveals your way to you one step at a time in the teachings and providences of your daily lives, asking only on your part that you yield yourselves up to His guidance. If, then, in anything you are convinced of sin, be sure that it is the voice of your Lord, and surrender it at once to His bidding, rejoicing with a great joy that He has begun thus to lead and guide you. Be perfectly pliable in His wise hands, go where He entices you, turn away from all from which He makes you shrink, obey Him perfectly; and He will lead you out swiftly and easily into a wonderful life of conformity to Himself, that will be a testimony to all around you, beyond what you yourself will ever know.

I knew a soul thus given up to follow the Lord whithersoever He might lead her, who in three short months traveled from the depths of darkness and despair into the realization and conscious experience of the most blessed union with the Lord Jesus Christ. Out of the midst of her darkness, she consecrated herself to the Lord, surrendering her will up altogether to Him, that He might work in her to will and to do of His own good pleasure. Immediately He began to speak to her by His Spirit in her heart, suggesting to her some little acts of service for Him, and calling her out of all un-Christ-like dispositions and ways. She recognized His voice, and yielded to Him each thing He asked for, following Him whithersoever He might lead her, with no fear but the one fear of disobeying Him. He led her rapidly on, day by day conforming her more and more to His will, and making her life such a testimony to those around her, that even some who had begun by opposing and disbelieving, were forced to acknowledge that it was of God, and were won to a similar surrender. And, finally, after three short months of this faithful following, it came to pass, so swiftly had she gone, that her Lord was able to reveal to her wondering soul some of the deepest secrets of His love, and to fulfill to her the marvelous promise of Acts 1:5, baptizing her with the Holy Ghost. Think you she has ever regretted her wholehearted following of Him? Or that aught but thankfulness and joy can ever fill her soul when she reviews the steps by which her feet had been led to this place of wondrous blessedness, even though some of them may have seemed at the time hard to take? Ah! dear soul, if thou wouldst know a like blessing, abandon thyself, like her, to the guidance of the Divine Master, and shrink from no surrender for which He may call.

> "The perfect way is hard to flesh,
>   It is not hard to love;
> If thou wert sick for want of God,
>   How swiftly wouldst thou move."

Surely thou canst trust Him! And if some things may be called for which look to thee of but little moment, and not worthy thy Lord's attention, remember that He sees not as man seeth, and that things small to thee may be in His eyes the key and the clue to the deepest springs of thy being. In order to moud thee into entire conformity to His will, He must have thee pliable in his hands, and this pliability is more quickly reached by yielding in the little things than even by the greater. Thy one great desire is to follow Him fully; canst thou not say then a continual "Yes, Lord!" to all His sweet commands, whether small or great, and trust Him to lead thee by the shortest road to thy fullest blessedness?

My dear friend, this, and nothing less than this, is what thy consecration meant, whether thou knew it or not. It meant inevitable obedience. It meant that the will of thy God was henceforth to be thy will under all circumstances and at all times. It meant that from that moment thou surrendered thy liberty of choice, and gave thyself up utterly into the control of thy Lord. It meant an hourly following of Him whithersoever He might lead thee, without any dream of turning back.

And now I appeal to thee to make good thy word. Let everything else go, that thou mayest live out, in a practical daily walk and conversation, the Divine life thou hast dwelling within thee. Thou art united to thy Lord by a wondrous tie; walk, then, as He walked, and show to the unbelieving world the blessed reality of His mighty power to save, by letting Him save thee to the very uttermost. Thou needst not fear to consent to this, for He is thy Savior; and His power is to do it all. He is not asking thee, in thy poor weakness, to do it thyself; He only asks thee to yield thyself to Him, that He may work in thee to will and to do by His own mighty power. Thy part is to yield thyself, His part is to work; and never, never will He give thee any command which is not accompanied by ample power to obey it. Take no thought for the morrow in this matter; but abandon thyself with a generous trust to thy loving Lord, who has promised never to call His own sheep out into any path, without Himself going before them to make the way easy and safe. Take each onward step as He makes it plain to thee. Bring all thy life in each of its details to Him to regulate and guide. Follow gladly and quickly the sweet suggestions of His Spirit in thy soul. And day by day thou wilt find Him bringing thee more and more into conformity with His will in all things; molding thee and fashioning thee, as thou art able to bear it, into a vessel unto His honor, sanctified and meet for His use, and fitted to every good work. So shall be given to thee the sweet joy of being an epistle of Christ known and read of all men; and thy light shall shine so brightly that men seeing, not thee, but thy good works, shall glorify, not thee, but thy Father which is in Heaven.

We are predestined to be "conformed to the image" of God's Son. This means, of course, not a likeness of bodily presence, but a likeness of character and nature. It means a similarity of thought, of feeling, of desire, of love, of hate. It means, that we are to think and act, according to our measure, as Christ would have thought and acted under our circumstances.

A little girl was once questioned what it meant to be a Christian. She replied, "It means to be just what Christ would be, if He was a little girl and lived in my house."

The secret of Christ's life was the pouring out of Himself for others; and if we are like Him, this will be the secret of our lives also. He saved others, but Himself He could not save. He "pleased not Himself," and therefore we are "not to please ourselves," but rather our neighbor, when it is for his good.

A thoughtful Hindu religionist, who visited England and America lately to examine into Christianity, said, as the result of his observations, "What Christians need is a little more of Christ's Christianity, and a little less of man's."

Man's Christianity teaches sacrifice to save ourselves; Christ's Christianity teaches sacrifice to save others. Man's Christianity produces the fruitless selfishness of too much of our religion. Christ's Christianity produces the blessed unselfishness of lives that are poured out for others, as was His.

In short, then, the one practical outcome of all that our book has been teaching us is simply this, that we are to be Christ-like Christians. And all our experiences amount to nothing if they do not produce this result. For "not every one that saith unto me, Lord, Lord, shall enter into the kingdom of heaven; but he that doeth the will of my Father which is in heaven."

XVII

The Joy of Obedience

I REMEMBER READING ONCE somewhere this sentence, "Perfect obedience would be perfect happiness, if only we had perfect confidence in the power we were obeying." I remember being struck with the saying, as the revelation of a possible, although hitherto undreamed-of way of happiness; and often afterward, through all the lawlessness and willfulness of my life, did that saying recur to me as the vision of a rest, and yet of a possible development, that would soothe and at the same time satisfy all my yearnings. Need I say that this rest has been revealed to me now, not as a vision, but as a reality; and that I have seen in the Lord Jesus, the Master to whom we may all yield up our implicit obedience, and, taking His yoke upon us, may find our perfect rest?

You little know, dear hesitating soul, of the joy you are missing. The Master has revealed Himself to you, and is calling for your complete surrender, and you shrink and hesitate. A measure of surrender you are willing to make, and think indeed it is fit and proper you should. But an utter abandonment, without any reserves, seems to you too much to be asked for. You are afraid of it. It involves too much, you think, and is too great a task. To be measurably obedient you desire; to be perfectly obedient appalls you.

And then, too, you see other souls who seem able to walk with easy consciences, in a far wider path than that which appears to be marked out for you, and you ask yourself why this need be. It seems strange, and perhaps hard to you, that you must do what they need not, and must leave undone what they have liberty to do.

Ah! dear Christian, this very difference between you is your privilege, though you do not yet know it. Your Lord says, "He that hath my commandments, and keepeth them, he it is that loveth Me; and he that loveth Me shall be loved of my Father, and I will love him, and will manifest Myself to him." You have His commandments; those you envy, have them not. You know the mind of your Lord about many things, in which, as yet, they are walking in darkness. Is not this a privilege? Is it a cause for regret that your soul is brought into such near and intimate relations with your Master, that He is able to tell you things which those who are further off may not know? Do you not realize what a tender degree of intimacy is implied in this?

There are many relations in life which require from the different parties only very moderate degrees of devotion. We may have really pleasant friendships with one another, and yet spend a large part of our lives in separate interests, and widely differing pursuits. When together, we may greatly enjoy one another's society, and find many congenial points; but separation is not any especial distress to us, and other and more intimate friendships do not interfere. There is not enough love between us, to give us either the right or the desire to enter into and share one another's most private affairs. A certain degree of reserve and distance is the suitable thing, we feel. But there are other relations in life where all this is changed. The friendship becomes love. The two hearts give themselves to one another, to be no longer two but one. A union of souls takes place, which makes all that belongs to one the property of the other. Separate interests and separate paths in life are no longer possible. Things which were lawful before become unlawful now, because of the nearness of the tie that binds. The reserve and distance suitable to mere friendship becomes fatal in love. Love gives all, and must have all in return. The wishes of one become binding obligations to the other, and the deepest desire of each heart is that it may know every secret wish or longing of the other, in order that it may fly on the wings of the wind to gratify it.

Do such as these chafe under this yoke which love imposes? Do they envy the cool, calm, reasonable friendships they see around them, and regret the nearness into which their souls are brought to their beloved one, because of the obligations it creates? Do they not rather glory in these very obligations, and inwardly pity, with a tender yet exulting joy, the poor far-off ones who dare not come so near? Is not every fresh revelation of the mind of one another a fresh delight and privilege, and is any path found hard which their love compels them to travel?

Ah! dear souls, if you have ever known this even for a few hours in any earthly relation; if you have ever loved a fellow human being enough to find sacrifice and service on their behalf a joy; if a whole-souled abandonment of your will to the will of another has ever gleamed across you as a blessed and longed-for privilege, or as a sweet and precious reality, then, by all the tender longing love of your heavenly Master, would I entreat you to let it be so toward God!

He loves you with more than the love of friendship. As a bridegroom rejoices over his bride, so does He rejoice over you, and nothing but a full surrender will satisfy Him. He has given you all, and He asks for all in return. The slightest reserve will grieve Him to the heart. He spared not Himself, and how can you spare yourself? For your sake He poured out in a lavish abandonment all that He had, and for His sake you must pour out all that you have without stint or measure.

Oh, be generous in your self-surrender! Meet His measureless devotion for you, with a measureless devotion to Him. Be glad and eager to throw yourself headlong into His dear arms, and to hand over the reins of government to Him. Whatever there is of you, let Him have it all. Give up forever everything that is separate from Him. Consent to resign from this time forward all liberty of choice; and glory in the blessed nearness of union which makes this enthusiasm of devotedness not only possible but necessary. Have you never longed to lavish your love and attention upon someone far off from you in position or circumstances, with whom you were not intimate enough for any closer approach? Have you not felt a capacity for self-surrender and devotedness, that has seemed to burn within you like a fire, and yet had no object upon which it dared to lavish itself? Have not your hands been full of alabaster boxes of ointment, very precious, which you have never been near enough to any heart to pour out? If, then, you are hearing the sweet voice of your Lord calling you into a place of nearness to Himself, which will require a separation from all else, and which will make this enthusiasm of devotedness not only possible, but necessary will you shrink or hesitate? Will you think it hard that He reveals to you more of His mind than He does to others, and that He will not allow you to be happy in anything which separates you from Himself? Do you want to go where He cannot go with you, or to have pursuits which He cannot share?

No! no, a thousand times, no! You will spring out to meet His dear will with an eager joy. Even His slightest wish will become a binding law to you, which it would fairly break your heart to disobey. You will glory in the very narrowness of the path He marks out for you, and will pity with an infinite pity the poor far-off ones who have missed this precious joy. The obligations of love will be to you its sweetest privileges; and the right you have acquired to lavish the uttermost abandonment of all that you have upon your Lord will seem to lift you into a region of unspeakable glory. The perfect happiness of perfect obedience will dawn upon your soul, and you will begin to know something of what Jesus meant when He said, "I delight to do thy will, O my God."

And do you think the joy in this will be all on your side? Has the Lord no joy in those who have thus surrendered themselves to Him, and who love to obey Him? Ah, my friends, we are not fit to speak of this but surely the Scriptures reveal to us glimpses of the delight, the satisfaction, the joy our Lord has in us, that ravish the soul with their marvelous suggestions of blessedness. That we should need Him is easy to comprehend; that He should need us seems incomprehensible. That our desire should be toward Him is a matter of course; but that His desire should be toward us passes the bounds of human belief. And yet, over and over He says it, and what can we do but believe Him? He has made our hearts capable of this supreme, overmastering affection, and has offered Himself as the object of it. It is infinitely precious to Him, and He says, "He that loveth me shall be loved of my Father, and I will love him, and will manifest myself to him." Continually at every heart He is knocking, and asking to be taken in as the supreme object of love. "Wilt thou have me," He says to the believer, "to be thy Beloved? Wilt thou follow me into suffering and loneliness, and endure hardness for my sake, and ask for no reward but my smile of approval, and my word of praise? Wilt thou throw thyself with an utter abandonment into my will? Wilt thou give up to me the absolute control of thyself and all that thou art? Wilt thou be content with pleasing me and me only? May I have my way with thee in all things? Wilt thou come into so close a union with me as to make a separation from the world necessary? Wilt thou accept me for thy only Lord, and leave all others, to cleave only unto Me?"

In a thousand ways He makes this offer of oneness with Himself to every believer. But all do not say "Yes," to Him. Other loves and other interests seem to them too precious to be cast aside. They do not miss of Heaven because of this. But they miss an unspeakable joy.

You, however, are not one of these. From the very first your soul has cried out eagerly and gladly to all His offers, "Yes, Lord; yes!" You are more than ready to pour out upon Him all your richest treasures of love and devotedness. You have brought to Him an enthusiasm of self-surrender that perhaps may disturb and distress the more prudent and moderate Christians around you. Your love makes necessary a separation from the world, which a lower love cannot even conceive of. Sacrifices and services are possible and sweet to you, which could not come into the grasp of a more half-hearted devotedness. The life upon which you have entered gives you the right to a lavish outpouring of your all upon your beloved One. Services, of which more distant souls know nothing, become now your sweetest privilege. Your Lord claims from you, because of your union with Him, far more than He claims of them. What to them is lawful, love has made unlawful for you. To you He can make known His secrets, and to you He looks for an instant response to every requirement of His love.

Oh, it is wonderful! the glorious, unspeakable privilege upon which you have entered! How little it will matter to you if men shall hate you, or shall separate you from their company, and shall reproach you and cast out your name as evil for His dear sake! You may well "rejoice in that day and leap for joy"; for behold your reward is great in Heaven, and if you are a partaker of His suffering, you shall be also of His glory.

In you He is seeing of the travail of His soul, and is satisfied. Your love and devotedness are His precious reward for all He has done for you. It is unspeakably sweet to Him. Do not be afraid then to let yourself go in a heart-whole devotedness to your Lord that can brook no reserves. Others may not approve, but He will, and that is enough. Do not stint or measure your obedience or your service. Let your heart and your hand be as free to serve Him, as His heart and His hand were to serve you. Let Him have all there is of you, body, soul, and spirit, time, talents, voice, everything. Lay your whole life open before Him that He may control it. Say to Him each day, "Lord, how shall I regulate this day so as to please Thee? Where shall I go? What shall I do? Whom shall I visit? What shall I say?" Give your intellect up into His control and say, "Lord, tell me how to think so as to please Thee?" Give Him your reading, your pursuits, your friendships, and say, "Lord, give me the insight to judge concerning all these things with Thy wisdom." Do not let there be a day nor an hour in which you are not intelligently doing His will, and following Him wholly. And this personal service to Him will give a halo to your life, and gild the most monotonous existence with a heavenly glow.

Have you ever grieved that the romance of youth is so soon lost in the hard realities of the world? Bring God thus into your life and into all its details, and a far grander enthusiasm will thrill your soul than the brightest days of youth could ever know, and nothing will seem hard or stern again. The meanest life will be glorified by this. Often, as I have watched a poor woman at her wash tub, and have thought of all the disheartening accessories of such a life, and have been tempted to wonder why such lives need to be, there has come over me, with a thrill of joy, the recollection of this possible glorification of it, and I have said to myself, Even this life, lived in Christ, and with Christ, following Him whithersoever He may lead, would be filled with an enthusiasm that would make every hour of it glorious. And I have gone on my way comforted to know that God's most wondrous blessings thus lie in the way of the poorest and the meanest lives. "For," says our Lord Himself, "whosoever," whether they be rich or poor, old or young, bond or free, "whosoever shall do the will of God, the same is my brother, and my sister, and my mother."

Pause a moment over these simple yet amazing words. His brother, and sister, and mother! What would we not have given to have been one of these! Oh, let me entreat of you, beloved Christian, to come, taste, and see for yourself how good the Lord is, and what wonderful things He has in store for those who "keep His commandments, and who do those things that are pleasing in His sight."

> *"And it shall come to pass, if thou shalt hearken diligently unto the voice of the Lord thy God, to observe and to do all His commandments which I command thee this day, that the Lord*

thy God will set thee on high, above all nations of the earth; and all these blessings shall come on thee, and overtake thee, if thou shalt hearken unto the voice of the Lord thy God.

"Blessed shalt thou be in the city, and blessed shalt thou be in the field.

"Blessed shall be the fruit of thy body, and the fruit of thy ground, and the fruit of thy cattle, the increase of thy kine, and the flocks of thy sheep.

"Blessed shall be thy basket and thy store.

"Blessed shalt thou be when thou comest in, and blessed shalt thou be when thou

goest out.

"The Lord shall cause thine enemies that shall rise up against thee to be smitten before thy face; they shall come out against thee one way, and flee before thee seven ways.

"The Lord shall command the blessing upon thee in thy storehouses, and in all that thou settest thine hand unto; and He shall bless thee in the land which the Lord thy God giveth thee.

"The Lord shall establish thee an holy people unto Himself, as He hath

sworn unto thee, if thou shalt keep the commandments of the Lord thy God, and walk in His ways.

"And all people of the earth shall see that thou art called by the name of the Lord, and they shall be afraid of thee.

"And the Lord shall make thee plenteous in goods, in the fruit of thy body, and in the fruit of thy cattle, in the fruit of thy ground, in the land which the Lord sware unto thy fathers to give thee.

"And the Lord shall make thee the head, and not the tail; and thou shalt be above only, and thou shalt not be beneath; if that thou hearken unto the commandments of the Lord thy God, which I command thee this day, to observe and to do them."

For the Israelites this was outward and temporal, for us it is inward and spiritual; and, as such, infinitely more glorious. May our surrendered wills leap out to embrace it in all its fullness!

XVIII

Oneness with Christ

ALL THE DEALINGS OF GOD with the soul of the believer are in order to bring him into oneness with Himself, that the prayer of our Lord may be fulfilled: "That they all may be one; as thou, Father, art in me and I in thee, that they also may be one in us."…"I in them, and thou in me, that they may be made perfect in one, and that the world may know that thou hast sent me, and hast loved them as thou hast loved me."

This soul-union was the glorious purpose in the heart of God for His people before the foundation of the world. It was the mystery hid from ages and generations. It was accomplished in the incarnation of Christ. It has been made known by the Scriptures. And it is realized as an actual experience by many of God's dear children.

But not by all. It is true of all, and God has not hidden it or made it hard, but the eyes of many are too dim and their hearts too unbelieving, and they fail to grasp it. And it is for the very purpose of bringing them into the personal and actual realization of this, that the Lord is stirring up believers everywhere at the present time to abandon themselves to Him, that He may work in them all the good pleasure of His will.

All the previous steps in the Christian life lead up to this. The Lord has made us for it; and until we have intelligently apprehended it, and have voluntarily consented to embrace it, the travail of His soul for us is not satisfied, nor have our hearts found their destined and final rest.

The usual course of Christian experience is pictured in the history of the disciples. First they were awakened to see their condition and their need, and they came to Christ and gave in their allegiance to Him. Then they followed Him, worked for Him, believed in Him; and yet, how unlike Him! seeking to be set up one above the other; running away from the cross; misunderstanding His mission and His Words; forsaking their Lord in time of danger; but still sent out to preach, recognized by Him as His disciples, possessing power to work for Him. They knew Christ only "after the flesh," as outside of them, their Lord and Master, but not yet their Life.

Then came Pentecost, and these disciples came to know Him as inwardly revealed;

as one with them in actual union, their very indwelling Life. Henceforth He was to them Christ within, working in them to will and to do of His good pleasure; delivering them by the law of the Spirit of His life from the bondage to the law of sin and death, under which they had been held. No longer was it between themselves and Him, a war of wills and a clashing of interest. One will alone animated them, and that was His will. One interest alone was dear to them, and that was His. They were made ONE with Him.

And surely all can recognize this picture, though perhaps as yet the final stage of it has not been fully reached. You may have left much to follow Christ, dear reader; you may have believed on him, and worked for Him, and loved Him, and yet may not be like Him. Allegiance you know, and confidence you know, but not yet union. There are two wills, two interests, two lives. You have not yet lost your own life that you may live only in His. Once it was I and not Christ; then it was I and Christ; perhaps now it is even Christ and I. But has it come yet to be Christ only, and not I at all?

Perhaps you do not understand what this oneness means. Some people think it consists in a great emotion or a wonderful feeling of oneness, and they turn inward to examine their emotions, thinking to decide by the state of these, what is the state of their interior union with God. But nowhere is the mistake of trusting to feelings greater than here.

Oneness with Christ must, in the very nature of things, consist in a Christ-like life and character. It is not what we feel, but what we are that settles the question. No matter how exalted or intense our emotions on the subject may be, if there is not a likeness of character with Christ, a unity of aim and purpose, a similarity of thought and of action, there can be no real oneness.

This is plain common sense, and it is Scriptural as well.

We speak of two people being one, and we mean that their purposes, and actions, and thoughts, and desires are alike. A friend may pour out upon us enthusiastic expressions of love, and unity and oneness, but if that friend's aims, and actions, and ways of looking at things are exactly opposite to ours, we cannot feel there is any real oneness between us, notwithstanding all our affection for one another. To be truly one with another, we must have the same likes and dislikes, the same joys and sorrows, the same hopes and fears. As someone says, we must look through one another's eyes, and think with one another's brains. This is, as I said above, only plain common sense.

And oneness with Christ can be judged by no other rule. It is out of the question to be one with Him in any other way than in the way of nature, and character, and life. Unless we are Christ-like in our thoughts and our ways, we are not one with Him, no matter how we feel.

I have seen Christians, with hardly one Christ-like attribute in their whole characters, who yet were so emotional and had such ecstatic feelings of love for Christ, as to think themselves justified in claiming the closest oneness with Him. I scarcely know a sadder sight. Surely our Lord meant to reach such cases when He said in Matthew 7:21, "Not every one that saith unto me, Lord, Lord, shall enter into the kingdom of heaven; but he that doeth the will of my Father which is in heaven." He was not making here any arbitrary statement of God's will, but a simple announcement of the nature of things. Of course it must be so. It is like saying, "No man can enter the ranks of astronomers who is not an astronomer." Emotions will not make a man an astronomer, but life and action. He must be one, not merely feel that he is one.

There is no escape from this inexorable nature of things, and especially here. Unless we are one with Christ as to character and life and action, we cannot be one with Him in any other way, for there is no other way. We must be "partakers of His nature" or we cannot be partakers of His life, for His life and His nature are one.

But emotional souls do not always recognize this. They feel so near Christ and so united to Him that they think it must be real; and overlooking the absolute necessity of Christ-likeness of character and walk, they are building their hopes and their confidence on their delightful emotions and exalted feelings, and think they must be one with Him, or they could not have such rich and holy experiences.

Now it is a psychological fact that these or similar emotions can be produced by other causes than a purely divine influence, and that they are largely dependent upon temperament and physical conditions. It is most dangerous, therefore, to make them a test of our spiritual union with Christ. It may result in just such a grievous self-deception as our Lord warns against in Luke 6:46-49, "And why call ye me, Lord, Lord, and do not the things which I say?" Our soul delights perhaps in calling Him, Lord, Lord, but are we doing the things which He said; for this, He tells us, is the important point, after all.

If, therefore, led by our feelings, we are saying in meetings, or among our friends, or even in our own heart before the Lord, that we are abiding in Him, let us take home to ourselves in solemn consideration these words of the Holy Ghost, "He that saith he abideth in Him, ought himself so to walk, even as He walked."

Unless we are thus walking, we cannot possibly be abiding in Him, no matter how much we may feel as if we were.

If you are really one with Christ you will be sweet to those who are cross to you; you will bear everything and make no complaints; when you are reviled you will not revile again; you will consent to be trampled on, as Christ was, and feel nothing but love in return; you will seek the honor of others rather than your own; you will take the lowest place, and be the servant of all, as Christ was; you will literally and truly love your enemies and do good to them that despitefully use you; you will, in short, live a Christ-like life, and manifest outwardly as well as feel inwardly a Christ-like spirit, and will walk among men as He walked among them. This, dear friends, is what it is to be one with Christ. And if all this is not your life according to your measure, then you are not one with Him, no matter how ecstatic or exalted your feelings may be.

To be one with Christ is too wonderful and solemn and mighty an experience to be reached by any overflow or exaltation of mere feeling. He was holy, and those who are one with Him will be holy also. There is no escape from this simple and obvious fact.

When our Lord tried to make us understand His oneness with God, He expressed it in such words as these, "I do always the things that please Him." "Whatsoever He saith unto me that I do." "The Son can do nothing of Himself, but what He seeth the Father do; for what things soever He doeth, these also doeth the Son likewise." "I can of mine own self do nothing; as I hear I judge, and my judgment is just; because I seek not mine own will, but the will of Him that sent me." "If I do not the works of my Father, believe me not. But if I do, though ye believe not me, believe the works; that ye may know and believe that the Father is in me and I in Him."

The test of oneness then, was the doing of the same works, and it is the test of oneness now. And if our Lord could say of Himself that if He did not the works of his Father, He did not ask to be believed, no matter what professions or claims He might make, surely His disciples must do no less.

It is forever true in the nature of things that "a good tree cannot bring forth evil fruit, neither can a corrupt tree bring forth good fruit." It is not that they will not, but they cannot. And a soul that is one with Christ will just as surely bring forth a Christ-like life, as a grape-vine will bring forth grapes and not thistles.

Not that I would be understood to object to emotions. On the contrary, I believe they are very precious gifts, when they are from God, and are to be greatly rejoiced in. But what I do object to is the making them a test or proof of spiritual states, either in ourselves or others, and depending on them as the foundation of our faith. Let them come or let them go, just as God pleases, and make no account of them either way. But always see to it that the really vital marks of oneness with Christ, the marks of likeness in character, and life, and walk, are ours, and all will be well. For "he that saith I know Him, and keepeth not His command-ments, is a liar, and the truth is not in Him. But whoso keepeth His Word, in him verily is the love of God perfected: hereby know we that we are in Him."

It may be, my dear reader, that the grief of your life has been the fact that you have so few good feelings. You try your hardest to get up the feelings which you hear others talking about, but they will not come. You pray for them fervently, and are often tempted to upbraid God because He does not grant them to you. And you are filled with an almost unbearable anguish because you think your want of emotion is a sign that there is not any interior union of your soul with Christ. You judge altogether by your feelings, and think there is no other way to judge.

Now my advice to you is to let your feelings go, and pay no regard to them whatever. They really have nothing to do with the matter. They are not the indicators of your spiritual state, but are merely the indicators of your temperament, or of your present physical condition. People in very low states of grace are often the subjects of very powerful emotional experiences. We all know this from the scenes we have heard of or witnessed at camp meetings and revivals. I myself had a colored servant once who would become unconscious under the power of her wonderful experiences, whenever there was a revival meeting at their church, who yet had hardly a token of any spiritual life about her at other times, and who was, in fact, not even moral. Now surely, if the Bible teaches nothing else, it does teach this, that a Christ-like life and walk must accompany any experience which is really born of His Spirit. It could not be otherwise in the very nature of things. But I fear some Christians have separated the two things so entirely in their conceptions as to have exalted their experiences at the expense of their walk, and have come to care far more about their emotions than about their character.

A certain colored congregation in one of the Southern States was a plague to the whole neighborhood by their open disregard of even the ordinary rules of morality; stealing, and lying, and cheating, without apparently a single prick of conscience on the subject. And yet their nightly meetings were times of the greatest emotion and "power." Someone finally spoke to the preacher about it, and begged him to preach a sermon on morality, which would lead his people to see their sins. "Ah, missus," he replied, "I knows dey's bad, but den it always brings a coldness like over de meetings when I preaches about dem things."

You are helpless as to your emotions, but character you can have if you will. You can be so filled with Christ as to be Christ-like, and if you are Christ-like, then you are one with Him in the only vital and essential way, even though your feelings may tell you that it is an impossibility.

Having thus settled what oneness with Christ really is, the next point for us to consider is how to reach it for ourselves.

We must first of all find out what are the facts in the case, and what is our own relation to these facts.

If you read such passages as 1 Corinthians 3:16, "Know ye not that ye are the temple of

God, and that the Spirit of God dwelleth in you?" and then look at the opening of the to see to whom these wonderful words are spoken, even to "babes in Christ," who were "yet carnal," and walked according to man, you will see that this soul-union of which I speak, this unspeakably glorious mystery of an indwelling God is the possession of even the weakest and most failing believer in Christ. So that it is not a new thing you are to ask for, but only to realize that which you already have. Of every believer in the Lord Jesus it is absolutely true that his "body is the temple of the Holy Ghost, which is in him, which he has of God."

It seems to me just in this way; as though Christ were living in a house, shut up in a far-off closet, unknown and unnoticed by the dwellers in the house, longing to make Himself known to them and be one with them in all their daily lives, and share in all their interests, but unwilling to force Himself upon their notice; as nothing but a voluntary companionship could meet or satisfy the needs of His love. The days pass by over that favored household, and they remain in ignorance of their marvelous privilege. They come and go about all their daily affairs with no thought of their wonderful Guest. Their plans are laid without reference to Him. His wisdom to guide, and His strength to protect, are all lost to them.

Lonely days and weeks are spent in sadness, which might have been full of the sweetness of His presence.

But suddenly the announcement is made, "The Lord is in the house!"

How will its owner receive the intelligence? Will he call out an eager thanksgiving, and throw wide open every door for the entrance of his glorious Guest; Or will he shrink and hesitate, afraid of His presence and seek to reserve some private corner for a refuge from His all-seeing eye?

Dear friend, I make the glad announcement to thee that the Lord is in thy heart. Since the day of thy conversion He has been dwelling there, but thou hast lived on in ignorance of it. Every moment during all that time might have been passed in the sunshine of His sweet presence, and every step has been taken under His advice. But because thou knew it not, and hast never looked for Him there, thy life has been lonely and full of failure. But now that I make the announcement to thee, how wilt thou receive it? Art thou glad to have Him? Wilt thou throw wide open every door to welcome Him in? Wilt thou joyfully and thankfully give up the government of thy life into His hands? Wilt thou consult Him about everything, and let Him decide each step for thee, and mark out every path? Wilt thou invite Him to thy innermost chambers, and make Him the sharer in thy most hidden life? Wilt thou say, "YES!" to all His longing for union with thee, and with a glad and eager abandonment, hand thyself and all that concerns thee over into His hands? If thou wilt, then shall thy soul begin to know something of the joy of union with Christ.

And yet, after all, this is but a faint picture of the blessed reality. For far more glorious than it would be to have Christ a dweller in the house or in the heart is it to be brought into such a real and actual union with Him as to be one with Him, one will, one purpose, one interest, one life. Human words cannot express such glory as this. And yet I want to express it. I want to make your souls so unutterably hungry to realize it, that day or night you cannot rest without it. Do you understand the words, one with Christ? Do you catch the slightest glimpse of their marvelous meaning? Does not your whole soul begin to exult over such a wondrous destiny? For it is a reality. It means to have no life but His life, to have no will but His will, to have no interests but His interests, to share His riches, to enter into His joys, to partake of His sorrows, to manifest His life, to have the same mind as He had, to think, and feel, and act, and walk as He did. Oh, who could have dreamed that such a destiny could have been ours!

Wilt thou have it, dear soul? Thy Lord will not force it on thee, for He wants thee as His companion and His friend, and a forced union would be incompatible with this. It must be voluntary on thy part.

The bride must say a willing "Yes" to her bridegroom, or the joy of their union is utterly wanting. Canst thou say a willing "Yes" to thy Lord?

It is such a simple transaction, and yet so real! The steps are but three. First, be convinced that the Scriptures teach this glorious indwelling of thy God; then surrender thy whole being to Him to be possessed by Him; and finally believe that He has taken possession, and is dwelling in thee. Begin to reckon thyself dead, and to reckon Christ as thy only life. Maintain this attitude of soul unwaveringly. Say, "I am crucified with Christ, nevertheless I live, yet not I, but Christ liveth in me," over and over day and night, until it becomes the habitual breathing of thy soul. Put off thy self-life by faith and in fact continually, and put on practically the life of Christ. Let this act become, by its constant repetition, the attitude of thy whole being. And as surely as thou dost this day by day, thou shalt find thyself continually bearing about in thy body the dying of the Lord Jesus, that the life also of Jesus may be made manifest in thy mortal flesh. Thou shalt learn to know what salvation means; and shalt have opened out to thy astonished gaze secrets of the Lord, of which thou hast hitherto hardly dreamed.

> How have I erred! God is my home
>   And God Himself is here.
> Why have I looked so far for Him,
>   Who is nowhere but near?
>
> Yet God is never so far off
>   As even to be near;
> He is within, our spirit is
>   The home He holds most dear.
>
> So all the while I thought myself
>   Homeless, forlorn, and weary;
> Missing my joy, I walked the earth,
>   Myself God's sanctuary.

XIX

"Although" and "Yet"

A Lesson in the Interior Life

IN MANY OF OUR STORE WINDOWS at Christmas time there stands a most significant picture. It is a dreary, desolate winter scene. There is a dark, stormy, wintry sky, bare trees, and brown grass and dead weeds, with patches of snow over them. On a leafless tree at one side of the picture is an empty and snow-covered nest, and on a branch near sits a little bird. All is cold, and dark, and desolate enough to daunt any bird, and drive it to some fairer clime, but this bird is sitting there in an attitude of perfect contentment, and has its little head bravely lifted up toward the sky, while a winter song is evidently about to burst forth from its tiny throat.

This picture, which always stands on my shelf, has preached me many a sermon. And the test is always the same, and finds its expression in the two words that stand at the head of this article, "Although" and "Yet."

"ALTHOUGH the fig tree shall not blossom, neither shall fruit be in the vines: the labor of the olive shall fail, and the field shall yield no meat; the flock shall be cut off from the fold, and there shall be no herd in the stall: YET I will rejoice in the Lord, I will joy in the God of my salvation."

There come times in many lives, when, like this bird in the winter, the soul finds itself bereft of every comfort both outward and inward; when all seems dark, and all seems wrong, even; when everything in which we have trusted seems to fail us; when the promises are apparently unfulfilled, and our prayers gain no response; when there seems nothing left to rest on in earth or Heaven. And it is at such times as these that the brave little bird with its message is needed. "Although" all is wrong everywhere, "yet" there is still one thing left to rejoice in, and that is God; the "God of our salvation," who changes not, but is the same good, loving, tender God yesterday, today, and forever. We can joy in Him always, whether we have anything else to rejoice in or not.

By rejoicing in Him, however, I do not mean rejoicing in ourselves, although I fear most people think this is really what is meant. It is their feelings or their revelations or their experiences that constitute the groundwork of their joy, and if none of these are satisfactory, they see no possibility of joy at all.

But the lesson the Lord is trying to teach us all the time is the lesson of self-effacement. He commands us to look away from self and all self's experiences, to crucify self and count it dead, to cease to be interested in self, and to know nothing and be interested in nothing but God.

The reason for this is that God has destined us for a higher life than the self-life. That just as He has destined the caterpillar to become the butterfly, and therefore has appointed the caterpillar life to die, in order that the butterfly life may take its place, so He has appointed our self-life to die in order that the divine life may become ours instead. The caterpillar effaces itself in its grub form that it may evolve or develop into its butterfly form. It dies that it may live. And just so must we.

Therefore, the one most essential thing in this stage of our existence must be the death to self and the resurrection to a life only in God. And it is for this reason that the lesson of joy in the Lord, and not in self, must be learned. Every advancing soul must come sooner or later to the place where it can trust God, the bare God, if I may be allowed the expression, simply and only because of what He is in Himself, and not because of His promises or His gifts. It must learn to have its joy in Him alone, and to rejoice in Him when all else in Heaven and earth shall seem to fail.

The only way in which this place can be reached, I believe, is by the soul being compelled to face in its own experience the loss of all things both inward and outward. I do not mean necessarily that all one's friends must die, or all one's money be lost: but I do mean that the soul shall find itself, from either inward or outward causes, desolate, and bereft, and empty of all consolation. It must come to the end of everything that is not God; and must have nothing else left to rest on within or without. It must experience just what the prophet meant when he wrote that "Although."

It must wade through the slough, and fall off of the precipice, and be swamped by the ocean, and at last find in the midst of them, and at the bottom of them, and behind them, the present, living, loving, omnipotent God! And then, and not until then, will it understand the prophet's exulting shout of triumph, and be able to join it: "YET I will rejoice in the Lord; I will joy in the God of my salvation."

And then, also, and not until then, will it know the full meaning of the verse that follows: "The Lord God is my strength, and He will make my feet like hind's feet, and He will make me to walk upon mine high places."

The soul often walks on what seem high places, which are, however, largely self-evolved and emotional, and have but little of God in them; and in moments of loss and failure and darkness, these high places become precipices of failure. But the high places to which the Lord brings the soul that rejoices only in Him can be touched by no darkness or loss, for their very foundations are laid in the midst of an utter loss and death of all that is not God.

If we want an unwavering experience, therefore, we can find it only in the Lord, apart from all else; apart from His gifts, apart from His blessings, apart from all that can change or be affected by the changing conditions of our earthly life.

The prayer which is answered today may seem to be unanswered tomorrow; the promises once so gloriously fulfilled may cease to be a reality to us; the spiritual blessing which was at one time such a joy may be utterly lost; and nothing of all we once trusted to and rested on may be left us, but the hungry and longing memory of it all. But when all else is gone, God is still left. Nothing changes Him. He is the same yesterday, today, and forever, and in Him is no variableness, neither shadow of turning. And the soul that finds its joy in Him alone can suffer no wavering.

It is grand to trust in the promises, but it is grander still to trust in the Promiser. The promises may be misunderstood or misapplied, and at the moment when we are leaning all our weight upon them, they may seem utterly to fail us. But no one ever trusted in the Promiser and was confounded.

The God who is behind His promises and is infinitely greater than His promises can never fail us in any emergency, and the soul that is stayed on Him cannot know anything but perfect peace.

The little child does not always understand its mother's promises, but it knows its mother, and its childlike trust is founded not on her word, but upon herself. And just so it is with those of us who have learned the lesson of this "Although" and "Yet." There may not be a prayer answered or a promise fulfilled to our own consciousness, but what of that? Behind the prayers and behind the promises, there is God, and He is enough. And to such a soul the simple words, GOD IS, answer every question and solve every doubt.

To the little trusting child the simple fact of the mother's existence is the answer to all its need. The mother may not make one single promise, or detail any plan, but she is, and that is enough for the child. The child rejoices in the mother; not in her promises, but in herself.

And to the child, as to us, there is behind all that changes and can change, the one unchangeable joy of the mother's existence. While the mother lives, the child must be cared for, and the child knows this, instinctively if not intelligently, and rejoices in knowing it. And while God lives, His children must be cared for as well, and His children ought to know this, and rejoice in it as instinctively and far more intelligently than the child of human parents. For what else can God do, being what He is? Neglect, indifference, forgetfulness, ignorance, are all impossible to Him. He knows everything, He cares about everything, He can manage everything; and He loves us; and what more could we ask? Therefore, come what may, we will lift our faces to our God, like our brave little bird teacher, and, in the midst of our darkest "Althoughs," will sing our glad and triumphant "Yet."

All of God's saints in all ages have done this. Job said, out of the depths of sorrow and trial which few can equal, "Though He slay me yet will I trust in Him."

David could say in the moment of his keenest anguish, "Yea, though I walk through the valley of the shadow of death," yet "I will fear no evil; for Thou art with me." And again he could say, "God is our refuge and strength, a very present help in trouble. Therefore, will not we fear, though the earth be removed, and though the mountains be carried into the midst of the sea; though the waters thereof roar and be troubled; though the mountains shake with the swelling thereof...God is in the midst of her; she shall not be moved; God shall help her, and that right early."

Paul could say in the midst of his sorrows, "We are troubled on every side, yet not distressed; we are perplexed, but not in despair; persecuted, but not forsaken; cast down, but not destroyed...for which cause we faint not; but though our outward man perish, yet the inward man is renewed day by day. For our light affliction, which is but for a moment, worketh for us a far more exceeding and eternal weight of glory; while we look, not at the things which are seen, but at the things which are not seen; for the things which are seen are temporal; but the things which are not seen are eternal."

All this and more can the soul say that learned this lesson of rejoicing in God alone.

Spiritual joy is not a thing, not a lump of joy, so to speak, stored away in one's heart to be looked at and rejoiced over. Joy is only the gladness that comes from the possession of something good, or the knowledge of something pleasant. And the Christian's joy is simply his gladness in knowing Christ, and in his possession of such a God and Savior. We do not on an earthly plane rejoice in our joy, but in the thing that causes our joy. And on the heavenly plane it is the same. We are to "rejoice in the Lord, and joy in the God of our salvation"; and this joy no man nor devil can take from us, and no earthly sorrows can touch.

A writer on the interior life says, in effect, that our spiritual pathway is divided into three regions, very different from one another, and yet each one a necessary stage in the onward progress. First, there is the region of beginnings, which is a time full of sensible joys and delights, of fervent aspirations, of emotional experiences, and of many secret manifestations of God. Then comes a vast extent of wilderness, full of temptation, and trial, and conflict, of the loss of sensible manifestations, of dryness, and of inward and outward darkness and distress. And then, finally, if this desert period is faithfully traversed, there comes on the further side of it a region of mountain heights of uninterrupted union and communion with God, of superhuman detachment from everything earthly, of infinite contentment with the Divine will, and of marvelous transformation into the image of Christ.

Whether this order is true or not, I cannot here discuss, but of one thing I am very sure, that to many souls who have tasted the joy of the "region of beginnings" here set forth, there has come afterward a period of desert experience at which they have been sorely amazed and perplexed. And I cannot but think such might, perhaps, in this explanation, find the answer to their trouble. They are being taught the lesson of detachment from all that is not God, in order that their souls may at last be brought into that interior union and oneness with Him which is set forth in the picture given of the third and last region of mountain heights of blessedness.

The soul's pathway is always through death to life. The caterpillar cannot in the nature of things become the butterfly in any other way than by dying to the one life in order to live in the other. And neither can we. Therefore, it may well be that this region of death and desolation must needs be passed through, if we would reach the calm mountain heights beyond. And if we know this, we can walk triumphantly through the darkest experience, sure that all is well, since God is God.

In the lives of many who read this paper there is, I feel sure, at least one of these desert "Althoughs," and in some lives there are many.

Dear friends, is the "Yet" there also? Have you learned the prophet's lesson? Is God enough for you? Can you sing and mean it,

"Thou, O Christ, art all I want,
    More than all in thee I find"?

If not, you need the little bird to speak to you. And the song that he sings, as he sits on that bare and leafless tree, with the winter storm howling around him, must become your song also.

"Though the rain may fall and the wind
be blowing,
    And cold and chill is the wintry blast;
Though the cloudier sky is still cloudier
growing,
    And the dead leaves tell that summer
is passed;
Yet my face I hold to the stormy heaven,
    My heart is as calm as a summer sea;
Glad to receive what my God hath given,
    Whate'er it be.

"When I feel the cold, I can say, 'He sends
it,'
    And His wind blows blessing I surely
know;
For I've never a want but that He attends
it;
    And my heart beats warm, though the
winds may blow
The soft sweet summer was warm and
glowing,

Bright were the blossoms on every
bough;
I trusted Him when the roses were
blowing,
I trust Him now.

"Small were my faith should it weakly
falter,
Now that the roses have ceased to blow;
Frail were the trust that now should
alter,
Doubting His love when the storm-
clouds grow.
If I trust Him once I must trust Him ever,
And His way is best, though I stand or
fall,
Through wind or storm He will leave me
never,
For He sends all."

XX

Kings and Their Kingdoms

Or, How to Reign in the Interior Life

"AND WHEN HE WAS DEMANDED of the Pharisees when the kingdom of God should come, he answered them and said, The kingdom of God cometh not with observation: neither shall they say, lo here! or, lo there! for, behold, the kingdom of God is within you."

The expressions "kingdom of God" and "kingdom of Heaven" are used in the Scripture concerning the divine life in the soul. They mean simply the place or condition where God rules, and where His will is done. It is an interior kingdom, not an exterior one. Its thrones are not outward thrones of human pomp and glory, but inward thrones of dominion and supremacy over the things of time and sense. Its kings are not clothed in royal robes of purple and fine linen, but with the interior garments of purity and truth. And its reign is not in outward show, but in inward power. Neither is it in one place rather than another, nor in one form of things above another. It is not, lo here, nor lo there, not in this mountain nor yet at Jerusalem, that we are to find Christ, and enter into His kingdom. It is not a matter of place at all, but one of condition. And in every place and under every name, and through every form, all who seek God and work righteousness shall find His kingdom within them.

But this is very little understood. In our childish fashion of literalism we have too much imbibed the idea that a kingdom must necessarily be in a particular place and with outward observation; and have therefore expected that the kingdom of heaven would mean for us an outward victory of heaven over earth in some particular place, or under some especial form; and that to sit on a throne with Christ would be to have an outward uplifting in power and glory before the face of all around us.

But as the inner sense of the Scripture unfolds to us, we see that this would be but a poor and superficial fulfilling of the real meaning of these wonderful symbols. And the vision of their true significance grows and strengthens before the "eyes that see," until at last we know that our Lord's words were truer than ever we had dreamed before, that the "kingdom of God cometh not with observation; neither shall they say, lo here! or, lo there! for, behold, the kingdom of God is within you."

In Daniel 2:44, we have the announcement of the kingdom, and in Isaiah 9:6, 7, the announcement of the King:—

"The God of heaven shall set up a kingdom which shall never be destroyed; and the kingdom shall not be left to other people, but it shall break in pieces and consume all these kingdoms, and it shall stand forever."

"For unto us a child is born, unto us a son is given: and the government shall be upon His shoulder; and His name shall be called Wonderful, Counselor, the mighty God, the everlasting Father, the Prince of Peace. Of the increase of His government and peace there shall be no end, upon the throne of David, and upon His kingdom, to order it, and to establish it with judgment and with justice from henceforth even forever. The zeal of the Lord of hosts will perform this."

This kingdom is to break in pieces and consume all other kingdoms by right of the law by which the inward always rules the outward. If there is peace within, no outward turmoil can affect the soul; but outward peace can never quiet an inward tempest. A happy heart can walk in triumphant indifference through a sea of external trouble; while internal anguish cannot find happiness in the most favorable surroundings. What a man is within himself makes or unmakes his joy, and not what he possesses outside of himself.

Someone said to Diogenes, "The king has degraded you." "Yes" replied Diogenes, triumphantly, "but I am not degraded!" No act of kings or emperors can degrade a soul that retains its own dignity; no tyrant can enslave a man who is inwardly free.

Therefore to have this divine kingdom set up within means that all other powers to conquer or enslave are broken, and the soul reigns triumphant over them all. Men and devils may try to hold such a one in bondage, but they are powerless before the might of this interior kingdom. No longer will fashion, or conventionality, or the fear of man, or the love of ease, or any other of the many tyrants to which Christians cringe and bow, rule a soul that has been raised to a throne in this inward kingdom. No sin or temptation can overcome, no sorrow can crush, no discouragement can hinder. Let a man or woman have been bound in ever so tyrannical chains of sinful habits, this kingdom will set them free. Circumstances make men kings in the outward life, but in this hidden life men become kings over circumstances. And the soul that has aforetime been the slave of a thousand outward things finds itself here utterly independent of them, every one.

For the King in this kingdom is One whom no circumstances can affect or baffle. He it is indeed who makes circumstances. And since the government is upon His shoulders, we cannot doubt that He will order the kingdom with a judgment and justice that will leave nothing for any subject in His kingdom to desire.

In the expression "the government shall be upon His shoulder," we have the whole secret of this wonderful kingdom. Upon His shoulder, not upon ours. The care is His, the burdens are His, the responsibility belongs to Him, the protection rests upon Him, the planning, and providing, and controlling, and guiding, all are in His hands. No one can question as to His perfect fulfillment of every requirement of His kingship. Therefore those who are in His kingdom are utterly delivered from any need to be anxious, or burdened, or perplexed, or troubled. And by this deliverance they become kings. The government is not upon their shoulders, and they have no business to interfere with it. Their King has assumed the whole responsibility, and if He can but see His subjects happy and prosperous, He is content Himself to bear all the weight and care of kingship. How often we speak of the responsibilities of earthly kings, and pity them for the burdens that kingship imposes. We recognize, even on an earthly plane, that to be a king means, or ought to mean, the bearing of the burdens of even the meanest of his subject. And even now, as I write, many hearts are aching with sympathy for the new Czar, who has assumed the grievous burden of the mighty Russian Empire.

From this instinctive sense of every human heart as to the rightful duties and responsibilities of kingship, we may learn what it means to be in a kingdom over which God is King, and where He has Himself declared all things shall be ordered with judgment and justice from henceforth and even forever. Surely no care or anxiety can ever enter here, if the heart but knows its kingdom and its King!

In John 18:36, our King tells us the tactics of His kingdom: "Jesus answered, My kingdom is not of this world: if my kingdom were of this world then would my servants fight, that I should not be delivered to the Jews; but now is my kingdom not from hence."

Earthly kings and earthly kingdoms gain and keep their supremacy by outward conflict; God's kingdom conquers by inward power. Earthly kings subdue enemies; God subdues enmity. His victories must be interior before they can be exterior. He does not subjugate, but he conquers. Even we, on our earthly plane, know something of this principle, and do not value any victory over another which only reaches the body and has not subdued the heart. No true mother cares for an outward obedience merely; nothing will satisfy her but the inward surrender. Unless the citadel of the heart is conquered, the conquest seem worthless. And with God how much more will this be the case, since we are told that "He seeth not as man seeth; for man looketh on the outward appearance, but the Lord looketh on the heart." We speak of "subduing hearts," and we mean, not that they are overpowered or forced into an unwilling and compulsory surrender, but that they are conquered by being won, and are willingly yielded up to another's control. And it is after this fashion and no other that God subdues. So that to read that "His kingdom ruleth over all" means that all hearts are won to His service in a glad and willing surrender.

For again I repeat, His reign must be inward before it can be outward. And in truth it is no reign at all, unless it is within. If we think of it a moment we shall see that this must be so in the very nature of things, and that it is impossible to conceive of God reigning in a kingdom where the subduing reaches no further than the outside actions of His subjects. His kingdom is not of this world, but is in a spiritual sphere, where its power is over the souls and not the bodies of men; and therefore only when the soul is conquered, can it be set up.

Understood in this light, how full of love and blessing do all those declarations and prophecies become, which tell us that God is to subdue His enemies under His feet, and is to rule them in righteousness and power! And how glorious with hope does the voice of that great multitude heard by John sound out, saying, "Alleluia! for the Lord God omnipotent reigneth!"

In confirmation of all this we have two passages descriptive of this kingdom, in Romans 14:17, and 1 Corinthians 4:20: "For the kingdom of God is not meat and drink, but righteousness and peace and joy in the Holy Ghost." "For the kingdom of God is not in word, but in power."

Not outward things, but inward. Not what a man eats and drinks, not where he lives, nor what is his nationality, nor the customs of his race, not even what he thinks nor what he says; but what are the inward characteristics of his nature, and the inward power of his spiritual life. For these alone constitute this kingdom of God. Not what I do, but what I am, is to decide whether I belong to it or not. And only as inward righteousness, and inward peace, and inward joy, and inward power are bestowed and experienced, can this kingdom be set up.

Therefore no outward subjugation can accomplish results like these, but only the interior work of the all-subduing Spirit of God.

I have been greatly instructed by the story of Ulysses, when he was sailing past the islands of the sirens. These sirens had the power of charming by their songs all who listened to them, and of inducing them to leap into the sea. To avert this danger, Ulysses filled the ears of his crew with wax, that they might not hear the fatal music, and bound himself to the mast with knotted cords; and thus they passed the isle in safety. But when Orpheus was obliged to sail by the same island, he gained a better victory, for he himself made sweeter music than that of the sirens, and enchanted his crew with more alluring songs; so that they passed the dangerous charmers not only with safety, but with disdain. Wax and knotted cords kept Ulysses and his crew from making the fatal leap; but inward delights enabled Orpheus and his crew to reign triumphant over the very source of temptation itself. And just so is it with the kingdom of which we speak. It needs no outward law to bind it, but reigns by right of its inward life. So that it is said of those who have entered it, "Against such there is no law."

For it is a kingdom of kings. The song we shall one day sing, nay, that we ought to be singing even now and here in this life, declare this: "Unto Him that loved us, and washed us from our sins in His own blood, and hath made us kings and priests unto God and His Father; to Him be glory and dominion for ever and ever. Amen" (Revelation 1:5, 6).

We who have entered this kingdom, or, rather, in whom this kingdom is set up, sit upon the throne with our King and share His dominion. The world was His footstool, and it becomes our footstool also. Over the things of time and sense He reigned triumphant by the power of a life lived in a plane above them and superior to them, and so may we. We are all of us familiar with the expression that such or such a person "rises superior to his surroundings," and we mean that there is in that soul a hidden power that controls its surroundings, instead of being controlled by them. Our King essentially rose superior to His surroundings; and it is given to us who are reigning with Him to do the same.

But, just as He was not a king in outward appearance, but only in inward power, so shall we be. He reigned, not in this, that He had all the treasures and riches of the world at His command, but that He had none of them, and could do without them. And so shall our reigning be. We shall not have all men bowing down to us, and all things bending to our will; but with all men opposing and all things adverse, we shall walk in a royal triumph of soul through the midst of them. We shall suffer the loss of all things, and by that loss be set forever free from their power to bind. We shall hide ourselves in the impregnable fortress of the will of our King, and shall reign there in a perpetual kingdom.

All this is contrary to man's thought of kingship. The only idea the human heart can compass is that outward circumstances must bend and bow to the soul that is seated on a throne with Christ. Friends must approve, enemies must be silenced, obstacles must be overcome, affairs must prosper, or there can be no reigning. If man had had the ordering of Daniel's business, or of that matter of the three Hebrew children in the burning fiery furnace, he would have said the only way of victory would be for the minds of the kings to have been so changed that Daniel should not have been cast into the den of lions, and the Hebrew children should have been kept out of the furnace. But God's way was infinitely grander. He suffered Daniel to be cast among the lions, in order that he might reign triumphant over them when in their very midst, and He allowed Shadrach, Meshach, and Abednego to be cast into the burning, fiery furnace, in order that they might walk through it without so much as the smell of fire upon them. He tells us, not that we shall walk in paths where there are no dragons and adders, but that we shall walk through the midst of dragons and adders, and shall "tread them under our feet."

And how much more glorious a kingdom is this than any outward rule or control could be! To be inwardly a king, while outwardly a slave, is one of the grandest heights of triumph of which our hearts can conceive. To be destitute, afflicted, tormented, to be stoned and torn asunder, and slain with the sword; to wander in sheepskins and goatskins, and in deserts and mountains, and in dens and caves of the earth, and yet to be through it all, kings in interior kingdoms of righteousness, peace and joy in the Holy Ghost, is surely a kingdom that none but God could give, and none but God-like souls receive.

A few such kings we have at some time or other seen or heard of in this world of ours, and all hearts have acknowledged their unconscious sway. One I read of among the brethren of the monastery of St. Cyr. Because of their piety, these brethren incurred the hatred of the monasteries around them, and the anger of their superiors, and were cast out as evil from their community. One of them was sent as prisoner to a monastery where his chief enemies dwelt, and was there subjected to the most cruel and degrading treatment.

Although he was of gentle birth, and had been an abbot in the community he had left, he was compelled to do the most menial work, was forced to carry a noisome burden on his back, and was driven out to beg with a placard on his bosom declaring him to be the vilest of the vile. But through it all the spirit of the saint reigned triumphant, and nothing disturbed his calm, or soured for a moment his Christ-like sweetness. For his persecutors he never had anything but words of kindness and smiles of love. And at last by the mighty power of the divine kingdom in which he lived, he subdued all hearts around him to himself, and became the trusted friend and adviser, and the beloved ruler over the very enemies who had once so delighted to persecute and revile him. "Blessed are the meek, for they shall inherit the earth." By his meekness he conquered and became king.

At one time a dangerous criminal was sent to the monastery for imprisonment. He was so violent that no bonds sufficed to bind him, and no strength could control him. At last he was taken to the cell of this brother from St. Cyr, and they were shut up together; even the stolid monks themselves recognizing in that divine meekness a power to conquer that surpassed all the powers with which they were acquainted. The saint received the violent man as a beloved brother, and smiled upon him with heavenly kindness. But the criminal returned it with abuse and violence. He broke the monk's furniture and destroyed his bed, he kicked him, and beat him, and tore his hair, and spat upon him. He exhausted himself in his violence against him. Through it all the monk made no resistance, and said no word but words of love; and when at length the criminal, worn out with his fury, paused to take breath, the beaten and outraged man looked upon his persecutor with a smile of ineffable love and tender compassion, as though he would gather him to his bosom and comfort him for his misery. It was more than the criminal could bear. Hatred, and revenge, and anger he could repay in kind, but against love and meekness like this he had no weapons, and his heart was conquered. He fell at the feet of the saint and washed them with his tears, as he entreated forgiveness for his cruelty, and vowed a lifelong loyalty to his service. And from that moment all trouble with that criminal was over. He followed the saint about like a loving and faithful dog, eager to do or to be anything the other might desire. And when the time of his imprisonment was over, and the gates of his prison were opened for his release, he could not be induced to go, because he could not bear to leave the man who had saved him by love.

Of such a nature is kingship in this kingdom of heaven.

Each soul can make the application for itself, without need of comment from me.

In Matthew 5, 6, and 7, we have the King of this kingdom describing the characteristics of His kingdom and giving the laws for His subjects. "Blessed are the poor in spirit," He says, "for theirs is the kingdom of heaven." Not the rich, or great, or wise, or learned, but the poor in spirit, the meek, the merciful, the pure in heart, those who mourn, and those who hunger and thirst, those who are persecuted, and reviled, and spoken evil against, all such belong to this kingdom. Gentleness, yieldingness, meekness, charity, are the characteristics of these kings, and they reign in the power of them.

One Christian asked another, "How can I make people respect me?" "I would command their respect," was the reply. And this meant, not that he should stand up and say in tones of authority, "Now I command you all to respect me," but that he should so act, and live, and be, that no one could help respecting him. Men sometimes win an outward show of respect and submission by an overbearing tyranny, but he who would rule the heart of his subjects must try other methods.

Our Lord developed this thought to some who wished to share His throne. He called them to Him, and said, "Ye know that they which are accounted to rule over the Gentiles exercise lordship over them; and their great ones exercise authority upon them. But so shall it not be among you: but whosoever will be great among you, shall be your minister: and whosoever of you will be the chiefest shall be servant of all. For even the Son of man came not to be ministered unto, but to minister, and to give his life a ransom for many."

From the human standpoint, that man alone reigns who is able to exercise lordship over those around him. From the divine standpoint the soul that serves is the soul that reigns. Not he who demands most receives this inward crowning, but he who gives up most.

What grander kingship can be conceived of than that which Christ sets forth in the sermon on the mount, "But I say unto you, that ye resist not evil; but whosoever shall smite thee on thy right cheek, turn to him the other also. And if any man will sue thee at the law and take away thy coat, let him have thy cloak also. And whosoever shall compel thee to go a mile, go with him twain."

Surely only a soul that is in harmony with God can mount such a throne of dominion as this!

But this is our destiny. We are made for this purpose. We are born of a kingly race, and are heirs to this ineffable kingdom; "heirs of God and joint heirs with Christ."

Would that we could realize this; and could see in every act of service or surrender to which we might find ourselves called, an upward step in the pathway that leads us to our kingdom and our throne!

I mean this in a very practical sense. I mean that the homely services of our daily lives, and the little sacrifices which each day demands, will be, if faithfully fulfilled, actual rounds in the ladder by which we are mounting to our thrones. I mean that if we are faithful over the "few things" of our earthly kingdom, we shall be made ruler over the "many things" of the heavenly kingdom.

He that follows Christ in this ministry of service and of suffering, will reign with Him in the glory of supreme self-sacrifice, and will be the "chiefest" in His divine kingdom of love. Knowing this, who would hesitate to "turn the other cheek," since by the turning a kingdom is to be won and a throne is to be gained?

Joseph was a type of all this. In slavery and in prison he reigned a king, as truly as when seated on Pharaoh's throne or riding in Pharaoh's chariot (see Genesis 39:6, 22, 23). He became the greatest by being the least, the chiefest by being servant of all.

Dear reader, art thou reigning after this fashion, and in this sort of a kingdom? Art thou the greatest in thy little world of home, or church, or social circle by being the least, and chiefest by being the servant of all? If not, thy kingdom is not Christ's kingdom, and thy throne is not one shared by Him.

To enter into the secrets of this interior kingdom and to partake of its heavenly power is no notional victory, no fancied supremacy. It is a real and actual reigning, which will cause thee as a matter of fact to "rise superior" to the world and the things of it, and to walk through it independent of its smiles or frowns, dwelling in a region of heavenly peace and heavenly triumph which earth can neither give nor take away. "For the kingdom of God is not in word but in power." It is not a talk but a fact; and those who are in it recognize their kingship and prove it by reigning.

But perhaps thou wilt say, "How can I enter into this kingdom, if I am not already in?" Let our Lord Himself answer thee: "At the same time came the disciples unto Jesus, saying, Who is the greatest in the kingdom of heaven? And Jesus called a little child unto him, and set him in the midst of them, and said, Verily I say unto you, Except ye be converted, and become as little children, ye shall not enter into the kingdom of heaven. Whosoever therefore shall humble himself as this little child, the same is greatest in the kingdom of heaven."

It is a kingdom of childlike hearts, and only such can enter it.

To be a "little child" means simply to be one. I cannot describe it better than this. We all have known little children in our lives, and have delighted ourselves in their simplicity and their trustfulness, their lighthearted carelessness, and their unquestioning obedience to those in authority over them. And to be the greatest in this divine kingdom means to have the most of this guileless, tender, trustful, self-forgetting, obedient heart of the child.

"Not every one that saith unto me, Lord, Lord, shall enter into the kingdom of heaven; but he that doeth the will of my Father which is in heaven."

It is not saying, but doing, that will avail us here. We must be a child, or we cannot sit on the child's throne. And to be a child means to do the Father's will, since the very essence of true childhood is the spirit of obedience united to the spirit of trust.

Become a little child, then, by laying aside all thy greatness, all thy self-assertion, all thy self-dependence, all thy wisdom, and all thy strength, and consenting to die to thy own self-life, be born again into the kingdom of God. The only way out of one life into another is by a death to one and a new birth into the other. It is the old story, therefore, reiterated so often and in so many different ways, of through death to life. Die, then, that you my live. Lose your own life that you may find Christ's life. The caterpillar can only enter into the butterfly's kingdom by dying to its caterpillar life, and emerging into the resurrection life of the butterfly; and just so can we also only enter into the kingdom of God by the way of a death out of the kingdom of self, and an emergence into the resurrection life of Christ. Let everything go, then, that belongs to the natural; all your own notions, and plans, and ways, and thoughts; and accept in their stead God's plans, and ways, and thoughts. Do this faithfully and do it persistently, and you shall come at last to sit on His throne, and to reign with Him in an interior kingdom which shall break in pieces and consume all other kingdoms, and shall stand for ever and ever.

There is no other way. This kingdom cannot be entered by pomp, and show, and greatness, and strength; but by littleness, and helplessness, and childlikeness, and babyhood, and death. He that humbleth himself, and he only, shall be exalted here; and to mount the throne with Christ requires that we shall first have followed Him in the suffering, and loss, and crucifixion. If we suffer with him, we shall also reign with Him. Not as an arbitrary reward for our suffering, but as the result that will follow in the very nature of things. Christ's loss must necessarily bring Christ's gain, Christ's death must bring Christ's resurrection, and to follow Him in the regeneration will surely and inevitably bring the soul that follows to His crown and His throne.

In a volume of sermons for children, I have found a vivid illustration of this royal kingdom:

"A little fellow from one of the Refuges in England had risked his life to save one of his comrades, and England's Queen had sent him a medal by the hand of one of England's earls. The little fellow was held forward by his comrades to receive it, for he was shy and nervous and tried to sidle away.

"Look at the noble chairman; he had driven down from his proper place in the House of Lords, where were gathered earls and dukes, and the men who had done well as lawyers, and judges, and statesmen, and warriors, and the Princes of the royal blood. Yet, all peer though he was, he was moved to the sincerest depths of his being as he murmured, 'I have the honor,' and pinned the life-saving medal on the child's jacket. His heart was full. He paused

to swallow down something that would rise in his throat before he could go on.

"There is the 'glory and honor' of successful statesmen, and warriors, and lawyers, but the glory of self-forgetful saving of life is a glory that excelleth, and that was the wondrous glory won by this boy. He had plunged into the stream and shared a drowning boy's risk, and that little hand, look at it there, steadying him by holding the table, had come out holding the saved.

"Why has self-forgetfulness such mighty power? How was it that a twelve-year-old boy could bow down an audience of grown men before him? What gave to that brow, that its stubby crown of carroty hair, a glory and honor more than the luster of gold and jewels? Why was it that that small body in its little breeches and jacket, wiping its tears on the rough little sleeve, could grip thousands of hearts and hold them all, and make them for the time loyal members of his kingdom?

"Why was all this so?

"It was so because that little boy in his measure had been like Christ, in the self-forgetful spirit of sacrifice for others. He had a bit of the same beauty we are all made on purpose to worship; the glory before which angels give a great shout, and all the company of heaven fall down and adore, saying with a loud voice, 'Worthy is the Lamb that was slain!'"

The "Lamb that was slain" is the mightiest King the world has ever known, and all who partake of His Spirit share in His kingdom.

And since this kingdom is not a place, but is character, those who have not the character cannot by any possibility be in it.

We pray daily, "Thy kingdom come." Do we know what we are praying for? Do we comprehend the change it will make in us if it comes in us? Are we willing to be so changed?

What is the kingdom of God but the rule of God? And what is the rule of God but the will of God? Therefore when we pray, "Thy will be done on earth as it is in heaven," we have touched the secret of it all.

A horde of savages might conquer a civilized kingdom by sheer brute force; but if they would conquer the civilization of that kingdom, they could only do so by submitting to its control. And just so is it with the kingdom of heaven. It yields its scepter to none but those who render obedience to its laws.

"To him that overcometh will I give to sit with me in my throne, even as I also overcame and am set down with my Father in his throne."

"He always reigns who sides with God," says an old writer. And again, "He who perfectly accepts the will of God, dwells in a perpetual kingdom."

Art thou reigning after this fashion and in this sort of a kingdom?

Art thou the "chiefest" by being the "servant of all"?

Art thou a king over thy circumstances, or do thy circumstances reign over thee?

Dost thou triumph over thy temptations, or do they triumph over thee?

Canst thou sit on an inward throne in the midst of outward defeat and loss?

Canst thou conquer by yielding, and become the greatest by being the least?

If thou canst answer Yes to all these questions, then thou art come into thy kingdom; and whatever thy outward lot may be, or the estimation in which men may hold thee, thou art in very truth among the number of those concerning whom our Lord declares "the same shall be called greatest in the kingdom of heaven."

XXI

The Chariots of God

Foundation Text.—Psalm 68:17.

CHARIOTS ARE FOR CONVEYANCE and progress. Earthly chariots carry the bodies of those who ride in them over all intervening distances or obstacles to the place of their destination, and God's chariots carry their souls. No words can express the glorious places to which that soul shall arrive who travels in the chariots of God. And our verse tells us they are "very many." All around us on every side they wait for us; but we, alas! We do not always see them. Earth's chariots are always visible, but God's chariots are invisible.

2 Kings 6:14-17 – "Therefore sent he thither horses, and chariots, and a great host: and they came by night, and compassed the city about. And when the servant of the man of God was risen early, and gone forth, behold, an host compassed the city both with horses and chariots. And his servant said unto him, Alas, my master! how shall we do? And he answered, Fear not: for they that be with us are more than they that be with them. And Elisha prayed, and said, Lord, I pray thee, open his eyes, that he may see. And the Lord opened the eyes of the young man; and he saw: and, behold, the mountain was full of horses and chariots of fire round about Elisha."

The king of Syria came up against the man of God with horses and chariots that were visible to every one, but God had chariots that could be seen by none save the eye of faith. The servant of the prophet could only see the outward and visible, and he cried, as so many have done since, "Alas, my Master! how shall we do?" But the prophet himself sat calmly within his house without fear, because his eyes were opened to see the invisible. And all that he asked for his servant was, "Lord, I pray thee open his eyes that he may see."

This is the prayer we need to pray for ourselves and for one another, "Lord, open our eyes that we may see." For the world all around us is full of God's horses and chariots, waiting to carry us to places of glorious victory.

But they do not look like chariots. They look instead like enemies, sufferings, trials, defeats, misunderstandings, disappointments, unkindnesses. They look like juggernaut cars of misery and wretchedness, that are only waiting to roll over us and crush us into the earth; but they really are chariots of triumph in which we may ride to those very heights of victory for which our souls have been longing and praying.

•••

Deuteronomy 32:12, 13 – "So the Lord alone did lead him, and there was no strange god with him. He made him ride on the high places of the earth, that he might eat the increase of the fields; and he made him to suck honey out of the rock, and oil out of the flinty rock..."

If we would "ride on the high places of the earth" we must get into the chariots that can take us there; and only the "chariots of God" are equal to such lofty riding as this.

•••

Isaiah 58:14 – " Then shalt thou delight thyself in the Lord; and I will cause thee to ride upon the high places of the earth, and feed thee with the heritage of Jacob thy father: for the mouth of the Lord hath spoken it."

We may make out of each event in our lives either a juggernaut car to crush us, or a chariot in which to ride to heights of victory. It all depends upon how we take them; whether we lie down under our trials and let them roll over and crush us, or whether we climb up into them as into a chariot, and make them carry us triumphantly onward and upward.

•••

> *2 Kings 2:11, 12 – "And it came to pass, as they still went on, and talked, that, behold, there appeared a chariot of fire, and horses of fire, and parted them both asunder; and Elijah went up by a whirlwind into heaven. And Elisha saw it, and he cried, My father, my father, the chariot of Israel, and the horsemen thereof. And he saw him no more: and he took hold of his own clothes, and rent them in two pieces."*

Whenever we mount into God's chariots the same thing happens to us spiritually that happened to Elisha. We shall have a translation. Not into the heavens above us, as Elisha did, but into the heaven within us, which after all is almost a grander translation than his. We shall be carried up away from the low earthly groveling plane of life, where everything hurts and everything is unhappy, up into the "heavenly places in Christ Jesus," where we shall ride in triumph over all below.

•••

Ephesians 2:6 – "And hath raised us up together, and made us sit together in heavenly places in Christ Jesus..."

These "heavenly places" are interior, not exterior, and the road that leads to them is interior also. But the chariot that carries the soul over this road is generally some outward loss, or trial or disappointment; some chastening that does not indeed seem for the present to be joyous, but grievous; but that nevertheless afterward yieldeth the peaceable fruits of righteousness to them that are exercised thereby.

•••

Hebrews 12:5-11 – "And ye have forgotten the exhortation which speaketh unto you as unto children, My son, despise not thou the chastening of the Lord, nor faint when thou art rebuked of him: For whom the Lord loveth he chasteneth, and scourgeth every son whom he receiveth. If ye endure chastening, God dealeth with you as with sons; for what son is he whom the father chasteneth not? But if ye be without chastisement, whereof all are partakers, then are ye bastards, and not sons. Furthermore we have had fathers of our flesh which corrected us, and we gave them reverence: shall we not much rather be in subjection unto the Father of spirits, and live? For they verily for a few days chastened us after their own pleasure; but he for our profit, that we might be partakers of his holiness. Now no chastening for the present seemeth to be joyous, but grievous: nevertheless afterward it yieldeth the peaceable fruit of righteousness unto them which are exercised thereby."

Look upon these chastenings, no matter how grievous they may be for the present, as God's chariots sent to carry your souls into the "high places" of spiritual achievement and uplifting, and you will find that they are after all "paved with love."

•••

Canticles 3:9, 10 – "King Solomon made himself a chariot of the wood of Lebanon. He made the pillars thereof of silver, the bottom thereof of gold, the covering of it of purple, the midst thereof being paved with love, for the daughters of Jerusalem."

Your own individual chariot may look very unlovely. It maybe a cross-grained relative or friend; it may be the result of human malice, or cruelty, or neglect; but every chariot sent by God must necessarily be paved with love, since

God is love, and God's love is the sweetest, softest, tenderest thing to rest one's self upon that was ever found by any soul anywhere. It is His love indeed that sends the chariot.

•••

Habakkuk 3:8, 12, 13 – "Was the Lord displeased against the rivers? was thine anger against the rivers? was thy wrath against the sea, that thou didst ride upon thine horses and thy chariots of salvation?... Thou didst march through the land in indignation, thou didst thresh the heathen in anger. Thou wentest forth for the salvation of thy people, even for salvation with thine anointed; thou woundedst the head out of the house of the wicked, by discovering the foundation unto the neck."

Here the prophet tells us that it was God's displeasure against the obstacles which beset the path of His people that made Him come to their rescue, riding in His "chariots of salvation." Everything becomes a "chariot of salvation" when God rides upon it.

The "clouds" that darken our skies and seem to shut out the shining of the sun of righteousness are, after all, if we only knew it, His chariots, into which we may mount with Him, and "ride prosperously" over all the darkness.

•••

Psalm 45:3, 4 – "Gird thy sword upon thy thigh, O most mighty, with thy glory and thy majesty. And in thy majesty ride prosperously because of truth and meekness and righteousness; and thy right hand shall teach thee terrible things."

Psalm 18:10 – "And he rode upon a cherub, and did fly: yea, he did fly upon the wings of the wind."

Deuteronomy 33:26 – "There is none like unto the God of Jeshurun, who rideth upon the heaven in thy help, and in his excellency on the sky."

A late writer has said that we cannot, by even the most vigorous and toilsome efforts, sweep away the clouds, but we can climb so high above them as to reach the clear atmosphere overhead; and he who rides with God rides upon the heavens far above all earthborn clouds.

•••

Psalm 68:32-34 – "Sing unto God, ye kingdoms of the earth; O sing praises unto the Lord; Selah: To him that rideth upon the heavens of heavens, which were of old; lo, he doth send out his voice, and that a mighty voice. Ascribe ye strength unto God: his excellency is over Israel, and his strength is in the clouds."

This may sound fanciful, but it is really exceedingly practical when we begin to act it out in our daily lives.

I knew a lady who had a very slow servant. She was an excellent girl in every other respect, and very valuable in the household, but her slowness was a constant source of irritation to her mistress, who was naturally quick, and who always chafed at slowness. The lady would consequently get out of temper with the girl twenty times a day, and twenty times a day would repent of her anger, and resolve to conquer it, but in vain. Her life was made miserable by the conflict. One day it occurred to her that she had for a long while been praying for patience, and that perhaps this slow servant was the very chariot the Lord had sent to carry her soul over into patience. She immediately accepted it as such, and from that time used the slowness of her servant as a chariot for her soul. And the result was a victory of patience that no slowness of anybody was ever after able to disturb.

Another instance: I knew a sister at one of our conventions who was put to sleep in a room with two others on account of the crowd. She wanted to sleep, but they wanted to talk, and the first night she was greatly disturbed, and lay there fretting and fuming long after the others had hushed and she might have slept. But the next day she heard something about God's chariots, and that night she accepted these talking sisters as her chariots to carry her over into sweetness and patience, and she lay there feeling peaceful and at rest. When, however, it grew very late, and she knew they all ought to be sleeping, she ventured to say slyly, "Sisters, I am lying here riding in a chariot," and the effect was instantaneous in producing perfect quiet. Her chariot had carried her over to victory, not only inwardly, but at last outwardly as well.

If we would ride in God's chariots, instead of in our own, we should find this to be the case continually.

•••

Isaiah 31:1-3 – "Woe to them that go down to Egypt for help; and stay on horses, and trust in chariots, because they are many; and in horsemen, because they are very strong; but they look not unto the Holy One of Israel, neither seek the Lord! Yet he also is wise, and will bring evil, and will not call back his words: but will arise against the house of the evildoers, and against the help of them that work iniquity. Now the Egyptians are men, and not God; and their horses flesh, and not spirit. When the Lord shall stretch out his hand, both he that helpeth shall fall, and he that is holpen shall fall down, and they all shall fail together."

Psalm 20:7, 8 – "Some trust in chariots, and some in horses: but we will remember the name of the Lord our God. They are brought down and fallen: but we are risen, and stand upright."

Our constant temptation is to trust in the "chariots of Egypt." We can see them; they are tangible and real, and they look so substantial; while God's chariots are invisible and intangible, and it is hard to believe they are there. Our eyes are not opened to see them.

•••

2 Kings 19:23 – "By thy messengers thou hast reproached the Lord, and hast said, With the multitude of my chariots I am come up to the height of the mountains, to the sides of Lebanon, and will cut down the tall cedar trees thereof, and the choice fir trees thereof: and I will enter into the lodgings of his borders, and into the forest of his Carmel."

We try to reach the high places with the "multitude of our chariots." We depend first on one thing, and then on another, to advance our spiritual condition and to gain our spiritual victories. We "go down to Egypt for help." And God is obliged often to destroy all our own chariots before he can bring us to the point of mounting into His.

•••

Micah 5:10 – "And it shall come to pass in that day, saith the Lord, that I will cut off thy horses out of the midst of thee, and I will destroy thy chariots…"

Haggai 2:22 – "And I will overthrow the throne of kingdoms, and I will destroy the strength of the kingdoms of the heathen; and I will overthrow the chariots, and those that ride in them; and the horses and their riders shall come down, every one by the sword of his brother."

We lean too much upon a dear friend to help us onward in the spiritual life, and the Lord is obliged to separate us from that friend. We feel that all our spiritual prosperity depends on our continuance under the ministry of a favorite preacher, and we are mysteriously removed. We look upon our prayer meeting or our Bible class as the chief source of our spiritual strength, and we are shut up from attending it. And the "chariot of God," which alone can carry us to the places where we hoped to be taken by the instrumentalities upon which we have been depending, is to be found in the very deprivations we have so mourned over. God must burn up with the fire of His love every chariot of our own that stands in the way of our mounting into His.

•••

Isaiah 66:15, 16 – "For, behold, the Lord will come with fire, and with his chariots like a whirlwind, to render his anger with fury, and his rebuke with flames of fire. For by fire and by his sword will the Lord plead with all flesh: and the slain of the Lord shall be many."

Let us be thankful, then, for every trial that will help to destroy our chariots, and will compel us to take refuge in the chariot of God, which stands ready and waiting beside us.

•••

Psalm 62:5-8 – "My soul, wait thou only upon God; for my expectation is from him. He only is my rock and my salvation: he is my defence; I shall not be moved. In God is my salvation and my glory: the rock of my strength, and my refuge, is in God. Trust in him at all times; ye people, pour out your heart before him: God is a refuge for us."

We have to be brought to the place where all other refuges fail us, before we can say, "He only." We say, "He and—something else." "He, and my experience," or "He, and my church relationships," or "He, and my Christian work"; and all that comes after the "and" must be taken away from us, or must be proved useless before we can come to the "He only." As long as visible chariots are at hand, the soul will not mount into the invisible ones.

•••

Psalm 68:4 – "Sing unto God, sing praises to his name: extol him that rideth upon the heavens by his name JAH, and rejoice before him."

If we want to ride with God "upon the heavens," we have to be brought to an end of all riding upon the earth.

•••

Psalm 68:24 – "They have seen thy goings,
O God; even the goings of my God, my King,
in the sanctuary."

To see God's "goings," we must get into the "sanctuary" of his presence; and to share in His "goings" and "go" with Him, we must abandon all earthly "goings."

•••

Proverbs 20:24 – "Man's goings are of
the Lord; how can a man then understand
his own way?"

Psalm 17:5 – "Hold up my goings in thy
paths, that my footsteps slip not."

Psalm 40:1, 2 – "I waited patiently for
the Lord; and he inclined unto me, and
heard my cry. He brought me up also out
of an horrible pit, out of the miry clay, and
set my feet upon a rock, and established my
goings."

When we mount into God's chariot our goings are "established," for no obstacles can hinder its triumphal course. All losses therefore are gains that bring us to this.

•••

Philippians 3:7-9 – "But what things were gain to me, those I counted loss for Christ. Yea doubtless, and I count all things but loss for the excellency of the knowledge of Christ Jesus my Lord: for whom I have suffered the loss of all things, and do count them but dung, that I may win Christ, And be found in him, not having mine own righteousness, which is of the law, but that which is through the faith of Christ, the righteousness which is of God by faith..."

Paul understood this, and he gloried in the losses which brought him such unspeakable gain.

•••

2 Corinthians 12:7-10 – "And lest I should be exalted above measure through the abundance of the revelations, there was given to me a thorn in the flesh, the messenger of Satan to buffet me, lest I should be exalted above measure. For this thing I besought the Lord thrice, that it might depart from me. And he said unto me, My grace is sufficient for thee: for my strength is made perfect in weakness. Most gladly therefore will I rather glory in my infirmities, that the power of Christ may rest upon me. Therefore I take pleasure in infirmities,

in reproaches, in necessities, in persecutions,
in distresses for Christ's sake: for when I am
weak, then am I strong."

Even the "thorn in the flesh," the messenger of Satan sent to buffet him, became only a chariot to his willing soul, that carried him to heights of triumph which he could have reached in no other way. To "take pleasure" in one's trials, what is this but turning them into the grandest of chariots?

Joseph had a revelation of his future triumphs and reigning, but the chariots that carried him there looked to the eye of sense like the bitterest failures and defeats. It was a strange road to a kingdom, through slavery and a prison, and yet by no other road could Joseph have reached his triumph. His dream, Genesis 37:5-10; His chariots, Genesis 37:19, 20, 27, 28; 39:19, 20; How he rode in his chariots, Genesis 39:1-6, 21-23; His triumph, Genesis 43:38-43.

And now a word as to how one is to mount into these chariots.

My answer would be simply this: Find out where God is in each one of them, and hide yourself in Him. Or, in other words, do what the little child does when trouble comest, who finds its mother and hides in her arms. The real chariot after all that takes us through triumphantly is the carrying of God.

> *Isaiah 46:4 – "And even to your old age I am he; and even to hoar hairs will I carry you: I have made, and I will bear; even I will carry, and will deliver you."*

The baby carried in the chariot of its mother's arms rides triumphantly through the hardest places, and does not even know they are hard.

•••

> *Isaiah 63:9 – "In all their affliction he was afflicted, and the angel of his presence saved them: in his love and in his pity he redeemed them; and he bare them, and carried them all the days of old."*

And how much more we, who are carried in the chariot of the "arms of God"!

Get into your chariot, then. Take each thing that is wrong in your lives as God's chariot for you. No matter who the builder of the wrong may be, whether men or devils, by the time it reaches your side it is God's chariot for you, and is meant to carry you to a heavenly place of triumph. Shut out all the second causes, and find the Lord in it. Say, "Lord, open my eyes that I may see, not the visible enemy, but thy unseen chariots of deliverance."

Accept His will in the trial, whatever it may be, and hide yourself in His arms of love. Say, "Thy will be done; Thy will be done!" over and over. Shut out every other thought but the one thought of submission to His will and of trust in His love. Make your trial thus your chariot, and you will find your soul "riding upon the heavens" with God in a way you never dreamed could be.

I have not a shadow of doubt that if all our eyes were opened today we would see our homes, and our places of business, and the streets we traverse, filled with the "chariots of God." There is no need for any one of us to walk for lack of chariots. That cross inmate of your household, who has hitherto made life a burden to you, and who has been the Juggernaut car to crush your soul into the dust, may henceforth be a glorious chariot to carry you to the heights of heavenly patience and long suffering. That misunderstanding, that mortification, that unkindness, that disappointment, that loss, that defeat, all these are chariots waiting to carry you to the very heights of victory you have so longed to reach.

Mount into them, then, with thankful hearts, and lose sight of all second causes in the shining of His love who will "carry you in His arms" safely and triumphantly over it all.

XXII

"Without Me Ye Can Do Nothing"

Concerning the Life of Divine Union in Its Practical Aspects

NOT LONG AGO I was driving with a Quaker preacher through our beautiful Philadelphia Park, when our conversation turned on the apparent fruitlessness of a great deal of the preaching in the church at the present time. We had spoken, of course, of the foundational cause in the absence of the power of the Holy Ghost, but we still felt that this could not account for it all, as we both of us knew many preachers really baptized with the Spirit, who yet seemed to have no fruit to their ministry. And then I suggested that one reason might be in the fact that so many ministers, when preaching or talking on religious subjects, put on a different tone and manner from the one they ordinarily use, and by this very manner remove religion so far from the range of ordinary life, as to fail of gaining any real hold on the hearts of the men and women whose whole lives are lived on the plane of ordinary and homely pleasures and duties. "Now, for instance," I said, "if in thy preaching from the Friends' gallery thee could use the same tone and manner as thy present one, how much more effectual and convincing thy preaching would be." "Oh, but I could not do that," was the reply, "because the preacher's gallery is so much more solemn a place than this."

"But why is it more solemn?" I asked. "Is it not the presence of God only that makes the gallery or the pulpit solemn, and have we not the presence of God equally here? Is it not just as solemn to live in our everyday life as it is to preach, and ought we not to do the one to His glory just as much as the other?" And then I added, as the subject seemed to open out before me, "I verily believe a large part of the difficulty lies in the unscriptural and unnatural divorce that has been brought about between our so-called religious life and our so-called temporal life; as if our religion were something apart from ourselves, a sort of outside garment that was to be put on and off according to our circumstances and purposes. On Sundays, for instance, and in church, our purpose is to seek God, and worship and serve Him, and therefore on Sundays we bring out our religious life and put it on in a suitably solemn manner, and live it with a strained gravity and decorum which deprives it of half its power. But on Mondays our purpose is to seek our own interests and serve them, and so we bring out our temporal life and put it on with a sense of relief, as from an unnatural bondage, and live it with ease and naturalness, and consequently with far more power."

The thoughts thus started remained with me and gathered strength. Not long afterward I was present at a meeting where the leader opened with reading John 15, and the words, "Without me ye can do nothing," struck me with amazement. Hundreds of times before I had read those words, and had thought that I understood them thoroughly. But now it seemed almost as though they must have been newly inserted in the Bible, so ablaze were they with wondrous meaning.

"There it is," I said to myself, "Jesus himself said so, that apart from Him we have no real life of any kind, whether we call it temporal or spiritual, and that, therefore, all living or doing that is without Him is of such a nature that God, who sees into the realities of things, calls it 'nothing.'" And then the question forced itself upon me as to whether any soul really believed this statement to be true; or, if believing it theoretically, whether anyone made it practical in their daily walk and life. And I saw, as in a flash almost, that the real secret of divine union lay quite as much in this practical aspect of it as in any interior revealings or experiences. For if I do nothing, literally nothing, apart from Christ, I am of course united to Him in a continual oneness that cannot be questioned or gainsaid; while if I live a large part of my daily life and perform a large part of my daily work apart from Him, I have no real union, no matter how exalted and delightful my emotions concerning it may be.

It is to consider this aspect of the subject, therefore, that the present paper is written. For I am very sure that the wide divorce made between things spiritual and things temporal, of which I have spoken, has done more than almost anything else to hinder a realized interior union with God, and to put all religion so outside of the pale of common life as to make it an almost unattainable thing to the ordinary mass of mankind. Moreover it has introduced an unnatural constraint and stiltedness into the experience of Christians that seems to shut them out from much of the free, happy, childlike ease that belongs of right to the children of God.

I feel, therefore, that it is of vital importance for us to understand the truth of this matter.

And the thought that makes it clearest to me is this, that the fact of our oneness with Christ contains the whole thing in a nutshell. If we are one with Him, then of course in the very nature of things we can do nothing without Him. For that which is one cannot act as being two. And if I therefore do anything without Christ, then I am not one with Him in that thing, and like a branch severed from the vine I am withered and worthless. It is as if the branch should recognize its connection with and dependence upon the vine for most of its growth, and fruit-bearing, and climbing, but should feel a capacity in itself to grow and climb over a certain fence or around the trunk of a certain tree, and should therefore sever its connection with the vine for this part of its living. Of course that which thus sought an independent life would wither and die in the very nature of things. And just so is it with us who are branches of Christ the true vine. No independent action, whether small or great, is possible to us without withering and death, any more than to the branch of the natural vine.

This will show us at once how fatal to the realized oneness with Christ, for which our souls hunger, is the divorce I have spoken of. We have all realized, more or less, that without Him we cannot live our religious life, but when it comes to living our so-called temporal life, to keeping house or transacting business, or making calls, or darning stockings, or sweeping a room, or trimming a bonnet, or entertaining company, who is there that even theoretically thinks such things as these are to be done for Christ, and can only be rightly done as we abide in Him and do them in His strength?

But if it is Christ working in the Christian who is to lead the prayer meeting, then, since Christ and the Christian are one, it must be also Christ working in and through the Christian who is to keep the house and make the bargain; and one duty is therefore in the very essence of things as religious as the other. It is the man that makes the action, not the action the man. And as much solemnity and sweetness will thus be brought into our everyday domestic and social affairs as into the so-called religious occasions of life, if we will only "acknowledge God in all our ways," and do whatever we do, even if it be only eating and drinking, to His glory.

If our religion is really our life, and not merely something extraneous tacked on to our life, it must necessarily go into everything in which we live; and no act, however human or natural it may be, can be taken out of its control and guidance.

If God is with us always, then He is just as much with us in our business times and our social times as in our religious times, and one moment is as solemn with His presence as another.

If it is a fact that in Him we "live and move and have our being," then it is also a fact, whether we know it or not, that without Him we cannot do anything. And facts are stubborn things, thank God, and do not alter for all our feelings.

In Psalm 127:1, 2, we have a very striking illustration of this truth. The Psalmist says, "Except the Lord build the house, they labor in vain that build it: except the Lord keep the city, the watchman waketh but in vain. It is vain for you to rise up early, to sit up late, to eat the bread of sorrows; for so He giveth His beloved sleep." The two things here spoken of as being done in vain, unless the Lord is in the doing of them, are purely secular things, so called; simple business matters on the human plane of life. And whatever spiritual lesson they were intended to teach gains its impressiveness only from this, that these statements concerning God's presence in temporal things were statements of patent and incontrovertible facts.

In truth the Bible is full of this fact, and the only wonder is how any believer in the Bible could have overlooked it. From the building of cities down to the numbering of the hairs of our head and the noting of a sparrow's fall, throughout the whole range of homely daily living, God is declared to be present and to be the mainspring of it all. Whatever we do, even if it be such a purely physical thing as eating and drinking, we are to do for Him and to His glory, and we are exhorted to so live and so walk in the light in everything, as to have it made manifest of our works, temporal as well as spiritual, that "they are wrought in God."

There is unspeakable comfort in this for every loving Christian heart, in that it turns all of life into a sacrament, and makes the kitchen, or the workshop, or the nursery, or the parlor, as sweet and solemn a place of service to the Lord, and as real a means of union with Him, as the prayer meeting, or the mission board, or the charitable visitation.

A dear young Christian mother and house-keeper came to me once with a sorely grieved heart, because of her engrossing temporal life. "There seems," she said, "to be nothing spiritual about my life from one week's end to the other. My large family of little children are so engrossing that day after day passes without my having a single moment for anything but simply attendance on them and on my necessary household duties, and I go to bed night after night sick at heart because I have felt separated from my Lord all day long, and have not been able to do anything for Him." I told her of what I have written above, and assured her that all would be changed if she would only see and acknowledge God in all these homely duties, and would recognize her utter dependence upon Him for the doing of them. Her heart received the good news with gladness, and months afterward she told me that from that moment life had become a transformed and glorified thing, with the abiding presence of the Lord, and with the sweetness of continual service to Him.

Another Christian, a young lady in a fashionable family, came to me also in similar grief that in so much of her life she was separated from God and had no sense of His presence. I told her she ought never to do anything that could cause such a separation; but she assured me that it was impossible to avoid it, as the things she meant were none of them wrong things. "For instance," she said, "it is plainly my duty to pay calls with my mother, and yet nothing seems to separate me so much from God as paying calls." "But how would it be," I asked, "if you paid the calls as service to the Lord and for His glory?" "What!" she exclaimed, "pay calls for God! I never heard of such a thing." "But why not?" I asked; "if it is right to pay calls at all it ought to be done for God, for we are commanded whatsoever we do to do it for His glory, and if it is not right you ought not to do it. As a Christian," I continued, "you must not do anything that you cannot do for Him." "I see! I see!" she exclaimed, after a little pause, "and it makes all life look so different! Nothing can separate me from Him that is not sin, but each act done to His glory, whatever it may be, will only draw me closer and make His presence more real."

These two instances will illustrate my meaning. And I feel sure there are thousands of other burdened and weary lives that would be similarly transformed if these truths were but realized and acted on.

An old spiritual writer says something to this effect, that in order to become a saint it is not always necessary to change our works, but only to put an interior purpose toward God in them all; that we must begin to do for His glory and in His strength that which before we did for self and in self's capacity; which means, after all, just what our Lord meant when He said, "Without me ye can do nothing."

There is another side of this truth also which is full of comfort, and which the Psalmist develops in the verses I have quoted. "It is vain," he says, "to rise up early, to sit up late, to eat the bread of sorrows." Or, in other words, "What is the use of all this worry and strain? For the work will after all amount to nothing unless God is in it, and if He is in it, what folly to fret or be burdened, since He of course, by the very fact of His presence, assumes the care and responsibility of it all."

Ah, it is vain indeed, and I would that all God's children knew it!

We mothers at least ought to know it, for our own ways with our children would teach us something of it every day we live, if we had but the "eyes to see."

How many mothers have risen early, and sat up, late, and eaten the bread of sorrows, just that they might give sleep to their beloved children. And how grieved their hearts would have been if, after all their pains, the children had refused to rest. I can appeal to some mother hearts, I am sure, as thoroughly understanding my meaning. Memories will arise of the flushed and rosy boy coming in at night, tired with his play or his work, with knees out and coat torn, and of the patient, loving toil to patch and mend it all, sitting up late and rising early, that the dearly loved cause of all the mischief might rest undisturbed in childhood's happy sleep. How "vain," and worse than vain, would it have been for that loved and cared-for darling to have himself also sat up late, and risen early, and eaten the bread of sorrows, when all the while his mother was doing it for him just that he might not have it to do.

And if this is true of mothers, how much more true must it be of Him who made the mothers, and who came among us in bodily form to bear our burdens, and carry our sorrows, and do our work, just that we might "enter into His rest."

Beloved, have we entered into this rest?

"For he that is entered into his rest, he also hath ceased from his own works as God did from His." That is, he has learned at last the lesson that without Christ or apart from Him he can do nothing, but that he can do all things through Christ strengthening him; and therefore he has laid aside all self-effort, and has abandoned himself to God that He may work in him both to will and to do of His good pleasure. This and this only is the rest that remaineth for the people of God.

Scientific men are seeking to resolve all forces in nature into one primal force. Unity of origin is the present cry of science. Light, heat, sound are all said to be the products of one force differently applied, and that force is motion. All things, say the scientists, can be resolved back to this. Whether they are right or wrong I cannot say; but the Bible reveals to us one grand primal force which is behind motion itself, and that is God-force. God is at the source of everything, God is the origin of everything, God is the explanation of everything. Without Him was not anything made that was made, and without Him is not anything done that is done.

Surely, then, it is not the announcement of any mystery, but the simple statement of a simple fact, when our Lord says, "Without me ye can do nothing."

Even of Himself He said, "I can of mine own self do nothing," and He meant that He and His Father were so one that any independent action was impossible. Surely it is the revelation of a glorious necessity existing between our souls and Christ that He should say we could do nothing without Him; for it means that He has made us so one with Himself that independent action is as impossible with us as toward Him, as it was with Him as toward His Father.

Dear Christian, dost thou not catch a glimpse here of a region of wondrous glory?

Let us believe, then, that without Him we can literally do nothing. We must believe it, for it is true. But let us recognize its truth, and act on it from this time forward. Let us make a hearty renunciation of all living apart from Christ, and let us begin from this moment to acknowledge Him in all our ways, and do everything, whatsoever we do, as service to Him and for His glory, depending upon Him alone for wisdom, and strength, and sweetness, and patience, and everything else that is necessary for the right accomplishing of all our living.

As I said before, it is not so much a change of acts that will be necessary, as a change of motive and of dependence. The house will be kept, or the children cared for, or the business transacted, perhaps, just the same as before as to the outward, but inwardly God will be acknowledged, and depended on, and served; and there will be all the difference between a life lived at ease in the glory of His presence, and a life lived painfully and with effort apart from Him. There will result also from this bringing of God into our affairs a wonderful accession of divine wisdom in the conduct of them, and a far greater quickness and dispatch in their accomplishment, a surprising increase in the fertility of resource, an ease in apprehending the true nature and bearing of things, and an enlargement on every side that will amaze the hitherto cramped and cabined soul.

I mean this literally. I mean that the house will be kept more nicely and with greater ease, the children will be trained more swiftly, the stockings will be darned more swiftly, the guest will be entertained more comfortably, the servants will be managed more easily, the bargain will be made more satisfactorily, and all life will move with far more sweetness and harmony. For God will be in every moment of it, and where He is all must go well.

Moreover the soul itself, in this natural and simple way, will acquire such a holy habit of "abiding in Christ" that at last His presence will become the most real thing in life to our consciousness, and an habitual, silent, and secret conversation with Him will be carried on that will yield a continual joy.

Sometimes the child of God asks eagerly and hungrily, "What is the shortest and quickest way by which I can reach the highest degree of union and communion with God, possible to human beings in this life?" No shorter or quicker way can be found than the one I have been declaring. By the homely path of everyday duties done thus in God and for God, the sublimest heights are reached. Not as a reward, however, but as an inevitable and natural result, for if we thus abide in Him and refuse to leave Him, where He is there shall we also be, and all that He is will be ours.

If, then, thou wouldst know, beloved reader, the interior divine union realized in thy soul, begin from this very day to put it outwardly in practice as I have suggested. Offer each moment of thy living and each act of thy doing to God, and say to Him continually, "Lord, I am doing this in Thee and for Thy glory. Thou art my strength, and my wisdom, and my all-sufficient supply for every need. I depend only upon Thee." Refuse utterly to live for a single moment or to perform a single act apart from Him. Persist in this until it becomes the established habit of thy soul. And sooner or later thou shalt surely know the longings of thy soul satisfied in the abiding presence of Christ, thy indwelling Life.

XXIII

The Life on Wings

THIS LIFE HID WITH CHRIST in God has many aspects, and can be considered under a great many different figures. One aspect has been a great help and inspiration to me. I think it may also help some other longing and hungry souls. It is what I call the life on wings.

Our Lord has not only told us to consider the "lilies of the field" (Matthew 6:28), but also the "birds of the air" (Matthew 8:20). I have found that these little winged creatures have some wonderful lessons for us. In one of the Psalms, the Psalmist, after specifying the darkness and bitterness of his life in this earthly sphere of trial, cries out, "Oh that I had wings like a dove! for then would I fly away, and be at rest. Lo, then would I wander far off, and remain in the wilderness. I would hasten my escape from the windy storm and tempest" (Psalm 55:68).

This cry for "wings" is as old as humanity. Our souls were made to "mount up with wings." They can never be satisfied with anything short of flying. The captive-born eagle feels within it the instinct of flight and is irritated and worried about its imprisonment, hardly knowing what it longs for. Our souls, too, are irritated and worried and cry out for freedom. We can never rest on earth, and we long to "fly away" from all that holds and hampers and imprisons us here.

In seeking an outward escape from our circumstances or from our miseries, restlessness and discontentment grow. At first we do not recognize that our only way of escape is to "mount up with wings" (Isaiah 40:31), and we try to "flee on horses," as the Israelites did, when oppressed by their trials (see Isaiah 30:16).

Our "horses" are the outward things on which we depend for relief, some change of circumstance, or some help from man. We mount on these and run east or west, north or south anywhere to get away from our trouble. In our ignorance we think that a change of our environment is all that is necessary to experience deliverance of our souls. But all such efforts to escape do not help. The soul is not made to "flee upon horses," but must make its flight always upon wings.

Moreover, as with the Israelites, these "horses" generally carry us out of one trouble only to land us in another. It is as the prophet

Amos says, "As if a man did flee from a lion, and a bear met him; or went into the house, and leaned his hand on the wall, and a serpent bit him" (Amos 5:19). How often have we also run from some "lion" in our pathway only to be met by a "bear." How often we have hidden ourselves in a place of supposed safety only to be bitten by a "serpent!" It is useless for the soul to hope to escape by running away from its troubles to any earthly refuge. There is not one that can give it deliverance.

Is there no way of escape for us, then, when in trouble or distress? Must we just plod wearily through it all and look for no relief? I rejoice to answer that there is a glorious way of escape for every one of us, if we will but mount up on wings and fly away from it all to God. It is not a way east or west or north or south, but it is a way upwards. "They that wait upon the Lord shall renew their strength; they shall mount up with wings as eagles; they shall run, and not be weary; and they shall walk, and not faint" (Isaiah 40:31).

All creatures that have wings can escape from every snare that is set from them, if only they will fly high enough. The soul that uses its wings can always find a sure "way to escape" from all that can hurt or trouble it.

What, then, are these wings? The secret is contained in the words, "They that wait upon the Lord." The soul that waits upon the Lord is the soul that is entirely surrendered to Him and trusts Him perfectly. Therefore, we might name our wings the wings of Surrender and of Trust. If we will only completely surrender ourselves to the Lord and trust Him perfectly, we will find our souls "mounting up with wings as eagles" to the "heavenly places" in Christ Jesus, where earthly annoyances or sorrows have no power to disturb us.

The wings of the soul carry it up into a spiritual plane of life, into the "life hid with Christ in God," which is a life utterly independent of circumstances, and one that no cage can imprison and no shackles bind.

The "things above" are the things the soul on wings cares about, not the "things on the earth." It views life and all its experiences from the high altitude of "heavenly places in Christ Jesus" (Ephesians 2:6). Things look very different according to the standpoint from which we view them. The caterpillar, as it creeps along the ground, must have a widely different "view" of the world around it, from that which the same caterpillar will have when its wings are developed, and it soars in the air above the very places where once it crawled. Similarly, the crawling soul must see things in a very different way from the soul that has "mounted up with wings." The mountaintop may blaze with sunshine when the valley below is shrouded in fog. The bird whose wings can carry him high enough may mount at will out of the gloom below into the joy of the sunlight above.

Once, while spending a winter in London, I did not see any genuine sunshine for three long months because of the dense clouds of smoke that hung over the city like a shroud. But many times I saw that above the smoke the sun was shining. Once or twice through a rift I had a glimpse of a bird, with sunshine on its wings, sailing above the fog in the clear blue of the sunlit sky. Not all the brooms in London could sweep away the fog. But could we only mount high enough, we would reach a region above it all.

This is what the soul on wings does. It overcomes the world through faith. To overcome means to "come over," not to be crushed under, and the soul on wings flies over the world and the things of it. These lose their power to hold or bind the spirit that can "come over" them on the wings of Surrender and Trust. That spirit is made in very truth "more than conqueror" (Romans 8:37).

Birds overcome the lower law of gravitation by the higher law of flight. The soul on wings overcomes the lower law of sin and misery and bondage by the higher law of spiritual flying. The "law of the spirit of life in Christ Jesus"

(Romans 8:2) must be a higher and more dominant law than the law of sin and death. Therefore, the soul that has mounted into this upper region of the life in Christ cannot fail to conquer and triumph.

But it may be asked how it is, then, that all Christians do not always triumph. I answer that it is because a great many Christians do not "mount up with wings" into this higher plane of life at all. They live on the same low level with their circumstances. Instead of flying over them, they try to fight them on their own earthly plane. On the earthly plane the soul is powerless. It has no weapons with which to conquer. Instead of overcoming (coming over) the trials and sorrows of the earthly life, it is overcome by them and crushed under them.

We all know, as I have said, that things look differently to us according to our "point of view." Trials assume a very different aspect when looked down upon from above than when viewed from their own level. What seems like an impassable wall on its own level becomes an insignificant line to the eyes that see it from the top of a mountain. The snares and sorrows that assume such immense proportion while we look at them on the earthly plane become insignificant when the soul has mounted on wings to the heavenly places above them.

A friend once illustrated the difference in her friends in the following way. She said, if all three came to a spiritual mountain which had to be crossed, the first one would tunnel through it with hard and wearisome labor. The second would meander around it in an indefinite fashion, hardly knowing where she was going, and yet, because her aim was right, would get around it at last. But the third, she said, would just flap her wings and fly right over. All of us must know something about this. If any of us in the past have tried to tunnel our way through the mountains that have stood across our pathway, or have been meandering around them, let us now resolve to spread our wings and "mount up" into the clear atmosphere of God's presence. There it will be easy to overcome, or come over, the highest mountain of them all.

I say, "spread our wings and mount up," because the largest wings ever known cannot lift a bird one inch upward unless they are used. We must use our wings, or they are of no help to us.

It is not worthwhile to say, "If I had wings I would flee." For we already have the wings; we should use them. The power to surrender and trust exists in every human soul, and only needs to be exercised. With these two wings we can "flee" to God at any moment. But, in order really to reach Him, we must actively use them. We must not merely want to use them, we must do it definitely and actively. A passive surrender or a passive trust will not do. I mean this very practically. We will not "mount up" very high, if we only surrender and trust in theory, or in our especially spiritual moments. We must do it definitely and practically, about each detail of daily life as it comes to us.

We must meet our disappointments, our betrayals, our persecutions, our malicious enemies, our provoking friends, our trials and temptations of every sort, with an active and experimental attitude of surrender and trust. We must spread our wings and "mount up" to the "heavenly places in Christ" above them all, where they will lose their power to harm or distress us. For from these high places we will see things through the eye of Christ, and all earth will be glorified in the heavenly vision.

> "The dove has neither claw nor sting,
>   Nor weapon for the fight;
> She owes her safety to the wing,
>   Her victory to flight.
> The Bridegroom opens His arms of love,
>   And in them folds the panting dove."

How changed our lives would be if we could only fly through the days on these wings of surrender and trust! Instead of stirring up strife and bitterness by trying to fight offending brothers and sisters, we should escape all strife by simply spreading our wings and mounting up to the heavenly region. There our eyes would see all things covered with a mantle of Christian love and pity.

Our souls were made to live in this upper atmosphere, and we stifle and choke on any lower level. Our eyes were made to look off from these heavenly heights, and our vision is distorted by any lower gazing. It is a great blessing, therefore, that our loving Father in heaven has mercifully arranged all the discipline of our lives with a view to teaching us to fly.

In Deuteronomy we have a picture of how this teaching is done: "As an eagle stirreth up her nest, fluttereth over her young, spreadeth abroad her wings, taketh them, beareth them on her wing: so the Lord alone did lead him, and there was no strange god with him" (Deuteronomy 32:11, 12).

The mother eagle teaches her little ones to fly by making their nest so uncomfortable that they are forced to leave it and commit themselves to the unknown world of air outside. God does the same to us. He stirs up our comfortable nests, pushes us over the edge of them, and we are forced to use our wings to save ourselves from fatal falling. Read your trials in this light, and see if you cannot begin to get a glimpse of their meaning. Your wings are being developed.

I knew a lady whose life was one long strain of trial, from a cruel, wicked, drunken husband. There was no possibility of human help, and in her despair she was driven to use her wings and fly to God. And during the long year of trial her wings grew so strong from constant flying, that at last, when the trials were at their hardest, it seemed to her as if her soul was carried over them on a beautiful rainbow and found itself in a peaceful resting place on the other side.

With this end in view we can surely accept with thankfulness every trial that compels us to use our wings, for only then can they grow strong and large and fit for the highest flying. Unused wings gradually wither and shrink and lose their flying power. If we had nothing in our lives that made flying necessary, we might at last lose all capacity to fly.

But you may ask, "Are there no hindrances to flying, even where the wings are strong, and the soul is trying hard to use them?" I answer, "Yes." A bird may be imprisoned in a cage; it may be tethered to the ground with a cord; it may be loaded with a weight that drags it down, or it may be entrapped in the "snare of the fowler" (Psalm 91:3). Hindrances may make it impossible for the soul to fly, until it has been set free from them by the mighty power of God.

One "snare of the fowler" that entraps many souls is the snare of doubt. The doubts look so plausible and often so humble that Christians walk into their "snare" without dreaming for a moment that it is a snare at all, until they find themselves caught and unable to fly. There is no more possibility of flying for the soul that doubts, than there is for the bird caught in the fowler's snare.

The reason for this is evident. One of our wings, namely the wing of trust, is entirely disabled by the slightest doubt. Just as it requires two wings to lift a bird in the air, it requires two wings to lift the soul. A great many people do everything but trust. They spread the wing of surrender, and use it vigorously. They wonder why they do not mount up, never dreaming that it is because all the while the wing of trust is hanging idle by their sides. It is because Christians use only one wing, that their efforts to fly are often so irregular and fruitless.

Look at a bird with a broken wing trying to fly, and you will get some idea of the kind of motion all one-sided flying must make. We must use both our wings, or not try to fly at all.

It may be that for some the "snare of the fowler" is some subtle form of sin, some hidden want of consecration. Where this is the case, the wing of trust may seem to be all right, but the wing of surrender hangs idly down. It is just as hopeless to try to fly with the wing of trust alone, as with the wing of surrender alone. Both wings must be used, or no flying is possible.

Or perhaps the soul may feel as if it were in a prison from which it cannot escape, and consequently is unable to mount up on wings. No earthly bars can ever imprison the soul. No walls however high, or bolts however strong, can imprison an eagle, so long as there is an open way upward. Earth's power can never hold the soul in prison while the upward way is kept open and free. Our enemies may build walls around us as high as they please, but they cannot build any barrier between us and God. If we "mount up with wings," we can fly higher than any of their walls can ever reach.

If we find ourselves imprisoned, we may be sure that it is not our earthly environment that constitutes our jail cell, for the soul's wings scorn all petty bars and walls of earth's making. The only thing that can really imprison the soul is something that hinders its upward flight. Isaiah 59:2 tells us "your iniquities have separated between you and your God, and your sins have hid His face from you, that He will not hear." Therefore, if our soul is imprisoned, it must be because some indulged sin has built a barrier between us and the Lord, and we cannot fly until this sin is given up and put out of the way.

But often, where there is no conscious sin, the soul is still unconsciously tethered to something of earth. It struggles in vain to fly. Some of my friends once got into a boat in Norway to row around one of the inlets there. They took their seats and began to row vigorously, but the boat made no headway. They put out more strength and rowed harder than before, but all in vain. The boat didn't move an inch. Then someone remembered that the boat had not been unmoored, and he exclaimed, "No wonder we could not get away, when we were trying to pull the whole continent of Europe after us!" Our souls are likewise often not unmoored from earthly things. We must cut ourselves loose. As an eagle might try to fly with a hundred-ton weight tied fast to its feet, the soul maw try to "mount up with wings" while a weight of earthly cares and anxieties is holding it down to earth.

When our Lord was trying to teach His disciples concerning this danger, He told them a parable of a great supper to which many who were invited failed to come because they were hindered by their earthly cares. One had bought a piece of land, another a yoke of oxen, and a third had married a wife. They felt that all these things needed their care.

Wives or oxen or land or even smaller things may be the cords that tether the soul from flying or the weight that holds it down. Let us then cut every cord and remove every barrier so our souls may find no hindrance to their mounting up with wings as eagles to heavenly places in Christ Jesus.

We are commanded to have our hearts filled with songs of rejoicing and to make inward melody to the Lord. But unless we mount up with wings this is impossible, for the only creature that can sing is the creature that flies. Though all the world should be desolate, Habakkuk 3:18 says, "Yet I will rejoice in the Lord, I will joy in the God of my salvation." Paul knew what it was to use his wings when he found himself "sorrowful, yet always rejoicing" (2 Corinthians 6:10). On the earthly plane all was dark to both, but on the heavenly plane all was brightest sunshine.

Do you know anything about this life on wings? Do you "mount up" continually to God, out of and above earth's cares and trials, to that higher plane of life where all is peace and triumph? Or, do you plod wearily along on foot through the midst of your trials and let them overwhelm you at every turn?

Let us guard against a mistake here. Do not think that by flying I mean very joyous emotions or feelings of exhilaration. There is a great deal of emotional flying that is not really flying at all. It is such flying as a feather accomplishes which is driven upward by a strong puff of wind, but flutters down again as soon as the wind ceases to blow. The flying I mean is a matter of principle, not a matter of emotion. It may be accompanied by very joyous emotions, but it does not depend on them. It depends only upon the facts of an entire surrender and an absolute trust. Everyone who will honestly use these two wings and will faithfully persist in using them will find that they have mounted up with wings as an eagle, no matter how empty of all emotion they may have felt themselves to be before.

For the promise is sure: "They that wait upon the Lord shall mount up with wings as eagles." Not "may perhaps mount up," but "shall." It is the inevitable result. May we each one prove it for ourselves!

"The lark soars singing from its nest,
    And tells aloud
His trust in God, and so is blest
    Let come what cloud.

"He has no store, he sows no seed,
    Yet sings aloud, and doth not heed.

Through cloudy day or scanty feed,
    He sings to shame
Men who forget in fear of need
    A Father's name.

"The heart that trusts forever sings,
And feels as light as it has wings;
A well of peace within it springs.
    Come good or ill,
Whate'er to-day or morrow bring,
    It is His will."

XXIV

"God with Us"

Or, The One Hundred and Thirty-Ninth Psalm

> *"Thus doth thy hospitable greatness lie*
> *Around us like a boundless sea;*
> *We cannot lose ourselves where all is home,*
> *Nor drift away from Thee."*

VERY FEW OF US understand the full meaning of the words in Matthew 1:23, "They shall call His name Emmanuel; which being interpreted is, God with us." In this short sentence is revealed to us the grandest fact the world can ever know; that God, the Almighty God, the Creator of Heaven and earth, is not a far-off Deity, dwelling in a Heaven of unapproachable glory, but is living with us right here in this world, in the midst of our poor, ignorant, helpless lives, as close to us as we are to ourselves. This seems so incredible to the human heart that we are very slow to believe it; but that the Bible teaches it as a fact, from cover to cover, cannot be denied by any honest mind. In the very beginning of Genesis we read of the "presence of the Lord God amongst the trees of the garden." And from that time on He is revealed to us always as in the most familiar and daily intercourse with His people everywhere.

In Exodus we find Him asking them to make Him a "sanctuary, that He might dwell among them." He is recorded as having "walked" with them in the wilderness, and as "taking up His abode" with them in the promised land. He taught them to rely on Him as an ever-present Friend and Helper, to consult Him about all their affairs, and to abandon the whole management of their lives to Him. And finally He came in Christ in bodily form and dwelt in the world as a man among men, making Himself bone of our bone and flesh of our flesh, taking upon Him our nature, and revealing to us, in the most tangible and real way possible, the grand, and blessed, and incomprehensible fact that He intended to be with us always, even unto the end of the world.

Whoever will believe this fact with all their hearts will find in it the solution of every difficulty of their lives.

I remember when I was a little girl and found myself in any trouble or perplexity, the coming in of my father or mother on the scene would always bring me immediate relief. The moment I heard the voice of one of them saying, "Daughter, I am here," that moment every burden dropped off and every anxiety was stilled. It was their simple presence that did it. They did not need to promise to relieve me, they did not need to tell me their plans of relief; the simple fact of their presence was all the assurance I required that everything now would be set straight and all would go well for me, and my only interest after their arrival was simply to see how they would do it all. Perhaps they were exceptional parents, to have created such confidence in their children's hearts. I think myself they were. But as our God is certainly an exceptional God, the application has absolute force, and His presence is literally all we need. It would be enough for us, even if we had not a single promise nor a single revelation of His plans. How often in the Bible He has stilled all questions and all fears by the simple announcement, "I will be with thee"; and who can doubt that in these words He meant to assure us that all His wisdom, and love, and omnipotent power would therefore, of course, be engaged on our side? Over and over again in my childhood have the magic words, "Oh, there is mother!" brought me immediate relief and comfort; and over and over again in my later years have almost the same words reverently spoken, "Oh, there is God!" brought me a far more blessed deliverance. With Him present, what could I have to fear? Since He has said, "I will never leave thee nor forsake thee," surely I may boldly say, "The Lord is my helper, and I will not fear what man shall do unto me." I remember to this day the inspiring sense of utter security that used to come to me with my earthly father's presence. I never feared anything when he was by. And surely with my Heavenly Father by, there can be no possible room for fear.

It is because of its practical help and comfort, therefore, that I desire to make this wonderful fact of "Emmanuel, God with us," clear and definite, for I am very sure but few, even of God's own children, really believe it. They may say they do, they may repeat a thousand times in the conventional, pious tone considered suitable to such a sentiment, "Oh, yes, we know that God is always present with us, but"—And in this "but" the whole story is told. There are no "buts" in the vocabulary of the soul that accepts His presence as a literal fact. Such a soul is joyously triumphant over every suggestion of fear or of doubt. It has God, and that is enough for it. His presence is its certain security and supply, always, and for everything.

Let me, then, beg my readers to turn with me for a while to the 139th Psalm, where we shall find a most blessed revelation of this truth.

The central thought of the Psalm is to be found in verses 7 to 12, "Whither shall I go from thy Spirit? Or whither shall I flee from thy presence? If I ascend up into heaven, thou art there: if I make my bed in hell, behold, thou art there. If I take the wings of the morning, and dwell in the uttermost parts of the sea; even there shall thy hand lead me, and thy right hand shall hold me. If I say, Surely the darkness shall cover me; even the night shall be light about me. Yea, the darkness hideth not from thee; but the night shineth as the day: the darkness and the light are both alike to thee. For thou hast possessed my reins: thou hast covered me in my mother's womb."

I cannot conceive of a more definite or sweeping declaration of His continual presence with us, wherever we may be or whatever we may do, than is contained in this passage. People talk about seeking to get into the presence of the Lord, but here we see that they cannot get out of it; that there is no place in the whole universe where He is not present; neither heaven, nor hell, nor the uttermost parts of the sea; and no darkness so great as to hide for one moment from Him. And the reason of this is, that He "has possessed our reins," which means that He is not only with us, but within us, and consequently must accompany us wherever we ourselves go.

We must accept it as true, therefore, that the words of our Lord, "Lo, I am with you always, even unto the end of the world," were the expression, not of a beautiful sentiment merely, but of an incontrovertible fact. He is with us, and we cannot get away from Him.

We may be in such thick darkness as to be utterly unable to see Him, and may think, probably often have thought, that, therefore, He does not see us. But our Psalm assures us that the darkness hideth not from Him, and that, in fact, darkness and light are both alike to Him. We are as present to His view and as plainly seen when our own souls are in the depths of spiritual darkness, as when they are basking in the brightest light. The darkness may hide Him from us, but it does not hide us from Him. Neither does any apparent spiritual distance or wandering take us out of His presence; not even if we go into the depths of sin in our wandering. In the uttermost parts of the sea, or wherever we may be, He is ever present to hold and to lead us. There is not a moment nor a place where we can be left without His care.

There are times in our lives when delirium makes us utterly unaware of the presence of our most careful and tender nurses. A child in delirium will cry out in anguish for its mother, and will harrow her heart by its piteous lamentations and appeals, when all the while she is holding its fevered hand, and bathing its aching head, and caring for it with all the untold tenderness of a mother's love. The darkness of disease has hidden the mother from the child, but has not hidden the child from the mother.

And just so it is with our God and us. The darkness of our doubts or our fears, of our sorrows or our despair, or even of our sins, cannot hide us from Him, although it may, and often does, hide Him from us. He has told us that the darkness and the light are both alike to Him; and if our faith will only lay hold of this as a fact, we will be enabled to pass through the darkest seasons in quiet trust, sure that all the while, though we cannot see nor feel Him, our God is caring for us, and will never leave nor forsake us.

Whether, however, this abiding presence of our God will be a joy to us or a sorrow, will depend upon what we know about Him. If we think of Him as a stern tyrant, intent only on His own glory, we shall be afraid of His continual presence. If we think of Him as a tender, loving Father, intent only on our blessing and happiness, we shall be glad and thankful to have Him thus ever with us. For the presence and the care of love can never mean anything but good to the one beloved.

The Psalm we are considering shows us that the presence of our God is the presence of love, and that it brings us an infinitude of comfort and rest. He says in verses 1 to 5, "O Lord, thou hast searched me, and known me. Thou knowest my downsitting and mine uprising; thou understandest my thought afar off. Thou compassest my path and my lying down, and art acquainted with all my ways. For there is not a word in my tongue, but lo, O Lord, thou knowest it altogether. Thou hast beset me behind and before, and laid thine hand upon me."

Our God knows us and understands us, and is acquainted with all our ways. No one else in all the world understands us. Our actions are misinterpreted, it may be, and our motives misjudged. Our natural characteristics are not taken into account, nor our inherited tendencies considered. No one makes allowances for our ill health; no one realizes how much we have to contend with. But our Father knows it all. He understands us, and His judgment of us takes into account every element, conscious or unconscious, that goes to make up our character and to control our actions. Only an all-comprehending love can be just, and our God is just. No wonder Faber can say:—

"There is no place where earth's sorrows
Are more felt than up in Heaven;
There is no place where earth's failings
Have such kindly judgment given."

Some of you have been afraid of His justice, perhaps, because you thought it would be against you. But do you not see now that it is all on your side, just as a mother's justice is, because "He knoweth our frame and remembereth that we are dust"? No human judge can ever do this; and to me this comprehension of God is one of my most blessed comforts. Often I do not understand myself; all within looks confused and hopelessly tangled. But then I remember that He has searched me, and that He knows me and understands the thoughts which so perplex me, and that, therefore, I may just leave the whole miserable tangle to Him to unravel. And my soul sinks down at once, as on downy pillows, into a place of the most blissful rest.

Then further, because of this complete knowledge and understanding of our needs, what comfort it is to be told that He knows our downsitting and our uprising; that He compasses our path, and takes note of our lying down. Just what a mother does for her foolish, careless, ignorant, but dearly loved little ones, this very thing does our God for us. When a mother is with her children she thinks of their comfort and well-being always before her own. They must have comfortable seats where no draught can reach them, no matter what amount of discomfort she may herself be compelled to endure. Their beds must be soft and their blankets warm, let hers be what they may. Their paths must be smooth and safe, even though she is obliged herself to walk in rough and dangerous ways. Her own comfort, as compared with that of her children, is of no account in a loving mother's eyes. And surely our God has not made the mothers in this world more capable of a self-sacrificing love than He is Himself. He must be better and greater on the line of love and self-sacrifice than any mother He ever made.

Then, since He has assured us that He knows our downsitting and our uprising, that He compasses our path and our lying down, we may be perfectly and blessedly sure that in even these little details of our lives we get the very best that His love, and wisdom, and power can compass. I mean this in a very literal sense. I mean that He cares for our literal seats and our literal beds, and sees that we, each one, have just that sort of a seat or that sort of a bed which is best for us and for our highest development. And just on this last point is where He is so much better than any mother can be. His love is a wise love, that sees the outcome of things, and cares more for our highest good than for that which is lower. So that, while a mother's weak love cannot see beyond the child's present comfort, and cannot bear to inflict or allow any discomfort, the strong, wise love of our God can bear to permit the present discomfort, for the sake of the future glory that is to result therefrom.

At home and abroad, therefore, let us commit the choosing of our seats, and of our beds, and of all the other little homely circumstances of our daily lives and surroundings, to the God who has thus assured us that He knows all about every one of them.

For we are told in our Psalm that He "besets" our path. We have some of us known what it was to be "beset" by unwelcome and unpleasant people or things. But we never have thought, perhaps, that we were beset by God, that He loves us so that He cannot leave us alone, and that no coldness nor rebuffs on our parts can drive Him away. Yet it is gloriously true! And, moreover, He besets us "behind" as well as before. Just as a mother does. She goes after her children and picks up all they have dropped, and clears away all the rubbish they have left behind them. We mothers begin this in the nursery with the blocks and playthings, and we go on with it all our lives long; seeking continually to set straight that which our children have left crooked behind them; often at the cost of much toil and trouble, but always with a love that makes the toil and trouble nothing in comparison to caring for the children we love. What good mother ever turned away the poor little tearful darling who came with a tangled knot for her unraveling, or refused to help the eager rosy boy to unwind his kite-strings? Suppose it has been their own fault that the knots and tangles have come, still her love can sympathize with and pity the very faults themselves, and all the more does she seek to atone for them.

All this and more does our God do for us from our earliest infancy, long even before we know enough to be conscious of it, until the very end of our earthly lives. We have seen Him before us perhaps, but we have never thought of Him as behind us as well. Yet it is a blessed fact that He is behind us all the time, longing to make crooked things straight, to untangle our tangled skeins, and to atone continually for the wrong we have done and the mistakes we have made. If any of us, therefore, have that in our past which has caused us anxiety or remorse, let us lift up our heads in a happy confidence from henceforth, that the God who is behind us will set it all straight somehow, if we will but commit it to Him, and can even make our very mistakes and misdoings work together for good. Ah! it is a grand thing to be "beset" by God.

Then again what depths of comfort there are in verses 14 to 16: "I will praise thee; for I am fearfully and wonderfully made: marvelous are Thy works; and that my soul knoweth right well. My substance was not hid from thee, when I was made in secret, and curiously wrought in the lowest parts of the earth. Thine eyes did see my substance, yet being unperfect; and in thy book all my members were written, which in continuance were fashioned, when as yet there was none of them."

One of the things which often troubles us more than we care to confess is our dislike of the way we have been put together. Our mental or moral "make-up" does not suit us. We think if we had only been created with less of this or more of that, if we were less impulsive or more enthusiastic, if we had been made more like someone else whom we admire, that then our chances of success would have been far greater; that we could have served God far more acceptably; and could have been more satisfactory in every way to ourselves and to Him. And we are tempted sometimes to think that with our miserable make-up, it is hopeless to expect to please Him.

If we really realized that God Himself had made us, we should see the folly of all this at once, but we secretly feel as if somehow He had not had much hand in the matter, but as if we had been put together in a haphazard sort of way, that had left our characters very much to chance. We believe in creation in the general, but not in the particular, when it comes to ourselves. But in this Psalm we see that God has presided over the creation of each one of us, superintending the smallest details; even, to speak figuratively, writing down what each "member" was to be, when as yet there was none of them. Therefore we, just as we are naturally, with just the characteristics that inhere in us by birth, are precisely what God would have us to be, and were planned out by His own hand to do the especial work that He has prepared for our doing. I mean, of course, our natural characteristics, not the perversion of them by sin on our parts.

There is something very glorifying to the Creator in this way of looking at it. Genius always seeks expression, and seeks, too, to express itself in as great a variety of forms and ways as possible. No true artist repeats himself, but each picture he paints, or statue he carves, is a new expression of his creative power. When we go to an exhibition of pictures, we should feel it a lowering of art if two were exactly alike; and just so is it with us who are "God's workmanship." His creative power is expressed differently in each one of us. And in the individual "make-up" which sometimes so troubles us, there is a manifestation of this power different from every other, and without which the day of exhibition, when we are, each one, to be to the praise of His glory, would be incomplete. All He asks of us is that, as He has had the making of us, so He may also have the managing, since He alone understands us, and is, therefore, the only one who can do it.

The man who makes an intricate machine is the best one to manage it and repair it; anyone else who meddles with it is apt to spoil it. And when we think of the intricacy of our inward machinery and the continual failure of our own management of it, we may well be thankful to hand it all over to the One who created it, and to leave it in His hands. We may be sure He will then make the best out of us that can be made, and that we, even we, with our "peculiar temperaments," and our apparently unfortunate characteristics, will be made vessels unto honor, sanctified and meet for the Master's use, and fitted to every good work.

I met once with a saying in an old Quaker writer which I have never forgotten: "Be content to be just what thy God has made thee." It has helped me to understand the point upon which I am dwelling; and I feel sure contentment with our own "make-up" is as essential a part of our submission to God as contentment with any other of the circumstances of our daily life. If we did not each one of us exist just as we are by nature, then one expression of God's creative power would be missing, and one part of His work would be left undone. And besides, to complain of ourselves is to complain of the One who has made us, and cannot but grieve Him. Let us be content, then, and only see to it that we let the Divine Potter make out of us the very best He can, and use us according to His own good pleasure.

Verses 17 and 18 bring out another view of God's continual presence with us, and that is, that He is always thinking about us, and that His thoughts are kind and loving thoughts, for the Psalmist calls them precious. "How precious also are thy thoughts unto me, O God! How great is the sum of them! If I should count them, they are more in number than the sand: when I awake, I am still with thee."

So many people are tempted to think that God is not paying any attention to them. They think that their interests and their affairs are altogether beneath His notice, and that they are too unworthy to hope for His attention. But they wrong Him grievously by such thoughts. A mother pays as much attention to her smallest infant as to her oldest children, and is as much interested in its little needs and pleasures as in theirs. I am not sure but she is more. Her thoughts dwell around the one who needs them most; and He who made the mother's heart will not Himself be less attentive to the needs and pleasures of the meanest and most helpless of His creatures. He even hears the young lions when they cry, and not a sparrow can fall to the ground without Him; therefore, we, who are of more value than many sparrows, need not be afraid of a moment's neglect.

In fact, the responsibilities of creating anything require an unintermitting care of it on the part of the Creator; and it is the glory of omnipotence that it can attend at once to the smallest details and to the grandest operations as well.

> "For greatness which is infinite makes room
>> For all things in its lap to lie;
> We should be crushed by a magnificence
>> Short of infinity."

I do not know why it is that we consider a man or woman weak who attends to large affairs to the neglect of little details, and then turn around and accuse our God of doing this very thing. But if any of my readers have hitherto been guilty of this folly, let it end now and here, and let each one from henceforth believe, without any questioning, that always and everywhere the "Lord thinketh upon me."

The remainder of the Psalm develops the perfect accord of thought between the soul and God, where this life of simple faith has been entered upon. Having learned the transforming fact of God's continual presence and unceasing care, the soul is brought into so profound a union with Him as to love what He loves, and hate what He hates; and eagerly appeals to Him to search it, and try it, that there may be no spot left anywhere in all its being which is out of harmony with Him.

In the sunlight of His presence darkness must flee, and the heart will soon feel that it cannot endure to have any corner shut away from His shining; for in His presence is "fullness of joy," and at His right hand "there are pleasures forevermore."

An old woman, living in a rather desolate part of England, made considerable money by selling ale and beer to chance travelers who passed her lonely cottage. But her conscience troubled her about it. She wanted to be a Christian and to go to Heaven when she died, but she had an inward feeling that if she did become a Christian she would have to give up her profitable business, and this she thought would be more than she could do; so that between the two things she was brought into great conflict.

But one night, at the meeting she attended, a preacher from a distance told about the sweet and blessed fact of God's continual presence with us, and of the joy this was sure to bring when it was known. Her soul was enraptured at the thought of such a possibility for her, and forgetting all about the beer, she began at once with a very simple faith to claim it as a blessed reality. Over and over again she exclaimed in her heart, as the preacher went on with his sermon, "Why, Lord Jesus, I didn't know as thee wast always with me! Why, Lord, how good it is to know that I have got thee all the time to live with me and take care of me! Why, Lord, I sha'n't never be lonely no more!" And when the meeting closed and she took her way home across the moors, all the time the happy refrain went on, "Ah, Lord Jesus, thee art going home with me tonight. Never mind, Lord Jesus, old Betty won't never let thee go again now, I knows I have got thee!"

As her faith thus laid hold of the fact of His presence she began to rejoice in it more and more, until finally, when she had reached her cottage door, her soul was full of delight. As she opened the door, the first object her eyes rested upon was a great pot of ale on the table ready for selling. At once it flashed into her mind, "The Lord will not like to have that ale in the house where He lives," and her whole heart responded eagerly, "That ale shall go." She knew the pot was heavy, and she kneeled beside it saying, "Lord, thee hast come home with me, and thee art going to live with me always in this cottage, and I know thee don't like this ale. Please give me strength to tip it over into the road." Strength was given, and the ale was soon running down the lane. Then the old woman came back into her cottage, and kneeling down again thanked the Lord for the strength given, and added, "Now, Lord, if there is anything else in this cottage that thee does not like, show it to me, and it shall be tipped out too."

Is not this a perfect illustration of the close of our Psalm? "Do not I hate them, O Lord, that hate thee? and am not I grieved with those that rise up against thee? I hate them with a perfect hatred; I count them mine enemies. Search me, O God, and know my heart; try me, and know my thoughts; and see if there be any wicked way in me, and lead me in the way everlasting."

Just as light drives out darkness, so does the realized presence of God drive out sin, and the soul that by faith abides in His presence knows a very real and wonderful deliverance.

And now I trust that some will ask, "How can I find this presence to be real to myself?" I will close, therefore, with a few practical directions.

First, convince yourself from the Scriptures that it is a fact. Facts must always be the foundation of our experiences, or the experiences are worthless. It is not the feeling that causes the fact, but the fact that produces the feeling. And what every soul needs in this case first of all, is to be convinced beyond question, from God's own words about it, that His continual presence with us is an unalterable fact.

Then, this point having been settled, the next thing to do is to make it real to ourselves by "practicing His presence," as an old writer expresses it, always and everywhere, and in everything. This means simply that you are to obey the Scripture command, and "in all your ways acknowledge Him," by saying over each hour and moment, "The Lord is here," and by doing everything you do, even if only eating and drinking, in His presence and for Him. Literally, "whether, therefore, ye eat or drink, or whatsoever ye do, do all to the glory of God."

By this continual "practice of His presence," the soul at last acquires a habit of faith; and it becomes, finally, as difficult to doubt His presence as it was at first to believe it.

No great effort is required for this, but simply an unwavering faith. It is not studied reasonings or elaborate meditations that will help you here. The soul must recognize, by an act of simple faith, that God is present, and must then accustom itself to a continual conversation with Him about all its affairs, in freedom and simplicity. He does not require great things of us. A little remembrance of His presence, a few words of love and confidence, a momentary lifting of the heart to Him from time to time as we go about our daily affairs, a constant appeal to Him in everything as to a present and loving friend and helper, an endeavor to live in a continual sense of His presence, and a letting of our hearts "dwell at ease" because of it,—this is all He asks; the least little remembrance is welcome to Him, and helps to make His presence real to us.

Whoever will be faithful in this exercise will soon be led into a blessed realization of all I have been trying to tell in this book, and of far more that I cannot tell; and will understand in a way beyond telling, those wonderful words concerning our Lord, "They shall call His name Emmanuel, which being interpreted is, God with us."

Hannah Whitall Smith

In 1870 Hannah Whitall Smith wrote what has become a classic of joyous Christianity, *The Christian's Secret of a Happy Life*. The title barely hints at the depths of that perceptive book. It is no shallow "four easy steps to successful living." Studiously, the writer defines the shape of a full and abundant life hid in God. Then she carefully reveals the difficulties to this way and finally charts the results of a life abandoned to God. What is the Christian's secret to a happy life? It is best summed up by her entitled "The Joy of Obedience." Joy comes through obedience to Christ, and joy results from obedience to Christ. Without obedience, joy is hollow and artificial.[1]

---

1 Foster, Richard J. *Celebration of Discipline,* p. 192. San Francisco: Harper & Row, 1988. Print.

ABOUT

SEA HARP TIMELESS

The Sea Harp Timeless series, by Sea Harp Press, is a collection of the greatest writings ever composed about Jesus of Nazareth, His Kingdom, His Holy Spirit, the Father of Heaven, the Early Church, the Christian life, one's inner life, and what it means to "abide." The men and women whose works we choose to comprise this series are those whose voices still rise above the march of time; whose words endure with a power only attributable to the workings of the Holy Spirit.

Our hope is that, by re-awakening the Body of Christ's interest in such "Christian classics," we may help the Church of today return to its simpler, more primitive roots. For, indeed, if a single thread is detectible across the centuries spanned by our Timeless series, it would run like this:

"We must all encounter Jesus, alive, every single day."

We pray that this offering, and the other works in this collection, will lead your heart to fresh, direct experience of Him; that the "best of the past" will find their home in you. May we ever seek to know Him better!

A B O U T
SEA HARP PRESS

Sea Harp is a specialty press with one overarching aim: in the words of Andrew Murray, to "be much occupied with Jesus, and believe much in Him, as the True Vine." Our mission is twofold: to reinvigorate the Church's reading of the best of the past, and to bring out fresh editions of both today's and tomorrow's classics — all for the purpose of personal encounter with Jesus Himself.

For every piece of media we consider publishing, we ask two fundamental questions:

- Is this work entirely about the person of Jesus of Nazareth?
- Would the Early Church have thought this work worthy of sharing?

We take our name from the original Hebrew word for the Sea of Galilee—*Kinneret*: כִּנֶּרֶת: meaning "harp"—which was given because of the harp-like shape of the shoreline around which Jesus ministered. It was, in less words, a place known as the Harp-Sea.

Thank you for joining us as we walk the Way with that most wonderful Man of Galilee.

the
SEA *of*
GALILEE

W W W . S E A H A R P . C O M

www.ingramcontent.com/pod-product-compliance
Lightning Source LLC
Chambersburg PA
CBHW031221090426
42740CB00009B/1261